The Complete Guide to

Coaching
at Work

To Venessa, with love and thanks
Perry

The Complete Guide to
Coaching at Work

Perry Zeus
& Suzanne Skiffington

The McGraw-Hill Companies, Inc.

Sydney New York San Francisco Auckland
Bangkok Bogotá Caracas Hong Kong
Kuala Lumpur Lisbon London Madrid
Mexico City Milan New Delhi San Juan
Seoul Singapore Taipei Toronto

McGraw·Hill Australia

A Division of The **McGraw·Hill** *Companies*

Reprinted 2003

National Library of Australia Cataloguing-in-Publication data:

Skiffington, Suzanne.
The complete guide to coaching at work.

Includes index
ISBN 0 074 70842 2.

1. Training – Handbooks, manuals, etc. 2. Organizational change. 3. Self-actualization (Psychology).
I. Zeus, Perry. II. Title

658.312404

Published in Australia by
McGraw-Hill Australia Pty Limited
Level 2, 82 Waterloo Road, North Ryde NSW 2113
Acquisitions Editor: Meiling Voon
Production Editor: Megan Lowe
Editor: Caroline Hunter
Designer: Kimberly Taliai, blue orange
Cover design: Lucy Bal
Typeset in Zurich Light Condensed 10.5/13.5pt by Kimberly Taliai, blue orange
Printed on 80gsm woodfree by **Pantech Limited, Hong Kong.**

About the authors

Dr S. M. Skiffington B.A., MCP, PhD, MAPS, MISH

Dr Suzanne Skiffington is the consulting psychologist and principal of S. M. Skiffington and Associates. She is one of Australia's leading specialists dealing with personal development within the corporate environment. During her early clinical experience she began developing performance enhancement techniques. She accepted a university research post in the study of human emotions, and taught in Australia's leading universities. Suzanne has since been retained as a private personal skills coach by numerous Australian and American business personalities. She now practises via her own global coaching business with some of the world's leading corporate professionals to enhance their personal and professional growth.

Perry Zeus Dip. B. Admin., Fellow VAAR

Since 1983, Perry has worked as a project and business development management consultant and in the last several years he has acted as a personal coach with clients to increase their personal effectiveness and performance levels. Perry's extensive background includes coaching senior managers in leadership development, and training health care professionals, sports coaches, educators, sales managers, executives, trainers and management consultants in how to be a successful personal coach. He has conducted coaching clinics in the United States, and has worked with a variety of professional groups and individuals (both in Australia and for several years in the United States) as a personal coach and mentor. His varied formal training includes financial accountancy, fine art, business management and counselling.

1 to 1 Coaching School

The 1 to 1 Coaching School (head office in Sydney), founded by Perry Zeus and Suzanne Skiffington, is a global Coach Training and service firm specialising in guiding senior business executives, businesses and organisations worldwide. The School exists to assist companies, individuals, government departments, education authorities, schools and local authorities to make a quantum leap in achieving sustained success.

Services include:

➤ *Coaching courses: seminars and workshops*   A portfolio of program formats is available, individually designed for clients. The firm provides guidance that will give genuine, long-lasting performance results. Also available are 'coach the coach' accreditation seminars and workshops.

➤ *Global Business Coaching Resource Network*   The Network is one of the most extraordinary business tools for any business or organisation, no matter what size or type. The Network provides its members with access to coaching support, services and resources. Other services include: a learning and development audit; an audit of existing coaching programs; an 'on-demand' pool of specialist master coaches at 'results-based-fees'; teleconferences; and televideophone and on-line chat and text sessions.

➤ *Lectures*   Suzanne and Perry speak on a variety of coaching, management and leadership topics, which are tailored to the needs of each conference or group and are delivered as key notes or presentations of up to two hours.

➤ *Master Coach Certification*   This certification is for qualified professionals desiring to work in, or already working in, the coaching profession who want to learn how to develop and enhance their coaching skills. The aim of the Masters Program is to help promote research into, and the development of, coaching as a discipline. Members' benefits include access to a coaching support network and the latest validated coaching tools.

For further information visit *http://www.1to1coachingschool.com*

Contents

Preface

Coaching is a conversation, a dialogue, whereby a coach and coachee interact in a dynamic exchange to achieve goals, enhance performance and move the coachee forward to greater success.

There is an intrinsic logic to the coaching process. There is also a logic behind organisations and businesses adopting coaching.

Coaching has probably existed as long as people have inhabited the earth. For centuries the world's athletes, painters and artists have employed personal coaches to develop and enhance their performance. Coaching in sports is familiar to us all, and indeed business, executive and life skills coaching derive many principles from sports psychology. In the 1960s, especially in the United States, the sports coaching model began to be adopted by the business world.

During the past 15 years or so, learning and development have become critical features of businesses and organisations as they confront rapid changes in the global marketplace. The traditional training model is under challenge on the grounds that it does not result in sustained behavioural change. New coaching models based on the principles of psychology and education have evolved to meet the needs of businesses and organisations worldwide. These models and coaching interventions have gradually filtered through to the business world, and today coaching for small business owners, corporations and public institutions is proliferating at an extraordinary rate.

Broadly speaking, this book is about three types of coaching: (i) business coaching, (ii) executive coaching and (iii) life skills coaching, particularly as it impacts on aspects of work performance. Although the distinctions between the three types of coaching are addressed in detail in Chapter 1, it is perhaps useful here to describe briefly how they differ.

Business coaching incorporates individual and executive team coaching in large corporations, including local authorities and public institutions, as well as coaching owners and managers of medium- to small-sized businesses and other organisations. Throughout the book we use the term 'business coaching' to refer to coaching in all types of organisations, whether they be profit or non-profit, government or non-government. An executive (or corporate) coach typically works with an individual executive, manager or team in large organisations to develop interpersonal or leadership skills. Finally, life skills coaches work with individuals in transition to develop aspects of their personal, interpersonal and spiritual lives.

However, separating life skills coaching from business and executive coaching is not always straightforward. Some coaches choose to deal with work-related issues only, while others incorporate life issues into business and executive coaching. Some coaches also choose to specialise in life skills issues. While life skills coaching is, by definition, more holistic than the other types of coaching, some areas typically addressed by life skills coaches clearly impact on careers and work performance. These include values, vision and purpose, home/work balance, relationships and health. Existential and spiritual issues can also be pertinent to business and executive coaching. With these interactions in mind, we have incorporated aspects of life skills coaching into those sections of executive and business coaching where we consider their impact warrants discussion.

Why have we written this book?

Some of the important aspects of coaching that we have addressed in this book include: the history of coaching, the different types of coaching, issues around self-awareness and the degree of self-exploration necessary for sustained behavioural change and the competencies of a coach as well as step-by-step models for various coaching processes.

This book can be used as a reference text and as an instructional 'how-to-coach' guide. We have incorporated relevant research in a non-academic, accessible style. Models for different types of coaching and the structure of a typical coaching cycle (individual and team) are set out in easy-to-follow steps, while exercises and case studies show how the theory applies to real life situations.

The models and exercises in this book are based on some of the fundamental premises, beliefs and values of coaching. These include:

➤ the belief in the human ability to change, while acknowledging that change can be difficult and therefore resisted

➤ the fact that people make the best choices available to them

➤ the notion that coaching is not a 'quick fix'—it is a journey where the process of learning is as important as the knowledge and skills gained.

Who should read this book?

The book is intended as a guide for:

1 *individuals*, because coaching is a way of relating that can be adopted at any level in the workplace, educational institutions, sporting arena and personal life

2 *small business owners* who simply do not have the time to undertake formal management or coaching training—some specific areas of relevance include how to better balance home and work life, how to handle staff relations and how to adopt a coaching role rather than a managing profile

3 *national and international corporations* wishing to retrain and establish a coaching culture—executives, managers, supervisors and team leaders can use the text to develop their roles in the workplace

4 *professionals* who intend to add coaching to their services or who wish to enhance their existing coaching skills

5 *trainers, management consultants and human resources personnel* who can refer to the book for professional guidance on how to develop their own skills and those of others in their workplace

Some courses for which the book may be suitable include: business management, psychology, counselling, education and personnel or people management.

Structure of the book

Part I provides an introduction to coaching. In Chapter 1 we outline the history of coaching and discuss the various types of coaching. We also examine the differences between coaching and allied disciplines such as counselling, mentoring, training and consulting. Chapter 2 presents a profile of a typical coach and discusses the personal qualities of a successful coach.

Part II addresses business coaching. In Chapter 3 we discuss businesses in the twenty-first century, the applications and benefits of business coaching, and the core competencies of a business coach, as well as some typical business coaching interventions and formats. Importantly, this chapter offers 'buyers' a checklist of criteria for choosing the right business coach. Chapter 4 examines executive coaching on a one-to-one individual basis, as well as executive team coaching. We review the literature on competencies for executive coaches and propose a step-by-step model for designing coaching interventions from the first meeting with management through to the completion of the coaching cycle. Typical coaching interventions such as coaching for leadership are outlined and discussed.

In Chapter 5 we discuss the role of the manager as coach. We look at specific roles of the manager/coach, including giving effective feedback, managing conflict, delegating and career coaching. We discuss and provide guidelines for carrying out executive alignment in order to encourage and establish a culture of coaching in an organisation. We also outline the 'coaching the coach' workshops that we conduct for managers to become coaches. Chapter 6 examines team coaching in the business and executive coaching arenas. We discuss some characteristics of a top performing team and some guidelines for the team coach. The chapter includes a step-by-step model and exercises for team coaching interventions. The role of the manager in coaching virtual teams is also addressed.

Part III is devoted to various coaching skills and coaching issues. Chapter 7 is an instructional chapter designed to assist coaches in the exploration of values, vision and purpose and their importance in goal setting. It is a practical guide to strategic goal setting and developing action plans. In Chapter 8 we detail communication skills such as listening, asking questions and understanding non-verbal signals. These interpersonal and communication skills are crucial to successful coaching.

As coaching is about learning, Chapter 9 overviews some models of learning and stresses the importance of establishing a learning culture in an organisation that truly values learning and growth. We discuss some of the features of the learning and development audits we conduct with larger organisations to recognise their learning strengths and weaknesses. The chapter also discusses preferred styles of learning and offers guidelines for coaches to deal with the differing learning styles of coachees. Chapter 10 examines the centrality of change in the coaching process, as well as some obstacles and resistance to change and how the coach can deal with these.

Part IV discusses three specific coaching areas. Chapter 11 addresses coaching issues and interventions in call centres. Chapter 12 concerns sales coaching and focuses on the notion of selling as a mental skill and coaching skills for the sales coach. Finally, Chapter 13 addresses career coaching and the coach's role in coaching individuals for their first job, job loss, career change and retirement coaching. The importance of career coaching in organisations is also discussed.

Increasingly, the term coaching is being absorbed into our vocabulary. Coaching as a unique, democratic style of exploring, learning and transferring knowledge and skills is fast becoming the preferred style of relating in business, education, public organisations and personal life.

PART ONE

An introduction to coaching

Definitions and distinctions

Key points

➤ What is coaching?

➤ The history of coaching

➤ Types of coaching

➤ What coaching is not

What is coaching?

We are all familiar with the term coaching, particularly in the context of sports coaching. Yet, although the technology of coaching is exploding into organisations and into our personal lives, many of us remain unclear about what coaching is and what the coaching process entails. For instance, coaching is sometimes seen as a style of facilitation or management and is occasionally used interchangeably with mentoring, consulting and even therapy. So what is coaching?

➤ *Coaching is essentially a conversation*—a dialogue between a coach and a coachee—within a productive, results-oriented context. Coaching involves helping individuals access what they know. They may never have asked themselves the questions, but they have the answers. A coach assists, supports and encourages individuals to find these answers.

➤ *Coaching is about learning*—yet a coach is not a teacher and does not necessarily know how to do things better than the coachee. A coach can observe patterns, set the stage for new actions and then work with the individual to put these new, more successful actions into place. Coaching involves learning. Through various coaching techniques such as listening, reflecting, asking questions and providing information, coachees become self-correcting (they learn how to correct their behaviour themselves) and self-generating (they generate their own questions and answers).

➤ *Coaching is more about asking the right questions than providing answers*. A coach engages in a collaborative alliance with the individual to establish and clarify purpose and goals and to develop a plan of action to achieve these goals.

Coaching is about change and transformation—about the human ability to grow, to alter maladaptive behaviours and to generate new, adaptive and successful actions. As most of us know, changing old patterns and habits can be difficult, even when we recognise that they are disadvantaging us or holding us back. A coach observes these habits, opens up new possibilities and supports us in the sometimes difficult process of change.

Coaching is about reinventing oneself—creating new stories, new identities and new futures. It recognises that the self is not a fixed entity, but is fluid and always in a state of becoming. Coaching is a journey where the journey is as important as the destination.

Coaching also operates on the emotional plane. Despite a plethora of books on emotional intelligence and a general recognition that interpersonal and personal skills are critical competencies in the workplace and home, there remains some suspicion and mistrust of 'emotions'. The word emotion conjures up images of vulnerability and weakness. Yet the very word emotion derives from the Latin *ex movrere*, meaning to move out. Every emotion includes a tendency to action; for example, one action tendency of anger is to hit out. A coach works with our emotions, for it is by recognising and understanding our feelings that different behavioural possibilities can be realised.

The history of coaching

It is generally agreed that the discipline of coaching is in its infancy. However, coaching has a lineage probably dating back to prehistory.

Features of coaching, such as clarifying values, and supporting, encouraging and planning new ways of action, are embedded in our everyday interactions and conversations with each other. On a more formal level, coaching derives many of its principles from psychology, especially sports psychology and education. The principles of coaching are therefore not new. Perhaps what is new is how coaching today (business, executive and life skills coaching) has become a synthesis or an amalgam of these disciplines, drawing also on philosophy and spirituality.

The origins of the terms 'executive coaching' and 'business coaching' can be traced to leadership development programs in the 1980s. Life skills coaching derives from education programs developed in New York in the 1960s. It is probably true to say that coaching remains an evolving 'art' or profession. Coaching competencies, tools and techniques are not yet standardised or formalised and niche areas for coaching continue to be uncovered and developed.

Sports psychology and coaching

Some of the basic principles of coaching derive from sports psychology, such as performing to our best, setting and reaching our goals, and becoming a successful team player. While traditional sports coaching tends to be based on a win–lose model, many contemporary sports coaches adopt an 'athletes first, winning second' philosophy. Such an approach is in harmony with the overall goals of coaching, which include:

➤ developing and encouraging the individual's *personal best*

➤ keeping the individual forward-focused and always aware of new opportunities for growth and development

➤ working through any obstacles to change and overcoming self-sabotaging or self-limiting beliefs

➤ maintaining a balance between professional and personal life.

However, sports psychology and coaching have more in common than broad-ranging aims and goals. Sports psychology delineates and emphasises aspects of human behaviour that are critical to the self-development that defines coaching. For example, some sports psychologists emphasise the importance of assessment. Butler, for instance, has developed a system of performance profiling for athletes, which illustrates the athlete's strengths and weaknesses in various technical and interpersonal areas as perceived by the individual and the coach. Many coaches, particularly those working within the business and executive arenas, employ a similar type of multi-rater assessment.

Sports psychology also recognises the importance of self-awareness both on the part of the athlete and the coach. Examining values, developing and maintaining vision, challenging beliefs that negatively impact on performance, coping with pressure and stress, and maintaining focus are other areas common to sports psychology and coaching.

Education and coaching

As already noted, coaching is about learning. Coaching today, although distinct from teaching, draws heavily on the principles of adult learning developed in the 1950s and 1960s. Some of these principles addressed by coaching are discussed in detail in Chapter 9, and include the assumptions that the self-concept of adults moves towards being self-directed rather than dependent on others and that adult learning is motivated by a need to manage real life issues more effectively. A critical role of the coach is to provide a safe, nurturing environment for the individual to grow and develop his or her own strategies and solutions.

Coaching is also influenced by constructivist learning theory. While an in-depth discussion of this theory is clearly outside the scope of this book, the following aspects bear particular relevance to coaching:

➤ The learner is always an active organism, not just responding to stimuli, but seeking them out and engaging and grappling with them in order to make sense of the world.

➤ Knowledge is generated internally, not just from external sources.

➤ Motivation is intrinsic. Coaches cannot motivate individuals. They examine and clarify the individual's values, purpose and vision, and collaboratively set goals that 'pull' the individual towards achieving them.

Types of coaching

Apart from sports coaching, coaching today can be divided into three main areas: *business coaching*, *executive coaching* and *life skills coaching*. Life skills issues impact on business and executive coaching and it is sometimes difficult to separate these areas. However, in the interests of clarity we address the three areas separately, and we discuss life skills coaching issues chiefly in relation to their impact on the business and executive arenas.

Life skills coaching

Historically, the concept of life skills coaching preceded that of business and executive coaching. Hence, although the emphasis of this book is on the latter, first we look briefly at the origins of life skills coaching, its development and contemporary profile.

Life skills coaching developed in New York in the 1960s. Life skills training was first introduced by Dr Winthrop Adkins and Dr Sidney Rosenberg as a model for anti-poverty group programs. They had concluded from their research that traditional education was inappropriate and ineffective for 'disadvantaged' adults and did not address the cognitive and emotional barriers to coping with life and with change. The life skills model was adopted in Canada as part of the New Start program, and the notion of problem solving was added to what had been essentially an interpersonal skills intervention. About this time the word 'coach' was chosen, and it was recognised that group facilitators required training in a wide range of skills and competencies.

There have been continual changes and developments in the life skills model over the past few decades in Canada, the United States and Australia. However, what is more relevant in the discussion is the degree to which life skills coaching has, from about the late 1980s, infiltrated into the private sector and become part of our everyday vocabulary. It has evolved into an individual relationship between a coach and a coachee to bring about life transforming experiences. Life skills coaching is about clarifying values and visions, and setting goals and new actions so that an individual may lead a more satisfying, successful and fulfilling life.

Such a broad definition suggests that life skills coaching has almost infinite applications. In a sense this is true. A coach can work with an individual to develop and improve virtually any aspect of that individual's life. Some examples of life skills coaching include: partnership coaching, retirement coaching, singles coaching, spiritual development coaching, migrant transition coaching, fitness coaching, wellness coaching, career coaching, transition coaching and quality of life coaching such as balancing life and work.

Some specific benefits of life skills coaching include:

➤ clarifying what you want from life—your purpose and vision

➤ setting more effective goals

➤ having someone 'on your side' to support and encourage you on your journey of change

➤ having someone to keep you focused, challenge you, keep you accountable and confront you when you are falling behind on your commitments

➤ having a sounding board for your ideas, plans and strategies.

Regardless of the type of coaching involved, the coach and the coachee develop a special collaborative synergy that moves the individual forward to more easily and quickly accomplish his or her dreams and ambitions.

Most life skills coaching contracts run over a period of three to six months. The sessions are usually weekly, and may be conducted in person, via the telephone, via e-mail, or by a combination of all three. Life skills coaches usually charge on a monthly basis.

 Case Study

Life skills coaching

R. W. is a 36-year-old male who manages an up-market retail fashion store. Although extremely successful at his work, he felt dissatisfied, 'stuck' and unfulfilled. He hired K. P., a life skills coach, to help him gain a fresh perspective on his life. During the sessions exploring R. W.'s goals and dreams, it became apparent that he really wanted to design men's clothes rather than sell them. The coach and R. W. examined in depth the beliefs and fears that held him back and together they proceeded to set goals and develop an action plan for him to achieve his life's purpose. Part of the short-term plan involved R. W. completing his final year of fashion design while continuing to manage the business. The longer-term goals included working with an established designer and eventually setting up his own business.

Business coaching

Business coaching can be applied to all types of businesses. It ranges from individual and executive team coaching in large corporations (including local authorities and public institutions), to coaching owners and managers of small- to medium-sized businesses and other organisations. More and more business owners/managers and organisations are hiring business coaches to help them develop, promote and grow their business, their staff and themselves.

Increasingly, business owners and managers find that they are so consumed by the day-to-day running of the business that they have no time to look at 'the big picture', develop their staff, increase value to customers and, importantly, balance their personal and working lives. Furthermore, most business owners do not have the time for formal management training and may lack the personal and communication skills required to deal effectively with their staff. Public institutions and government departments are being 'corporatised' and have to adapt to the demands of the marketplace in ways that require complex interpersonal and strategic skills.

Some areas in which business coaches work include:

➤ interpersonal and communication skills—how to get the best out of your staff

➤ time management

➤ balancing work and personal life issues

➤ staff development and dealing with conflict

➤ identifying gaps and obstacles to efficiency

➤ strategic thinking and business planning

➤ increasing productivity

➤ increasing market share

➤ customer service development.

 Case Study

Business group coaching

B. M. is a female business coach with offices in the central business district. She specialises in working with retailers and other small business owners/managers. She conducts weekly, roundtable group coaching sessions with six to eight individuals, usually over a period of three months. The sessions focus on issues common to all group members, such as how to develop staff, how to balance work and personal life demands, how to improve customer service and how to establish strategic business development goals and action plans.

Executive coaching

Executive coaching is a collaborative, individualised relationship between an executive and a coach, the aims of which are to bring about sustained behavioural change and to transform the quality of the executive's working and personal life. Although executive coaching always focuses on the individual's working life, coaching sessions frequently centre on interpersonal development, personal change and transformation.

The term 'executive coaching' developed as an outgrowth of executive leadership programs in the late 1980s. Tobias suggests that the term simply implies a repackaging of certain practices previously subsumed under consulting or counselling, although, like us, he distinguishes between the three disciplines.

Executive coaches work with individuals or teams within large organisations. Some areas of individual executive coaching include: leadership development; interpersonal and communication skills; career coaching to enhance personal satisfaction and career opportunities; specific skills coaching; developing 'superstars'; and executive strategic planning as well as problem solving. Executive coaching can also focus on building a top performing team, working with individuals to become more effective team players and coaching executives/managers to be coaches.

There are various styles of executive coaching, depending on the aims of the coaching sessions, the goals of the executive and the types of interventions employed. We have adopted the classificatory system employed by the Center for Creative Leadership. As each of these coaching roles is discussed in more detail in Chapter 4, only a brief synopsis is given here. According to this model, coaching occurs on a continuum of four coaching roles:

➤ *coaching for skills* focuses on an executive's current task—for example, presentation and negotiation skills

➤ *coaching for performance* is focused more broadly on an executive's effectiveness in a present job—for example, establishing a 'people development program' to enhance staff satisfaction and productivity

➤ *coaching for development* is focused on an executive's new or future career

➤ *coaching for the executive's agenda* focuses on the executive's larger work and/or personal agenda.

Coaching for performance

A. S. is a newly appointed senior executive in an advertising company. One of his goals is to establish an effective, efficient feedback system that includes regular appraisals and monthly review meetings with all departments. He and the executive coach initially worked together on strategies to enrol all staff in the process. This included data gathering, brainstorming sessions with department heads and a pilot study. Coaching sessions then focused on expanding the program and delegating responsibility for it to the general manager and human resources personnel.

What coaching is not

Coaching compared with therapy

Coaching has its roots in psychology. It draws from psychological theory and, in many cases, from psychological practices. Coaching is imbued with notions from humanistic psychology—a science created by Abraham Maslow which is concerned with higher human values, self-development and self-understanding. Coaching involves examining and clarifying an individual's needs and values and working with these to develop goals that will lead to personal and professional development.

Existential issues, such as identifying purpose and meaning in life, alleviating suffering and enabling the individual to live a more fulfilled and joyful life, are central to the coaching process. A successful coach 'nurtures' the client and offers what psychologist Carl Rogers calls 'unconditional acceptance and warmth'. Olalla claims that the most important aspect of coaching is being accepted, respected and taken care of, rather than the exchange of information between the coach and coachee.

Although coaching is not therapy, many coaches trained in psychology adopt or borrow from various therapy models. The most commonly employed models include:

➤ *Solution-focused therapy*   Perhaps the closest therapy model to coaching is brief therapy or solution-focused therapy, which focuses on the problem, rephrases it, presents alternative possibilities, develops goals and then develops an action plan to meet these goals. As with coaching, this type of therapy is based on the belief that answers reside in the individual's own repertoire of skills and is always framed within a context of human competency and our ability to change and adapt.

➤ *Transactional analysis (TA)*   Developed by Eric Berne, TA helps people identify their ego states (parent, adult and child) and evaluate and improve ways in which they function in order to achieve an adaptive, mature and realistic attitude to life. It is used in coaching for time structuring, problem solving and resolving conflicts.

➤ *Neurolinguistic programming (NLP)*   A technique rather than a therapy, NLP is the study of what works in thinking, language and behaviour. It is used as a coaching intervention in organisations to enhance learning abilities, set goals, improve relationships and manage thoughts and emotions more effectively.

➤ *Constructivist therapy*   Based on constructivist learning principles, constructivist or narrative therapy is seen as a problem-dissolving system and a means of rewriting an individual's story and biography. It is used in organisations to move individuals towards a more workable, powerful story. For instance, executives are encouraged to write their story in order to celebrate their gifts and abilities. Individuals transform their inner reality, become more mindful and are better able to dictate their own stories.

➤ *Psychodynamic therapy*   Largely influenced by Freud, this therapy uses interpretation, explores unconscious motivation and searches for deep causes (usually in a person's early life) for presenting problems. In the United States particularly, many coaches are trained in psychodynamic therapy. This therapy emphasises the importance of assessing the underlying dynamics surrounding certain behaviours, such as an executive's tendency to overcontrol or an individual's difficulties with intimacy. Yet all take pains to distinguish psychoanalytic therapy from coaching. Levinson, for example, cautions that it is important for coaches to avoid becoming psychotherapeutic, because time does not allow them to develop and deal with the transference (unconsciously making a current relationship an extension of an earlier one). He also claims that executive coaching requires the ability on the part of the coach to differentiate coaching from therapy while using basic psychological skills and insights. Other authors, such as Kilburg, claim that coaching shares some but not all of the characteristics of psychotherapeutic interventions.

The following table shows some of the similarities and differences between coaching and therapy.

Similarities	Differences
➤ Both use assessment.	➤ Therapists are less self-disclosing than coaches, so the power differential is less in a coaching relationship.
➤ Both investigate and clarify values.	➤ Therapists rarely give advice, whereas coaches are free to make suggestions, advise, make requests and confront the individual.
➤ Both are client centred.	➤ Therapists tend to focus on the resolution of old pains and old issues, whereas coaches acknowledge their historical impact but do not explore these in-depth. Coaches are more inclined to reflect pro-active behaviours and move the person forward out of their feelings and into action.
➤ Both listen and reflect.	➤ Therapy tends to deal with dysfunction, either vague or specific, whereas coaching moves a functional person on to greater success and refers clients on for clinical issues.
➤ Both help individuals recognise the potential destructiveness of their actions and feelings.	➤ Therapy tends to focus on past-related feelings, whereas coaching is about setting goals and forward action.
➤ Both recognise strengths and weaknesses.	➤ Therapy explores resistance and negative transference, whereas coaching attempts to rephrase complaints into goals.
➤ Both seek to situate the individual in a context of adult development.	➤ Therapy is about progress, whereas coaching is about performance.

Whereas we have differentiated therapy and coaching, some practitioners assume the title of 'corporate therapist'. Corporate therapy is an extension of occupational clinical psychology in that it focuses on troubled employees and executives as well as troubled organisations. Specific areas where corporate therapists work include: culture transformation, helping executives better understand customers, team building, executive coaching, recruitment and screening, and easing the trauma of downsizing.

 Case Study

Referring on for therapy

M. Y. is a 42-year-old senior manager in a large service industry. She has been targeted for promotion and has been engaged in a coaching relationship (coaching for development) for three months. The coach has always been aware that M. Y. has difficulties at home and that her marriage is under strain. During one coaching session, she informed the coach that domestic violence

Case Study

was an issue for her and that she wanted to work with the coach on ways to deal with her husband. The coach, also a trained clinical psychologist and competent to deal with the matter, decided that it was outside her mandate as a coach, and referred M. Y. to a colleague who was a family therapist. M. Y. and the coach continued their coaching sessions focusing on developing the requisite skills and competencies for M. Y.'s future position.

Coaching compared with workplace counselling

Workplace counselling is another discipline closely allied to, and sometimes confused with, coaching. Counselling in the workplace usually involves turning around underperformance by resolving a particular problem. Such problems can involve stress, anxiety, poor quality work, absenteeism and frequently missed deadlines. While a workplace counsellor may adopt a coaching role, there are some critical differences between the traditional model of counselling and coaching, including:

➤ The purpose of counselling is to get problem employees to recognise the gaps between their actual and the desired performance, identify the source of the problem and develop an action plan to address it. Coaching is a process of continual development by which employees gain the skills and abilities they need to develop professionally and personally and perform better at work and in their personal lives.

➤ Counselling looks for causes behind the problem or performance deficit, whereas coaching emphasises new competencies and new actions.

➤ The traditional counselling model generally follows a remedial approach, emphasising deficits and the problems of not meeting a set, required conduct or standard. Coaching emphasises strengths and achievements.

➤ Counselling generally involves minimal assessment, whereas the coaching model interfaces with learning and development tools (e.g. 360-degree feedback) and behavioural diagnostic assessment tools introduced at the beginning of the coaching intervention.

➤ Traditional counselling focuses on exploring reactive problems and behaviours, whereas coaching is pro-active and looks to recognise and avert problems before they arise.

➤ Counselling is usually needs based and occasional, whereas coaching generally involves an initial ongoing contract of three to six months.

Coaching compared with training

Organisations throughout the world spend billions of dollars on training programs each year. Yet research conducted at the Center for Creative Leadership suggests that only 8 to 12 per cent of those who attend training courses translate new skills and knowledge into measurable performance improvement or business results. Essentially, this is because most training programs do not allow for the skills to be put into practice, and there is no feedback or ongoing support. Subsequently, when an employee's skill level deteriorates during the initial trying out of new skills, there are no support mechanisms in place, so the individual reverts to the previous behaviours.

Some differences between training and coaching include:

➤ The training agenda is fixed and set by the trainer, whereas in coaching, the individual sets the agenda, which can be fluid and flexible.

➤ Change comes from the outside in training, whereas coaching works with the client to clarify values and enhance intrinsic motivation.

➤ Some trainees benefit from a training program while others do not. By contrast, the coaching intervention is personalised and geared towards the individual's needs and aspirations.

➤ Trainees are frequently assigned to a training course, whereas, ideally, coaching is voluntary.

➤ Training rarely involves feedback, whereas the coaching process includes ongoing feedback and continuous learning.

➤ Training tends to reinforce a traditional, hierarchical style of management, whereas coaching is a more democratic, collaborative process.

➤ Coaching is about sustained behavioural change, whereas training tends not to bring about major shifts in thinking and action.

These differences should not obscure the fact that a coach can function in a trainer/teacher role and that a trainer/teacher can adopt some of the essential ingredients of successful coaching.

These roles overlap when the following principles are adhered to:

➤ emphasise learner independence and choice

➤ emphasise and develop intrinsic motivation

➤ encourage and develop natural curiosity

➤ develop higher-order abilities.

Training versus coaching

P. D. is the human resources manager (and former training manager for eight years) of a regional insurance company. He is instituting a personal development program for senior staff. As the program is to be outsourced, P. D. has interviewed an experienced coach and two training organisations that did not offer coaching services. He had not updated himself on the process and benefits of coaching, and during the interview it was clear to the coach that he did not understand the differences between training and coaching. More importantly, he did not want to know about coaching. It was evident that he felt somewhat threatened and confronted by the concept of coaching and could only view it as opposition to his training background and programs.

Coaching compared with management consulting

Management consultants hail from a variety of professional backgrounds, including training and development specialists, human resources specialists and industrial and organisational psychologists. Increasingly, many consultants are adding coaching to their services. Although the primary function of most management consultants is to work at an organisational level, more and more consultants report that their clients are requesting individual, one-on-one work. Some of the specific requests include assistance with performance appraisals and dealing with organisational change, particularly in the context of downsizing. As these areas lend themselves particularly well to the coaching model, coaching can be seen as the next evolutionary stage of consulting.

While there are some major differences between management consulting and coaching, the professions share many similarities. In one sense, all coaches are consultants, whereas few consultants are coaches. The similarities and differences between the two roles include:

Similarities	Differences
➤ Both aim to support organisational change.	➤ Coaching can be conducted outside of a consulting relationship.
➤ Both solve problems, set goals and design an action plan.	➤ Consultants tend to be experts within a specific industry or business, whereas a coach's expertise is in the domain of conversation, communication, interpersonal skills and emotions. The coach does not have to be an expert in the business field.
➤ Both can design and facilitate workshops and work with teams.	➤ Consultants' services are information based, whereas coaching revolves around relationships.
➤ Both can be seen as a quick-fix, remedial intervention for a targeted individual, rather than for a problem that is deep-seated in an organisation.	➤ Consultants are frequently expected to provide answers, whereas coaches evoke answers from the individual.
	➤ Consultants gather and analyse data, write reports and make recommendations that are frequently systemic and based on the needs of the organisation. They are rarely employed to deal with individuals during the period of transition and change. On the other hand, coaches work with individuals during and after organisational change.
	➤ Consultants can tend to prescribe 'canned' or 'commercial' solutions, whereas coaching is more personalised and concerned with the individual's needs, values and goals.
	➤ Consultants generally focus on work aspects, whereas coaching is more holistic and considers other aspects of an individual's life.
	➤ Consultants tend to deal with specific problems, whereas coaches are more forward looking and always ready to create and take advantage of opportunities.

Management consulting versus coaching

A large information technology organisation decided to institute a pilot program for managers to adopt a coaching style. A medium-sized management consulting firm which was already contracted to the organisation assumed responsibility for the task. Although the consulting firm's staff had also labelled themselves as coaches, they had no formal training in the discipline. Because they lacked the requisite coaching expertise, the consultants established a 'coaching' program that essentially involved training, advice giving and old-style counselling techniques. As a result, the outcome of the pilot program was disappointing and it was not rolled-out into the organisation.

Coaching compared with mentoring

Mentoring is also frequently confused with, or referred to interchangeably with, coaching. Some definitions of mentoring might help to differentiate the two processes. According to Lewis, mentoring is a natural way of passing on knowledge, skills and experiences to others by someone who is usually older and wiser with broad life experiences and specific expertise.

Other definitions of mentoring include:

> 'one who offers knowledge, insight, perspective or wisdom that is especially useful to the other person' (Shea 1996)

> 'a career friend, knowledgeable about your field who advises and encourages' (Rolfe-Flett 1996)

Traditionally, mentoring was a hierarchical relationship involving a wise senior who dispensed wisdom, knowledge and advice to a grateful but essentially powerless junior. Modern mentoring relationships, however, are based on a more mutual, equal and collaborative learning alliance. These features also apply to the coaching relationship and, indeed, there are numerous similarities between mentoring and coaching. Some of the similarities and differences are listed below.

Similarities	Differences
➤ Both require well-developed interpersonal skills.	➤ Mentoring invents a future based on the expertise and wisdom of another, whereas coaching is about inventing a future from the individual's own possibilities.
➤ Both require the ability to generate trust, to support commitment and to generate new actions through the use of listening and speaking skills.	➤ Mentors are recognised as experts in their field.
➤ Both shorten the learning curve.	➤ Mentoring is usually more specifically career focused in terms of career advancement.
➤ Both aim for the individual to improve his or her performance and be more productive.	➤ Mentors usually have experience at senior management level, and have a broad knowledge of organisational structure, policies, power and culture.
➤ Both encourage the individual to stretch, but can provide support if the person falters or gets out of his or her depth.	➤ Mentors freely give advice and opinions regarding strategies and policies, whereas coaching is about evoking answers from the individual.
➤ Both provide support without removing responsibility.	➤ Mentors have considerable power and influence to advance the individual's career and advocate promotion.
➤ Both require a degree of organisational know-how.	➤ Mentors convey and instill the standards, norms and values of the profession/organisation. Coaching is more about exploring and developing the individual's own values, vision and standards.
➤ Both focus on learning and development to enhance skills and competencies.	
➤ Both stimulate personal growth to develop new expertise.	
➤ Both can function as a career guide to review career goals and identify values, vision and career strengths.	
➤ Both are role models.	

While there are obvious distinctions between mentoring and coaching, they share much in common, including some of the competencies necessary for success in both disciplines. Perhaps the simplest way to define the connection between the two roles is to view coaching as a style of relationship that can be employed in mentoring. Furthermore, once the coach and individual have completed the formal coaching intervention (setting goals; developing and successfully carrying out an action plan), the coach may move to a role akin to that of a mentor. That is, the coach and individual might meet on a monthly or bimonthly basis, with the coach's role to guide and support the individual on his or her journey, offering professional advice and providing a trustworthy sounding board.

Case Study

The coach as mentor

E. B., an executive coach, worked with D. S., a senior manager in a banking corporation, for a period of six months. During this time, the coaching alliance focused on establishing goals, strategies and action plans to enhance D. S.'s leadership and team-building skills. At the end of the formal coaching sessions, E. B. and D. S. continued to meet on a monthly or bimonthly basis. No formal coaching sessions were conducted, but rather, D. S. would seek professional guidance and support on any work issues he was dealing with at the time. The 'mentoring' relationship extended over a period of two years.

Who can coach?

Key points

➤ Characteristics of a successful coach

➤ Life skills coaching

Characteristics of a successful coach

In the first section of this chapter we examine some of the core competencies or personal attributes generic to successful business, executive and life skills coaching. These qualities can guide potential coaches in their self-development agenda and provide a checklist for practising coaches. The second section offers some specific guidelines and selection criteria for individuals choosing a life skills coach. The core competencies and selection criteria for business and executive coaches are discussed in Chapters 3 and 4, respectively.

What is the profile of a typical coach?

A recent poll in the United States by Harriet Salinger and Judy Feld suggests that the majority of coaches are female, belong to the 'baby-boomers' generation and come from a variety of professional backgrounds including psychology, human resources, management consulting, teaching and health care. Each group of professionals brings something unique to the coaching situation. Psychologists, for example, have a large tool kit they can employ to bring about sustained behavioural change, while human resources personnel bring their assessment and performance evaluation skills. Management consultants have specialist organisational skills and project management experience; teachers possess an extensive knowledge of adult learning and development principles; and health practitioners understand the connection between mind and body. Other professional groups such as lawyers and doctors bring a specialist understanding of the niche areas they work in.

What motivates a person to become a coach?

While curiosity, altruism and challenge may serve as possible motivators for aspiring coaches, many professionals who plan to assume a coaching role often idealise and romanticise the profession. They may see themselves as guiding, advising and dispensing wisdom to all who cross their paths. If they choose to work in the corporate arena, they may imagine a life of glamour and excitement, dealing with high-powered and important people. Some common reasons for becoming a coach include: recognition, financial gain, entrepreneurial spirit, independence, self-worth and career change.

Before embarking on a coaching career, it is important to understand the nature and purpose of coaching. Prospective coaches should test their reality level and expectations of what coaching is and is not, and whether or not it is suitable for them. Coaching can be different things to different people. It is a relatively new profession and does not have a traditional career path. A prospective coach needs to define coaching and ascertain its uniqueness.

Some characteristics of the coaching profession include:

➤ Coaching is a service business.

➤ Coaches work in a wide variety of niche areas.

➤ Client relationships are at the heart of the business.

➤ Coaches come from a broad spectrum of professions, unlike other traditional professional groups.

➤ Coaches tend to be outsiders working on the inside.

One way for prospective coaches to develop more realistic expectations of coaching and their suitability for the role is to talk to other coaches about their motivations and the competencies, rewards, challenges and limitations of the profession. The most effective and useful way of going about this exercise is to arrange an interview, either in person or by telephone, with several professional coaches. Prior to the interviews, it is useful to research the topic and prepare a list of questions and topics for discussion.

Some other factors to consider when deciding on a career in coaching include:

➤ *Self-concept*   Self-concept is made up of self-awareness and knowledge of our strengths and limitations, our cognitive style (thoughts and perceptions), our style of interacting with others and our adaptability to change. How we view ourselves generally indicates how others view us.

➤ *Interests*   Clearly, a coach has to be people oriented, curious about what motivates people, and aware of and intrigued by subtle nuances of feelings and behaviours. A genuine interest in people's careers, lifestyles, goals and visions is a good starting point for a coach.

➤ *Abilities*   While many coaching skills and competencies can be learned, some natural abilities augur well for a successful coaching career. These include mental agility, strong problem-solving skills and a high level of interpersonal functioning (e.g. sensitivity, empathy and insight).

The role of values in coaching

Our value systems define our standards of what is good and bad, right and wrong, worthwhile or worthless. Coaching is not synonymous with counselling, teaching or preaching, yet as with these professions, values lie at the core of the relationship between the coach and the coachee. In order to establish goals and action plans that are congruent with the coachee's aspirations and vision, the coach has to address extensively the values of the coachee. Goals have their basis in personal values.

Occasionally, we lose touch with our values and act in ways that are inconsistent with them. At times a coach has to clarify and sometimes challenge a coachee's values. If these values are not challenged, coachees may not really consider how they hold some values higher than others or even what some of their values are. At times a coach may have to openly and honestly challenge coachees when their belief systems and values are patently interfering with goal attainment.

In the coaching relationship, the coach's own values are brought sharply into focus. Coaches cannot exclude their own values and beliefs and remain non-committal or 'value free'. While coaches have an ethical obligation not to impose their values on a coachee, it is important nonetheless to discuss openly the importance of values in the coaching relationship.

There are several issues regarding a coach's values and how these might impact on the coaching relationship. For instance, the coach could make value judgments about the coachee's personality and interpersonal style. If these judgments are negative, it could prove difficult to establish rapport and trust. The coach may disagree with the coachee's choices or goals, and may not be able to offer the necessary unconditional support to achieve these goals. Finally, the coach may experience a conflict of interest when the values and goals of an organisation conflict with the coachee's values or with the coach's own values.

Obviously, the question of values and the ethical issues surrounding them are a matter of individual integrity and choice.

Personal qualities of a successful coach

There is no such thing as an ideal or perfect coach. Knowledge is a continuous process. We are constantly re-evaluating ourselves in terms of what we know and what we need to know to continue our journey of self-growth. In our experience, we have found a consistent need for follow-up seminars and workshops for individuals to continue their professional development and advancement.

Yet, not everyone can be a coach. While many coaching skills can be acquired through training and practice, research and experience suggest 10 personal qualities that characterise an effective, successful coach. These are outlined below.

1 A capacity for self-awareness

While we are not advocating that coaches undergo intensive analysis, to be a successful coach clearly entails a considerable degree of self-knowledge and self-acceptance. The greater our awareness, the greater our possibilities for choice and freedom. As with any profession that involves working with and 'helping' others, an awareness of our own motives for coaching is crucial.

Coaching demands that we be motivated by a genuine interest in and concern for our fellow human beings, as exemplified in the humanistic tradition associated with psychologists Abraham Maslow and Carl Rogers. Such a world view entails a belief that reason can triumph over fear, and that people are resourceful, competent, capable of self-direction and able to live fulfilling and productive lives. A coach who is motivated and inspired by these beliefs can guide and support individuals to develop their capacities and stimulate constructive, lasting change. Curiosity, challenge and altruism may also serve as possible motivators. It is perhaps useful to note several possible harmful motives for helping others as identified by Nelson-Jones. These include unresolved emotional pain, do-gooding, seeking intimacy, expediency and true believerism.

Some examples of self-awareness include:

➤ a capacity for self-observation and self-reflection

➤ recognition of what is immutable, what is beyond our control and what we can change

➤ an ability to monitor our own reactions, emotions and behaviours and the impact they are having during coaching interventions

➤ a realistic understanding of our own strengths and weaknesses

➤ a knowledge of our own motives and needs (e.g. the need to be liked, the need for control, the need to be seen as an expert and to give advice, unresolved emotional issues, etc.)

➤ recognition of our own prejudices

➤ the ability to accept criticism and feedback without becoming defensive

➤ awareness of transference situations (where the coachee unconsciously projects onto the coach qualities belonging to a significant other in his or her life, often a parent figure) and countertransference situations (where the coach overidentifies with the coachee)

➤ knowledge of our own fears and anxieties about coaching, such as fear of failure, confrontation, challenge or success.

2 A capacity to inspire others

A coach will not be able to inspire coachees to do in their lives what he or she is unable or unwilling to accomplish in his or her own life. A coach is aware of coachees' developmental needs and inspires them to identify their passions and values, strive to attain their highest goals and fulfil their destinies.

A successful coach elicits discipline and intensity through an individual's inner motivation rather than outside pressure. It is the coach's faith that enables the individual to develop his or her own potential. The coach enables coachees to work through any restrictions or constraints that prevent them from achieving their goals.

Not everyone has the natural ability to inspire. Some individuals may excel at nurturing and supporting others through a life they may consider difficult and painful. To inspire is to lead through example and through the belief that life is rich, meaningful and challenging. A winning coach inspires and encourages risk-taking and establishes a safety net for those who falter or fail. Failure is feedback—an opportunity to grow. Coaches and coachees who are not willing to risk failure risk stagnating instead. A truly inspiring, transformational coach will:

➤ live and act according to stated values and beliefs

➤ operate from a model of 'strengths' rather than deficits

➤ recognise strengths where others see weaknesses

➤ build insight and motivation so coachees can determine and focus on the goals that 'pull' them towards action and truly reflect their values, dreams and aspirations

➤ help individuals recognise previously unseen possibilities that exist within their current life circumstances

➤ continue to set higher standards for himself or herself and others

➤ provide a role model

➤ challenge and take individuals out of their 'comfort zone' to achieve greater success and satisfaction

➤ be willing to accept responsibility for setbacks and failures

➤ show a commitment to competence

➤ demonstrate the ability to inspire commitment to change in the individual, and promote persistence to ensure that the end result is sustained learning and behavioural change

➤ reveal a passion to help others learn, grow and perform to their maximum potential.

3 A capacity to build relationships

A coach is someone who is seen as being accessible, friendly and trustworthy and who treats coaching as a high priority. Coaches must be supportive and approachable and be seen to give 100 per cent of themselves. They must be totally focused on the task and non-attached to the outcome. The success of coaching depends to a great extent on the nature of the relationship between the coach and the coachee.

Coaches should encourage independent, healthy individuals who can make choices and determine the quality of relationships they desire. As coaching frequently centres on the coachee's relationship building skills (personal or work-related), the coach provides a model for building effective and sustainable partnerships. A good coach will:

➤ take time to get to know the individual

➤ build rapport, trust and openness

➤ establish credibility by a strong belief in his or her purpose, and show strength in adversity

➤ establish confidentiality of the relationship

➤ show patience and have reasonable expectations, understanding that personal growth is sometimes slow, uneven and perhaps difficult

➤ earn the trust and belief of the individual in order to provide the necessary amount of support and challenge

➤ resist the urge to deliver insights and allow the individual to discover his or her own insights/answers

➤ offer unconditional support and appreciation of the individual's uniqueness and worth

➤ encourage mutual discussion and problem solving.

4 A capacity to be flexible

Unlike a trainer with a set curriculum, a coach's agenda is flexible. Together with the coachee, the coach establishes priorities and goals and develops an action plan to achieve behavioural change. Yet this agenda is not set in stone and an effective coach can adapt and go 'off course' to meet the changing needs of the individual. The coachee's priorities, not those of the coach, determine the agenda.

A coach has the capacity to move at someone else's pace and to know when to switch strategies to suit the individual. A successful coach is also able to adjust to the various ways individuals cope with information, change and feedback. For instance, in some circumstances change may be rapid, and the coachee may make a 'breakthrough' early in the process. At other times change may be slow and erratic, and the coach will require patience and persistence to maintain his or her own momentum and to support and encourage the coachee during a difficult period of growth.

Some examples of flexibility include being able to:

➤ recognise when to be supportive or challenging, tough or compassionate

➤ adjust easily to the agenda of the coachee

➤ recognise different personal styles and adapt to these styles

➤ vary the style of coaching to suit the individual

➤ receive feedback and make changes in attitude and behaviour

➤ be self-confident and appropriately humble.

5 A capacity to communicate

Many individuals undertake coaching when they have difficulties relating to co-workers, peers and clients. Others seek personal coaches to guide and support them through various transitions, including relationship or partnership difficulties. A coach should possess a strong range of inter-personal and communication skills and show sensitivity and patience with the anxieties of others.

A coach empathises with the coachee, showing an appreciation and understanding of his or her world view, values, fears and dreams. A coach listens, asks provocative and timely questions, gives clear, straightforward feedback and elicits regular feedback. Importantly, a coach must be willing to communicate truthfully, and clearly identify unacceptable performance despite any defensiveness on the part of the coachees and any fear of embarrassing them or their not liking it.

Some requisite interpersonal skills include:

➤ *Authenticity*   Coaches are sincere and honest. They attempt to *be* what they think and say. They do not hide behind masks or roles and are willing to self-disclose when it will facilitate the coachee's self-exploration and self-awareness.

➤ *Empathy*   A coach can experience and understand the world of the coachee and meet his or her needs with concern and understanding. Yet such empathy is non-possessive.

➤ *Unconditional support*   The coach appreciates the individual's uniqueness and worth.

➤ *Insight*   A successful coach has the ability to perceive, understand and generalise from personal experience and professional sources.

➤ *Curiosity*   A coach is genuinely interested in human nature and is sensitive to the personal wellbeing of others.

➤ *Ability to listen*   A coach listens more than he or she talks. The coach asks questions, reflects, clarifies and gives feedback.

➤ *Ability to use humour*   Coaches should be able to laugh at themselves and their idiosyncrasies and to be light-hearted.

➤ *Ability to tolerate ambiguity*   Coaches require the ability to cope with unfamiliar territory, with paradox and uncertainty underscored by a trust in self and the process of coaching.

➤ *Courage and willingness to offer feedback*   Coaches provide ongoing feedback, both positive and negative, for the purpose of helping their clients change and grow.

➤ *Ability to confront others*   A coach does not hesitate to challenge coachees regarding their unused potential for the good of the individual and the organisation.

6 A capacity to be forward-looking

Coaching is about action. Self-exploration, insight and self-awareness always occur in the context of action: What can we do to achieve this goal or change this behaviour? What will the coachee do with this new understanding? A coach does not stall at the starting post or get bogged down examining feelings, objections or fears of failure. Even if coachees are initially unsuccessful, a good coach keeps them active and at the same time looks for blocks where they may be stuck and where they are being ineffective. The coach believes that people have the necessary intelligence, creativity and drive to move forward and succeed, but that they may require help accessing it. Forward-looking coaches:

➤ emphasise the here and now

➤ are future oriented, recognising the past only as it impinges on the present

➤ identify openings that will allow a meaningful result in the shortest period of time

➤ act even when uncertain of the outcome

➤ work with the coachee to establish stretch goals and action plans

➤ are goal oriented and outcome oriented

➤ encourage the coachee to accept responsibility for his or her own future development.

7 A capacity for discipline

Change is sometimes painful. Regardless of the ultimate outcome and benefits, individuals frequently resist change, fearing what they might lose in the process. Coaching is about development, growth and change. A coach shows dedication and stamina, and a disciplined focus on goals and action plans that will ultimately effect the desired, sustained behavioural change. Discipline is manifested through the following:

➤ focusing intently on achieving the goals, tempered by an empathic awareness of the coachee's insecurities and blockages regarding change

➤ focusing on the task at hand, despite setbacks and the possibility of failure

➤ resisting pressures from self, the coachee or management for 'a quick fix'

➤ recognising circumstances when a coachee may not be able to change, and being willing to support the coachee to focus his or her energies elsewhere

➤ adhering to the structure of the coaching sessions

➤ always matching and adjusting to the coachee's pace of learning and change.

8 A capacity to manage professional boundaries

Coaching is not a panacea for everyone and not all individuals are suitable candidates for coaching. It is important to select individuals for coaching and to establish 'a good fit' between the coach and the coachee. Some individuals may not be open to learning and change, and coaching, therefore, may not be the most effective response.

A coach cannot be all things to all people. No coach knows enough about everything to help everyone. Good coaches are always aware of their capabilities and limitations and display the following characteristics:

➤ the ability to recognise whether coaching is the best option for the particular individual

➤ the ability to appreciate whether change is within the control of the individual and will lead to the desired results, such as more satisfying relationships, a balanced lifestyle, career enhancement, and so on

➤ the ability to know when not to take on a client

➤ the ability to recognise when the coaching issue is beyond their competence.

9 A capacity to diagnose issues and find solutions

A coach has to gather information regarding the coachee in order to determine the specific needs that require addressing. While assessment and interviewing techniques are learned skills, successful coaches exhibit certain qualities that allow them to use this information creatively in order to diagnose problems or issues and provide exciting solutions. These qualities include:

➤ a genuine sense of enquiry

➤ intuition as to what is 'wrong' and what can be done

➤ an ability to apply theory to practical situations

➤ creativity—offering fresh perspectives and new insights

➤ unique and novel problem-solving abilities.

10 A capacity for business

Coaches not only sell an intangible product, they also sell themselves. In an increasingly competitive marketplace, coaches are selected for the quality of their services as well as for their ability to articulate the need for, and the specific benefits of, their coaching programs. In order to sell themselves successfully and succeed in business, coaches require:

➤ ambition and a strong drive to be successful

➤ a strong belief in themselves and their products

- the ability to be a self-starter—the ability to make things happen
- a 'contagious' enthusiasm for coaching
- a 'can do' confident attitude
- energy—the stamina to complete the task
- resilience and determination in the face of rejection
- the willingness to take on new risks and challenges and enter the unknown
- a creative 'entrepreneurial spirit' that constantly challenges and inspires them to develop newer and more successful selling strategies
- a commitment to a vision and business goals
- a competitive desire to win new business.

As a coach, at some time or another, the above qualities will be called upon. To improve the likelihood of business success, it would be useful for prospective coaches to take an inventory of these qualities so that they can identify their strengths and weaknesses.

Life skills coaching

How to choose the right life skills coach

The emphasis of this book is on business and executive coaching. Yet, increasingly, many professionals are turning to coaches for help with life skills issues that impact on their work performance. Some business and executive coaches are equipped to coach in areas that are more aligned to personal life than working life, while others prefer to concentrate on work issues. The boundaries are not clearly defined. For example, some coaches work with professionals on life skills areas as they affect business and careers; others work with individuals to achieve a balance between life and work; and others may choose to specialise in life skills issues.

Before choosing the right life coach, it is necessary first to undergo a process of self-appraisal and ask 'What do I need from a coach?' You may ask questions such as: How can I have a more satisfying relationship with my partner? How can I better balance work and recreation or leisure time? How can I achieve in retirement the goals that have eluded me in my working life? How can I further develop my spiritual side?

The following case study illustrates the role of a life skills coach in the life of a successful professional lawyer. At this stage of her career, B. H. does not recognise a need for a coach to develop or enhance her work skills. However, she accepts that she could benefit from a specialist coach to assist her in those aspects of her life that are impacting indirectly on her work performance.

Case Study

Coaching for relationships

B. H. is a single, 42-year-old senior partner in a successful city law firm. She is financially secure and owns her own city apartment close to the firm's offices. However, for the past few years she has felt increasingly out of touch with her family and friends and lacking a spiritual base. She has decided, at this stage of her career, to take charge and better balance her professional and personal life. She has short-listed two life skills coaches—one is a singles coach and the other is a spiritual coach. Some of the issues and questions she wishes to deal with include: How can I find equality in romantic relationships? Is Mr Right a romantic fallacy? Why is it difficult for accomplished women to find an equal partnership? How can I find time to get in contact with my spiritual self? Some of the criteria B. H. has listed for a coach include openness, frankness, sensitivity and flexible availability.

Coaching is currently unregulated. Individuals, therefore, have no professional criteria on which to choose a suitable life skills coach. We suggest the following guidelines, shown in Figure 2.1.

Credentials

> What is the coach's professional training and background?

> How much experience does the coach have in my particular area of interest?

> Does the coach have training in counselling skills?

> Can the coach clearly articulate the differences between counselling and coaching?

> Would the coach recognise 'a clinical issue' and does the coach have the necessary resources to refer out for therapy?

Skills

  ▸ Which coaching models does the coach use?

  ▸ Does the coach have an understanding of adult learning principles, and advocate self-learning and independence?

  ▸ Does the coach have goal setting and action planning skills?

  ▸ How will the coach identify my needs?

  ▸ How will the coach establish goals?

  ▸ Is the action plan consistent with my lifestyle?

Interpersonal skills

  ▸ Do I feel comfortable with the coach, or vulnerable and unsure?

  ▸ Does the coach exhibit maturity, humour, sincerity and trustworthiness?

  ▸ Does the coach show flexibility and a balance between supporting and challenging me?

Contract

  ▸ What is the cost of the coaching sessions?

  ▸ Are the sessions held in suitable conditions?

  ▸ Is there an agreed upon time frame for coaching with regular re-evaluations built into the process?

  ▸ Is there any homework?

  ▸ How will success be measured?

Ethics

  ▸ Is the coach bound by a code of ethics?

  ▸ Can the coach ensure complete confidentiality?

  ▸ Do I have any redress if I am dissatisfied with the coaching services?

Figure 2.1   Some questions to ask a life skills coach

Coaching assessment audit

This brief checklist exercise is useful for practising coaches, potential coaches and clients who are in the process of hiring or appraising a coach. For each of the listed coaching attributes, select the answer that best describes how frequently the coach displays the following competencies.

Checklist

Coaching competencies	Usually	Sometimes	Never
A capacity for self-awareness	☐	☐	☐
A capacity to inspire others	☐	☐	☐
A capacity to build relationships	☐	☐	☐
A capacity to be flexible	☐	☐	☐
A capacity to communicate	☐	☐	☐
A capacity to be forward-looking	☐	☐	☐
A capacity for discipline	☐	☐	☐
A capacity to manage professional boundaries	☐	☐	☐
A capacity to diagnose issues and find solutions	☐	☐	☐
A capacity for business	☐	☐	☐

PART TWO
Coaching in the workplace

Business coaching

Key points

- ➤ The growth of business coaching
- ➤ People and business
- ➤ Some benefits of business coaching
- ➤ Some key business coaching applications
- ➤ Businesses in the twenty-first century
- ➤ Customer satisfaction
- ➤ Strategic planning and coaching
- ➤ Negotiation and coaching
- ➤ Finding the right business coach
- ➤ Coaching tools for the business coach

The growth of business coaching

Businesses today are facing changes that are happening at an incredibly exponential rate. Change has overtaken every company, and some writers claim that the notion of programs to institute and deal with organisational change is artificial and 'faddish'. Change *is* the business environment, not some external program.

Business owners have to perform a difficult and sometimes seemingly impossible juggling act. They have to hire high-performing, self-motivated staff, manage the day-to-day affairs of the company, plan for the future and keep customers, employees and investors satisfied. Increasingly, businesses are finding it difficult to achieve, gain and maintain a competitive advantage. This is borne out by the fact that one-third of the Fortune 500 companies from 1970 had disappeared by 1983, and today, only 13 of the original top 50 Fortune 500 companies remain. In the United States, 50 per cent of small new companies close down within four years, 70 per cent in eight years and 98 per cent within 11 years. Of all new companies, 50 per cent fold within the first five years. These rather astounding figures are not unique to the United States. Bankruptcies in Canada have doubled during the past few years and the average life span of companies in Japan and most of Europe is now 12.5 years. Clearly, many current business strategies and competencies are inadequate to meet the rapidly changing global marketplace.

It is no surprise then, that more and more companies and organisations, both public and private, are turning to business coaches to help them navigate through the constant changes and demands of the marketplace. Business coaching is now a widely accepted term, with increasing numbers of businesses recognising its benefits and applications. Business coaching can be applied to all types of businesses. As mentioned earlier, it ranges from one-on-one executive coaching and team coaching in large corporations and public organisations, to coaching managers and owners of small- to medium-sized companies in both individual and group formats. Our coaching practice has a specialist business coaching unit. Our work has ranged, for example, from working for global organisations and coaching their individual executives for leadership skills, to coaching dentists and medical practitioners to improve customer service, and helping small Web-development companies to increase their market share.

Business coaching has emerged as a critical activity to support individual and team development and provide new directions in customer satisfaction, productivity and overall organisational effectiveness. It is a professional service for organisations wishing to master continuing change and achieve their business objectives. Like other competitive individuals such as athletes who hire a personal coach to improve and enhance their performance, players in the business game are appreciating that they too require coaching in acquiring, maintaining and updating their skills and competencies.

Globally, more and more businesses and organisations are demanding coaching support, coaching resources and services. Through our Global Business Coaching Resource Network, we are increasingly asked to provide master specialist coaches and conduct learning and development audits of companies and organisations. Businesses of all types are recognising the need to audit and assess the strengths and weaknesses in their organisational learning structures, to benchmark their learning and development capabilities and to enhance their coaching skills.

Coaching, as we reiterate throughout this book, is about change, and change entails learning. Learning is not just about obtaining knowledge; it requires being able to demonstrate this knowledge by taking action. The business coach's role is to observe and provide an objective perspective on the issues and problems—on what is working and what is not working. A coach is not affected by internal company politics and can recognise patterns and anticipate negative trends before the owner or manager does. The coach asks questions in a manner that facilitates a discussion of possibilities and opportunities, and guides and supports individuals through the process of personal and organisational performance and development.

Business coaches aim to develop more competent, effective and productive individuals. Business coaching is transformational. Whereas training impacts on people's ability to do the job, they often continue to 'push and pull the same wagon'. Coaches move business owners and leaders into an 'adult' mode of operation.

People and business

People *are* the business and people, not processes, contribute the most to the success or failure of an organisation. The potential of any business is a function of the people in the business. Yet, many organisations and businesses emphasise learning in relation to process or systems change and give scant attention to the emotional states of those surviving the changes. The 'human factor' in many companies is frequently ignored, resulting in insecure, demoralised staff lacking in vision and enthusiasm. Many companies put a great deal of effort into financial deals but neglect communication, compatibility and trust—and all these factors affect productivity.

Systems and people

A medium-sized call centre was experiencing problems after introducing a new incoming call system. There were constant complaints from inbound callers, staff complained about the unworkability of the new system and the general standard of service had deteriorated. The call centre employed a telephony consulting company, which in turn engaged P. Z. to coach their consulting technical support people on how to coach the end users (i.e. team leaders and agents). However, it quickly became clear to P. Z. that the problem was not related to systems or procedures but was in fact a 'people' issue. The new system had resulted in several staff being laid off and the remaining staff felt insecure and resentful because they had not been consulted about the changes. Consequently, the coaching intervention also focused on working with the staff to accept change, and encouraging and supporting management to adopt a more participative, consultative style of management.

As we emphasise throughout this book, self-knowledge and self-awareness play a crucial role in being a successful coach and a successful business person. Coaching is about developing character, personal maturity, ethics and vision. It is about an individual becoming the best human being possible. The foundation of the business coaching experience lies in the coachee's discovery of his or her true self and building a sense of community within a company and with clients. Applying such wisdom to business is likely to result in good client and employee relationships, as well as increased market share and productivity.

It is becoming increasingly apparent that our model for organisational change and growth is fundamentally flawed. Traditional methods of team building and bonding have failed to create a genuine sense of camaraderie, common cause and shared vision. For example, recent surveys have found that many line workers, managers and executives live in fear in their work lives—they fear failure and loss of their jobs—and only 35 per cent of workers feel that the level of trust between managers and senior managers is satisfactory. The organisation of the twenty-first century has to become a team of people with well-developed interpersonal and communication skills. These individuals should understand and appreciate differences, trust and support each other and work with commitment and energy. Business coaching can play a vital part in these transformational changes and can result in:

➤ increased productivity

➤ a happier, more creative work environment

➤ highly satisfied customers

➤ a trusting, supportive climate.

Some benefits of business coaching

The benefits of business coaching are numerous, and range from reducing hours at work and developing stronger relationships with clients, to expanding and developing a wider market base. For convenience, we have grouped the benefits of business coaching into two categories: strategic or bottom-line benefits and personal or interpersonal benefits (see Figure 3.1). Of course, these categories overlap in that interpersonal relationships as well as intrapersonal skills are central to any business enterprise.

Some key business coaching applications

As mentioned above, business coaching is applicable to all types of businesses and takes myriad forms. The following list, therefore, is in no way intended to be exhaustive. We are simply highlighting some of the major areas in which we are most frequently called on to carry out coaching interventions.

➤ Strategic planning: see section later in this chapter for detailed coaching guidelines.

➤ Goal setting and action planning: companies frequently choose a course of action but are unable to operationalise their goals. The business coach is invaluable in helping business managers to clarify and prioritise their goals, and develop strategies and plans to achieve them.

➤ Identifying and coaching 'hidden employees': in the Information Age, increasing numbers of 'invisible' technical and support people are vital to many organisations. Coaches can assist managers to identify and reward such workers, foster a sense of appreciation, belonging and worth, and develop leadership principles that encourage commitment and motivation among them.

Strategic benefits

- Attract more business
- Improve customer service
- Provide structure, guidance and focus
- Monitor and evaluate actions
- Guide individuals to adopt better solutions—streamlining processes and procedures to ensure productivity and customer satisfaction
- Promote initiative and accountability—encourage and support managers and others to take responsibility for the entire organisation, not just their own jobs
- Motivate and sustain momentum
- Provide non-biased, objective advice on business decisions
- Increase awareness of resources and when to use them
- Broaden the scope of available information, ideas and solutions.

Interpersonal benefits

- Unearth and tap potential and creativity
- Coordinate career and personal life
- Increase the ability to cope with and welcome change and transitions
- Improve concentration, confidence, relaxation and decision making
- Remove performance fears and anxieties
- Eliminate unhealthy work stressors.

Figure 3.1 Strategic and interpersonal benefits of business coaching

➤ Managing in the computer age: previous styles of leadership were based on the control of information. However, in an age when employees have instant access to so much data, this approach is obsolete. Coaches can assist managers to develop skills and competencies to meet the challenges of the Information Age, such as working with or as part of a virtual team, sharing information and acting as a resource person.

➤ Networking, enlisting the support of other business owners and sharing ideas and resources.

➤ Identifying and eliminating procedures and systems that stifle staff.

➤ Helping owners and managers interface with senior management, the board and investors.

➤ Improving negotiation skills with both internal staff and external clients and customers.

➤ Identifying new market targets and future investment opportunities.

➤ Assisting with effective time management by improving an individual's time allocation and encouraging them to become more focused and organised.

Business coaching

R. M. is a 45-year-old mother of two who owns a small niche advertising company. Although financially successful, she found herself working six to seven days a week and spending minimal time with her family. While working with a business coach, R. M. recognised that her poor time-management skills and her unwillingness to delegate were two of the major causes of her work overload. As a result of coaching, she developed more effective ways to allocate her time and hired another part-time employee. Such a move allowed her to work only a five-day week and freed her to concentrate on identifying and targeting new clients. At a six-month follow-up, R. M. and her family were happier and more united and her client base was gradually expanding.

Businesses in the twenty-first century

During lectures and presentations, we are sometimes asked how coaching will affect and define organisational structures in the twenty-first century. It is generally accepted that the globalisation of the world economy has created modes of marketing and production that demand new and different organisational structures. Organisations with a strong tradition of learning and social cooperation will no doubt be the first to discover and implement twenty-first century practices. People and organisations who are unable or unwilling to learn, or who are driven by suspicion and fear based on class, ethnicity, kinship or other factors, will face major difficulties in adopting and adjusting to the necessary organisational changes.

We agree with LeKander that future, optimal forms of organisations may well be network structures that share the advantages of both large and small companies. The future probably belongs to those who have the 'social capital' and 'cognitive capital' to join the networked economy. Briefly, social capital involves trust and social cooperation. Companies with this resource, for example, can economise substantially on transaction costs that otherwise require detailed contract and enforcement mechanisms. Trust arises not from rational calculation but from religion, ethics and social culture. Through learning we can develop a predisposition to trust. Cognitive capital is the skill of learning and knowing, as shown through taking effective action and the ability to think through the processes of dialogue and communication.

Businesses and organisations of the future therefore require a new paradigm. Issues such as competency, sincerity, trust and reliability will have to be taken into account before we enter into any transaction. Companies that employ business coaches to develop and enhance their social and cognitive capital will more easily:

➤ make strong connections between customers and performers (or providers)

➤ discard layers of management, organisational barriers and complexity that are counter-productive

➤ create learning organisations capable of dealing with rapid change.

Business as change

We are contacted frequently by businesses whose major concern is that, despite structural and process changes in their organisations, there is no discernible increase in productivity. Interestingly, researchers have found that organisations with increased productivity are the ones in which managers go beyond structural change and create a sense of 'collective responsibility'. It is the way people interact and how they perceive joint undertakings that impacts most on productivity levels.

Case Study

Coaching for accountability

K. C. is the senior manager of a large national manufacturing company. The company was losing market share, staff morale was low and customer complaints were at an all time high. On the advice of a friend who had benefited from business coaching, K. C. somewhat reluctantly hired a coach. Rather than looking at interpersonal issues, the coach focused on guiding and supporting K. C. and key personnel through a series of structural changes that were aimed at increasing accountability and a sense of belonging. Managers from various departments were given broader responsibilities and were included in strategic planning sessions for all units. Previously, each business unit conducted its own staff meetings. The coach encouraged management to conduct a weekly staff meeting attended by various representatives from each unit. The coach also introduced the concept of a role-play situation where, at each meeting, a member(s) of one unit would act out some issue that was proving contentious and creating disharmony between units. The role-plays allowed each group to become more understanding of the demands and responsibilities of the other sectors. Finally, a solid team structure was introduced and rewards and incentives were based on team performance rather than individual performance.

An interesting approach to developing collective responsibility is that of open book management, which involves companies sharing information with their employees. In a business literate culture, employees become more effective if they know about some business fundamentals and processes in their company. There is a shared setting of goals and rewards, shared decision making, and employees share in business outcomes, both negative and positive. The result of open book management is that employees begin to think and care like owners.

The business world is defined by change. However, when dealing with change, many companies only pay attention to its implementation, and then midway through the process, things fall apart and regressive tendencies surface. The real challenge of change is not just to come up with a brilliant idea or strategy, but to implement it so that it is alive in the company and defines the company's culture. Change is no longer the domain of CEOs and human resource personnel. It is an issue of personal responsibility.

One way to implement change successfully is to deal with the 'transitions' that change involves. Transitions are more than just gradual changes; they are a psychological process. Coaching is critical in guiding people through transitions. Transitions involve three phases:

1   letting go of the old identity, reality and strategy

2   crossing the wilderness between the old way and the new (if this is not done, people get lost in the neutral zone and can become unfocused, confused and anxious)

3   making a new beginning and functioning effectively in a new way.

Unless individuals are coached and guided through such periods, companies often lose good staff, old problems resurface and anxiety undermines work performance, teamwork and communication. Stress levels rise and the company suffers increased absenteeism and high health care costs.

 Case Study

Coaching on personnel selection

L. G. is a business coach who specialises in working with newly hired staff and in dealing with interpersonal conflict within companies. She was employed by a small manufacturing company because it had difficulty retaining key staff. She found that staff were hired purely on their technical expertise and that scant attention was paid to personality factors or interpersonal skills. Together with the owner/manager, L. G. established a list

Case Study

of job competencies as well as desirable personality traits and work styles for each key position. Subsequent potential employees were screened against this profile and a 'goodness of fit' was determined. In addition, L. G. worked with the owner and key personnel to develop the notion of a 'work community' where trust and interpersonal skills were recognised as valuable resources integral to the success of the business.

Customer satisfaction

Many organisations are redesigning and redefining themselves in order to gain a competitive advantage, reduce costs and enhance consumer satisfaction. Much of this revolution focuses on improving the quality of the products and services provided. Yet, many companies only talk about customer service improvement, or it only translates as a gimmick to get employees to be 'nice' and customers to be 'happy'. However, many products are similar and the only way to beat the competition is to establish and meet the customers' needs before the opposition does.

Many businesses today are manager oriented rather than customer centred. When managers are accountable for individual units, rather than being involved in managing strategy processes across the company, they have a tendency to lose sight of the big picture and of the company's overall aims and vision. They can get caught up in the everyday running of particular sections or units and, as a result, collective responsibility for customer satisfaction remains in the realm of rhetoric.

Case Study

Coaching for customer satisfaction

V. T. is a business coach employed by a medium-sized IT company that was gradually losing its market share to the opposition. Despite the senior manager's rhetoric about customer service, the company showed little recognition or appreciation of consumers' needs and expectations. The marker research department was understaffed, and there was little data available on various customer groups and market segments. Customers were rarely canvassed for ideas and opinions about product development. In discussions with the senior manager, it became apparent that he and other key senior personnel were out of touch with customers and spent very little

Case Study

time interacting with them. Customers had somehow become secondary to processes and procedures. Furthermore, the majority of marketing strategies were aimed at attracting new customers, and scant attention was paid to retaining them. V. T.'s initial coaching sessions focused on working with the senior manager to redefine his notion of 'customer satisfaction' and to recognise that much of the company's policies were governed by the needs of management rather than those of customers. It was only when his attitude was transformed that he and the coach could work together on actually improving marketing strategies and delivering true customer satisfaction.

An interesting approach to customer satisfaction, and one that lends itself to coaching extremely well, is to recognise customer satisfaction as a linguistic phenomenon. Customer satisfaction is defined as a spoken or written declaration made by a customer in conversation with the business provider or others. It is a process and not just an evaluation at the end of a business transaction. It is a function of several variables that include:

➤ interactions with customers

➤ promises made in those conversations—much stress in organisations is directly related to overcommitting and an inability to monitor the status of the promises

➤ customers' expectations generated in these conversations—often, in our enthusiasm to please, we make promises that are beyond our capacity to fulfil, and consequently, customers can only feel dissatisfied when we fail to deliver

➤ actions we take consistent with the generated expectations.

Business coaches can assist the business owner to view business as a series of human interactions and commitments. In the future, acquiring and applying knowledge will become the key competitive advantage in business. It is through conversation that we manage and communicate knowledge, so developing and maintaining relationships is central to customer satisfaction and customer retention. Through conversations we learn what our customers want, and we can be creative and innovative in anticipating and meeting their changing demands.

The communication between the customer and the provider, as described in the linguistic model of customer satisfaction, mirrors the interaction between the coach and coachee/business owner. For instance, both alliances centre on sharing information, listening to the other's concerns, making a commitment to their demands and expectations, establishing goals and action plans to meet these expectations, and evaluating goal achievement and satisfaction.

Business coaching can also assist the business owner to:

➤ understand that business can be viewed as a conversation involving four linguistic actions: (a) request or offer, (b) negotiate and promise, (c) complete the exchange or work and (d) indicate acceptance and completion of the exchange

➤ improve team effectiveness by streamlining communication processes and interpersonal communication

➤ increase the level of trust and cooperation across business units

➤ understand and be pro-active in assessing breakdowns in organisational business processes

➤ discuss and understand the impact of beliefs about customers and service. Some of these beliefs include:

'The response you get is a measure of the service you provide.'

'Whatever your customer says and does is a benefit to your business.'

'There is no failure, only feedback.'

'There is a solution to every problem.' (Knight 1995)

Strategic planning and coaching

Strategic planning is a crucial factor in the survival and success of any business. However, strategic plans do not amount to anything unless there is a compelling vision driving and guiding them. A recent survey by Kepner Tregoe Inc. of Princeton, New Jersey, found that 49 per cent of American workers did not believe that their company had a plan, and 51 per cent of managers did not understand the decisions made by top management.

Strategic planning skills have been identified as an intellectual competency of top grade performers. The skills involve remaining knowledgeable about the competitive environment, market and trade dynamics, product services, technology trends and patterns of customer behaviour. Other aspects of these skills include contributing to the strategic efforts of the team and predicting where the particular industry is going in the next few years.

Early approaches to strategic planning looked at long-range plans and strategies. More recently, the notion of 'logical incrementalism', which allows for a more evolutionary, flexible approach to planning, has become popular. Yet even incremental change and successful and innovative strategic plans can lag behind other changes in business and marketing, and transformational change may be necessary. Transformational change and creative strategic planning are more likely to occur within those companies that emphasise leadership, innovation and strong market forces. Such companies are characterised by the following:

➤ They are led by visionary, enthusiastic champions.

➤ They know their customers.

➤ They unlock the potential of their staff.

➤ They deliver products and services that exceed customers' expectations (promise less and deliver more).

➤ They continually introduce differentiated products and services.

Business coaches can help a company define and clarify its direction and set long-term goals, including new target market and market strategies. Together, the coach and business owner examine and develop the company's attitude to some of the following issues:

1 *Customers and quality*   Does the business regard customers as a nuisance, or does it have a high regard for customer service and satisfaction? What plans can be set in place to enhance service and satisfaction?

2 *Staff*   Are staff empowered and given authority and autonomy? Are they part of the strategic planning process? Are their contributions encouraged and valued? If not, what can be done to change the situation?

3 *Innovation*   Does management encourage experimentation? Is a certain degree of failure tolerated or is there a cautious tendency to rely on tried and trusted methods of the past?

4 *Colleagues*   Are the predominant attitudes of colleagues those of cooperation, trust and teamwork or are individualism and competition promoted?

The business coach does not have to be an expert in the industry in which he or she is working. However, it is mandatory that the coach be familiar with the basic principles of strategic planning and how these can be applied to a specific company or organisation. One effective method to employ in any planning process is a SWOT analysis, whereby the business owner and coach analyse the company in terms of its *s*trengths, *w*eaknesses, *o*pportunities and *t*hreats.

Strengths (advantages) include what the company does well and the areas in which it is currently successful. For example:

➤ competencies in key technical areas

➤ proven marketing skills

➤ a market niche.

Weaknesses are any internal or external processes that contribute to customer dissatisfaction, low staff morale or decreased productivity. For example:

➤ no clear strategic direction

➤ ineffective internal communication systems

➤ lack of leadership in management.

Opportunities include any areas in which the business can expand. For example:

➤ new markets

➤ new staff

➤ product diversification.

Threats can include any factors that might impact negatively on the success and growth of the business. For example:

➤ lower-cost foreign competitors

➤ changes in buyer taste and demands

➤ costly regulatory and contractual requirements.

Having conducted a SWOT analysis, the coach and owner are in an ideal position to draw up a strategic plan to move the business forward. The following six-step model provides guidelines for doing this (see also Figure 3.2):

Step one Develop a statement of purpose, mission, vision and values. The document should clearly set out the following: what business you are in; why you are in this business; what you represent as a company; and where you want to position yourself in the future.

Step two   Circulate the document to everyone in the company, and ask them to make suggestions for improvement. Participative management ensures that the vision and future plans for the company are owned by everyone and are not just seen as a directive from above.

Step three   Allocate resources and support systems to ensure that the desired changes and plans are put into effect and that individuals are able to cope with the transitions involved. Such resources might include training, coaching and team building.

Step four   Conduct goal-setting sessions in all business units and include all staff. Establishing goals for each business unit clarifies what the company wishes to achieve and how this relates to the company's vision of the future.

Step five   Strategy sessions should be held to create action plans to accomplish the agreed upon goals. Goals may be short term, medium term or long term. The action plans should detail issues such as accountability, how success is to be monitored and measured, the time frames for reaching the goals, and contingency plans to cope with sudden or unexpected changes in the marketplace.

Step six   Although strategy development clearly demands reflection and careful planning sessions, some companies spend too much time in discussion and making long-term plans rather than taking action. To avoid getting caught up in, and sometimes delayed and disadvantaged by, elaborate planning, it is wise to also establish short-term compelling goals. Individuals can thereby experience success and build momentum towards realising long-term goals and vision.

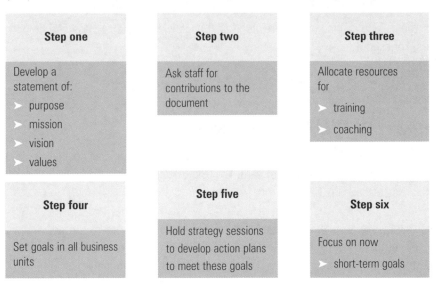

Figure 3.2   A six-step model for strategic planning

Group coaching for small businesses

S. C. is a business coach who owns his own business and specialises in group business coaching. He conducts weekly, two-hour group coaching sessions for six business owners in the local area. Coaching topics include strategic planning, networking skills and how to deal with difficult employees. The business owners work together in a spirit of collaboration—for instance, over a six-week period, a session is devoted exclusively to each participant's unique business situation and strategic planning needs. Using SWOT analysis and the guiding principles discussed in the six-step model, S. C. facilitates the group in drawing up a strategic business plan for each business owner. The free exchange of ideas, information and resources develops trust and cooperation. Importantly, it focuses and guides each participant in the process of structuring and acting on strategic business plans.

Negotiation and coaching

The ability to negotiate, either within the company or externally with customers/suppliers, is a crucial skill for business owners and managers. Negotiation, like strategic planning, has been identified as a competency of top grade performers. It involves being thoroughly prepared for the negotiating situation and knowing everything possible about the other person—his or her negotiating style, needs, leverage and vulnerabilities.

Yet, even armed with this knowledge, negotiation can be difficult, and some claim, inherently stressful. In negotiating situations, we sometimes become charged with emotion, our mind becomes clouded and we fail to process information efficiently. The end result is often unnecessary compromise or negotiation failure. We can capitulate because we are trying too hard to please the client, or because the client is exerting pressure as a result of changes in market conditions, such as more competition or tighter margins. In addition, there can be a polarisation of personalities, whereby both negotiators are inflexible and believe that they are indisputably in the right.

Common obstacles to successful negotiation include:

➤ fear of losing, which can lead to aggressive posturing or making concessions prematurely

➤ lack of appreciation and empathy for the position and point of view of the other person—criticising (either aloud or silently) and 'demonising' the opposition

➤ excessive talking, due to nervousness or a need to control and dominate the situation

➤ lack of preparation and knowledge about the other's needs and bargaining potential

➤ lack of flexibility in style—inability to match the negotiation and personality style of the other person

➤ emotional responses rather than a rational and logical approach

➤ closed mindedness—determining beforehand how to act and what to say and being unable or unwilling to adapt to the demands of the situation.

In our coaching work with small businesses and executives in large organisations, we have developed a negotiation model that isolates certain personal skills crucial to a successful outcome. This is shown in Figure 3.3. Of the personal skills listed in the figure, the three most critical for negotiation are self-awareness, emotional competence and communication skills. We discuss these three briefly below.

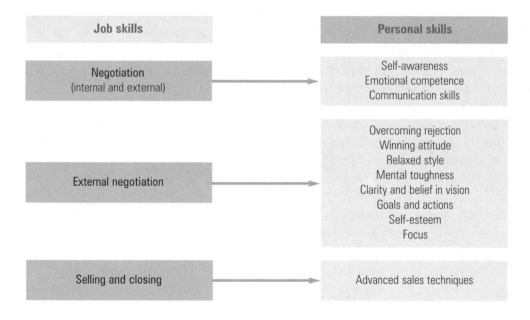

Figure 3.3   Coaching for negotiation—a model

Self-awareness

Self-awareness is an important facet of negotiating, both within the company with colleagues and other business units, and externally with customers, clients and service providers. Negotiation can occur in a trusting, supportive, relaxed and cooperative environment or in a suspicious, tense and obstructive climate. As coaches, we have found it necessary to work with coachees to determine their attitude to negotiation and how this contributes to or obstructs successful negotiation. For instance, is the individual usually cooperative, competitive or adaptable in a negotiating role? Some classic modes of negotiation include:

➤ *competing*, where the outcome is win or lose

➤ *compromising*, where a win–win outcome is likely, but not optimal

➤ *cooperating*, where both parties engage in joint problem solving so that there is a win–win outcome

➤ *accommodating*, where one negotiator capitulates and loses.

Individuals have to be aware of their negotiation philosophy and likely reactive style. The coach can facilitate self-knowledge by asking coachees to rate themselves where they fall on various dimensions and then collaboratively developing strategies to enhance or minimise these tendencies. These dimensions include:

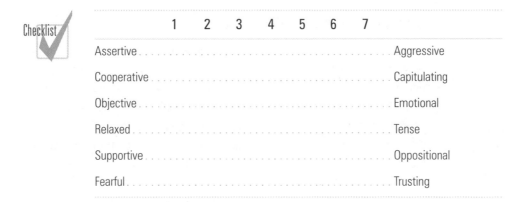

Checklist	1	2	3	4	5	6	7	
Assertive								Aggressive
Cooperative								Capitulating
Objective								Emotional
Relaxed								Tense
Supportive								Oppositional
Fearful								Trusting

In addition to coaching for self-awareness, the coach can assist the negotiator to understand and appreciate the style of the other party involved in the negotiation. Neurolinguistic programming (NLP) techniques, such as matching the other's pace and emotions, can be discussed and rehearsed in coaching sessions.

Emotional competence

In coaching for negotiation skills, the coach has to work with the coachee to develop emotional control. As noted above, negotiation is more likely to have a satisfactory outcome if it is conducted in a rational rather than an emotional climate. The issue of emotional control centres on the ability of the coachee to separate his or her ego from the product or object of negotiation. Sometimes such implied objectivity may be difficult—for instance, if the individual has been involved in the designing or packaging of a product and the packaging is unpopular. Yet this separation is vital if negotiations are not to get bogged down by damaged egos and wounded pride.

Communication skills

Although coaching for communication skills is discussed in depth in Chapter 8, it is perhaps useful here to highlight some salient features of communication as they apply in a negotiation context. Building rapport quickly and easily is a vital negotiating skill. The coach can guide the coachee in the use of non-verbal signals that can set the stage for a constructive and relaxed encounter. Role-plays and rehearsals should focus on the use of the voice—pitch, tone, volume, pace and rhythm. The coachee should be aware of the impact of his or her appearance and what information it conveys. Finally, listening and questioning skills, as well as the use of silence, should be examined and developed.

Case Study

Coaching for negotiation skills

R. W. is a 37-year-old manager in a large financial services company. He was recently promoted to a position that involves frequent and often critical negotiations. Senior management employed a business coach to work with R. W. because he was experiencing difficulties in his new role. Although well schooled in the techniques of negotiation (he had attended an intensive training program prior to assuming his new job), clients complained that he was too confrontational, even sometimes intimidating. First, the coach worked with R. W. to develop some appreciation of the other negotiator's position—R. W. tended to view all the 'opposition' as intractable, exploitative and inflexible. Second, the coach and R. W. discussed the possibility and benefits of aiming for a win–win outcome and how this could be achieved without capitulating. The third focus of the coaching alliance

Case Study

was to modify R. W.'s aggressive stance as portrayed in his verbal and non-verbal behaviours. This involved role-plays of negotiation scenarios where R. W. played the 'opposition' as well as himself. Although initially hesitant, even scornful of the 'soft approach' advocated by the coach, R. W. gradually recognised and appreciated its potential. Over a period of two months he successfully modified his negotiating style and vindicated management's choice and belief in his capabilities.

Finding the right business coach

There are certain qualities that characterise successful coaches. These are discussed in Chapter 2 and include self-awareness, the ability to inspire and the ability to diagnose issues and find solutions. However, while many personal attributes and skills are generic to all types of coaching, business coaching demands additional coaching competencies and expertise.

What to look for in a business coach

1   *Interpersonal competencies*   Is the coach able to generate trust; enable and support commitment; generate new actions through speaking and listening skills; observe and intervene and manage moods and emotions to allow for new possible actions to take place?

2   *Commitment to customer service*   Does the coach have a genuine commitment to your customers? Particularly, does the coach have a working model of 'customer satisfaction'?

3   *Strategic planning skills*   Does the coach have a knowledge of, and experience in, long-term and short-term strategic planning? Can he or she relate this experience to your specific business?

4   *Exclusivity*   Is the coach working with any of your direct competitors? It could be useful to contract with the coach so that that he or she will not take on a competitor as a client as long as your coaching agreement is in effect.

5   *Availability*   Is the coach available so that you can check in regularly? Some coaches offer on-site individual coaching, telephone coaching or e-mail coaching. Choose which format best suits your needs and make sure the coach is available on your terms.

6   *Business expertise*   Does the coach have an understanding of your business? For example, if you are a family business owner/manager, you should determine whether the coach understands the unique stresses involved in running a family business and can work with you to deal effectively with family dynamics and other family business issues.

7   *Credentials, training and experience*   Where was the coach trained? Can the coach differentiate between coaching and counselling issues? What is the coach's experience in your particular niche area? What does the coach know about your organisation's values and vision?

Skills

Although there are numerous coaching skills, the questions below serve to highlight some of the requisite skills of a successful business coach.

➤   What tools and processes does the coach employ? Do they have proven validity? Are they relevant to your company?

➤   Does the coach know how you best learn, for example, by reflection or activity?

➤   Does the coach have creative insights to offer you about yourself and your organisation?

➤   Does the coach exhibit creative problem-solving abilities?

➤   Does the coach have the requisite skills in goal setting and action planning?

➤   How will your performance be benchmarked?

Personal qualities

The personal qualities of a successful coach are discussed in Chapter 2. However, the following questions can assist in determining whether the coach is able to meet your specific personal and organisational needs.

➤   Will the coach's personal style fit in with your organisation?

➤   Is the coaching work driven by your personal and organisational needs rather than by the coach's agenda or needs?

➤   Does the coach show the confidence and flexibility to deal with top executives in the organisation?

➤   Does the coach have the ability to relate to individuals at all levels of your organisation?

➤   Is the coach trustworthy and sincere?

➤   Is the coach flexible regarding session times?

Contract

A coaching contract should encompass the following points:

➤ Does the coach negotiate openly and directly regarding what coaching services will be provided and what they entail?

➤ Is there an agreed upon trial period of coaching, with regular reviews?

➤ What is the cost of coaching? Are there any hidden costs? What is the system of payment?

Ethics

Coaching is, as yet, an unregulated profession, so prospective clients should determine the coach's ethical stance. Some questions to ask include:

➤ Is the coach bound by a code of ethics?

➤ What are the parameters of confidentiality? (Will the coach be meeting with others in your organisation, for example your boss or team mates? Is there a system of formal reporting? How frequently? To whom? What information is contained in these reports?)

Coaching tools for the business coach

Developing rapport and establishing trust and reliability are core features of any successful coaching alliance. Yet, as mentioned above, coaching in the business arena demands expertise beyond interpersonal skills. The coach has to build a relationship with the business owner/manager that will assist the individual to be receptive to recommended strategies and directions.

In order to establish a receptive learning climate, the coach first has to build a profile of the person he or she is working with in the business setting. We have developed the following profile based on personality, leadership, cognitive style and communication style as part of a structured interview to assess coachees on several dimensions. The profile is, in many regards, a preliminary form of 'investigation'. Our experience shows that formal questionnaires are an important starting point for opening up discussion on issues and influences that otherwise can remain unrecognised. However, a significant amount of valuable information about the client is also gathered during 'structured' dialogue and conversation.

Personality profile

Rate yourself on the following dimensions:

	1	2	3	4	5	6	7	
High self-awareness								Low self-awareness
Conservative								Non-conformist
Bold								Hesitant
Diffident								Self-confident
People oriented								Task oriented
Passive								Dominating
Careful								Risk-taking
Pragmatic								Idealistic
Assertive								Tentative
Tolerant								Impatient
Optimistic								Pessimistic
Emotional								Logical

Leadership profile

Rate yourself on the following dimensions:

	1	2	3	4	5	6	7	
Visionary								Pragmatic
Confrontational								Laissez-faire
Security-oriented								Innovative
Remote								Influencing
Low key								Charismatic
Hierarchical								Empowering
Individualist								Team player
Flexible								Rigid
Reluctant								Enthusiastic
Initiator								Follows through

Checklist

Cognitive style

Rate yourself on the following dimensions:

	1	2	3	4	5	6	7	
Curious								Narrow-focused
Feelings-oriented								Analytical
Factual								Imaginative
Cautious								Likes challenge
Results-oriented								Process-oriented
Self-sufficient								Solicits ideas
Internal locus of control								External locus of control
Easily distracted								Focused
Persevering								Easily bored
Thoughtful, considered								Makes decisions quickly
Rapid processor of data								Gradual processor of data
Likes big picture								Interested in details
Solicits feedback								Avoids appraisal

Communication style

Rate yourself on the following dimensions:

	1	2	3	4	5	6	7	

Gregarious . . . . Shy

Flamboyant . . . . Reserved

Poised . . . . Casual

Spontaneous . . . . Controlled

Animated . . . . Withdrawn

Self-disclosing . . . . Non-self-disclosing

Trusting . . . . Guarded

Good eye contact . . . . Little eye contact

Friendly . . . . Distant/aloof

Varies voice pitch . . . . Speaks in a
                                                                                                       monotone

Individual profile summary

Name: . . . .   Coach: . . . .

Personality traits . . . .

Leadership qualities . . . .

Cognitive style . . . .

Communication style . . . .

The profile the business coach constructs is a useful and necessary prelude as a means of getting to know the person he or she is coaching. Together, the coach and coachee discuss the profile and determine how it impacts on the business in general, business goals and future directions. Typically, the business person employs the coach to help with a specific issue or problem. From discussions, careful questioning and information gathering, the coach determines which issue or issues demand immediate attention. In order to develop recommendations and enlist the coachee's commitment and enthusiasm, the following model or plan is useful.

Guidelines for coaches making recommendations to clients

Issues ————————➤ Options ————————➤ Recommendations ————————➤ Goals

STAGE ONE Describe the issue or problem as you see it to the client

1 Summarise the issue succinctly and non-judgmentally

2 How does it impact on the business, in the present, short term and long term?

3 How do the individual's personal strengths and weaknesses affect the issue?

4 Is the issue a structural/organisational one?

5 Are there business opportunities the company is not exploiting?

6 To what extent do interpersonal factors contribute?

 ➤ What is the company's human potential?

 ➤ How do key personnel interact with each other?

 ➤ What is the level of trust, cooperation and support in the company?

STAGE TWO Options

1 List all possible options to the coachee.

2 What are the costs and benefits for all the options?

3 Solicit the client's options.

4 Prioritise the options and get a consensus.

5 Do a SWOT analysis of each of the major options.

STAGE THREE Recommendations

1 Describe the overall recommendations.

2 What are the benefits of the recommendations?

3 What are the disadvantages of the recommendations?

4 Elicit the coachee's response/feedback/objections and discuss.

STAGE FOUR Establish goals

1 Agree on a goal or a hierarchy of goals for the short term, medium term and long term.

2 Establish a time frame for the goals to be met.

3 Determine the parameters for success.

4 Establish monitoring, evaluation and feedback procedures.

Executive coaching

Key points

- ➤ The growth of executive coaching
- ➤ What is executive coaching?
- ➤ Types of executive coaching
- ➤ Executive derailment
- ➤ Some typical goals and benefits of executive coaching
- ➤ Successful versus unsuccessful outcomes in coaching
- ➤ Self-awareness in executive coaching
- ➤ Assessment in executive coaching
- ➤ Some coaching tools, techniques and interventions
- ➤ Coaching intervention for leadership
- ➤ Some competencies for executive coaches
- ➤ How to choose the right corporate coach
- ➤ A six-step model for executive coaching
- ➤ Life issues in executive coaching

The growth of executive coaching

While some authors suggest that executive coaching has turned into an industry overnight, the process, in fact, has been far more gradual. Executive coaching is an outgrowth of executive development programs, and the term was first used in 1985 to describe leadership development courses. Although executive coaching has been gaining widespread acceptance on the part of consulting firms since the early 1990s, it is only during the latter part of that decade that it flourished, with businesses and organisations hiring personal coaches in unprecedented numbers.

There are several reasons for the growing recognition of the need for and benefits of executive coaching. These include:

➤ an increase in executive stress and executive derailment

➤ corporate leaders today require more complex people skills

➤ executives today are subject to better and more frequent assessments of their personal skills

➤ many executives still employ a command-and-control style of management, with a resulting lack of loyalty and commitment by staff

➤ up to 60 per cent of managers assume managerial positions without any training in how to manage people

➤ training alone has proved inadequate in providing executives with the skills they need— evidence shows that a critical factor in the transfer of skills is the opportunity to practise and gain constructive feedback, and a study in the private sector found that training alone increased productivity by 22.4 per cent, whereas training and follow-up coaching increased productivity by 88 per cent

➤ with an improved economy, many companies are moving away from downsizing and de-layering, and are looking at multiskilling

➤ by necessity, in many organisations a competitive attitude has been replaced by the need to function as a collaborative team member and leader.

What is executive coaching?

There are various definitions of executive coaching, each highlighting different aspects of the process. Kilburg (1996) provides a useful and widely used definition of what is involved in executive coaching:

> 'executive coaching is defined as a helping relationship between a client who has managerial authority and responsibility in an organization and a consultant who uses a wide variety of behavioral techniques and methods to help the client achieve a mutually identified set of goals to improve his or her performance and, consequently, to improve the effectiveness of the client's organization within a formally defined coaching agreement'.

Coaching is essentially a highly personalised form of learning. It entails individually helping executives to learn and to make the most of that learning in order to bring about effective action, performance improvement and/or personal growth, as well as better business results for the organisation. Executive coaching is concerned with designing and facilitating change and continuous improvement. As such, it involves understanding and capitalising on an individual's strengths, as well as recognising and overcoming his or her weaknesses. Some of the features, misconceptions and concerns about coaching are show in Table 4.1.

Types of executive coaching

There are several forms of executive coaching, with various coaches determining their own typology. Perhaps the most comprehensive and useful categories are those developed by the Center for Creative Leadership. These include the following four classes:

1 Coaching for skills

In coaching for skills, the coaching process is specifically focused on the executive's current task. The coach helps the coachee learn specific skills, attitudes and behaviours that will directly improve work performance. Some typical skills include making a successful presentation, leading a successful team meeting, negotiating and delegating.

Features

1 It is typically a series of one-on-one interactions designed to meet the individual needs of the client, but generally focuses on personal awareness and targeted skills to improve work performance.

2 It is a process to provide executives with valid information to enable them to make well-informed choices.

3 It recognises that no two executives are alike and that each person has a unique knowledge base and learning pace and style.

4 It is a consultative, relationship-based service provided by coaches who serve as advisers and sounding boards.

5 It is about moving the executive towards increased versatility and effectiveness.

6 It involves a coach being an active resource for an executive and exploring, developing and maximising his or her potential.

Misconceptions and concerns

1 Coaching is in danger of becoming the next fad.

2 Some organisations confuse coaching with mentoring or various forms of training.

3 It is an overutilised growth industry where many self-styled and unskilled individuals are hanging out their shingles.

4 The area is unlicensed and unregulated and hence it is difficult to establish competencies and standards of practice.

5 It is often not thought through or managed very well.

6 Some management consultants are adding 'coach' to their business cards without the requisite skill and knowledge base (for example, goal setting and strategic planning).

7 Many therapists and counsellors who take on executive coaching do not have the necessary corporate expertise, and tend to keep clients in the 'feelings zone' rather than helping them to move forward towards their goals.

8 Some organisations and coaches believe that coaching can be successful in a vacuum, and fail to appreciate the necessity for establishing a culture of coaching within the organisation. As a result, many expensive and resource intensive coaching programs fail.

Table 4.1   Some features, misconceptions and concerns about executive coaching

Coaching for skills

S. E. is an executive in a large national service industry. Part of her job involves holding weekly meetings with senior managers from several departments. Increasingly, she has found that she is losing control of the meetings and rarely accomplishes the stated goals or agenda. During conversations with her coach, it became apparent that she had difficulties organising and presenting information in a logical, coherent and interesting fashion. Together, S. E. and the coach devised a program (10 weekly sessions) that involved mind-mapping techniques and videotaping simulated meetings using mind-mapping methods of planning and ordering information. Coaching for skills increased her ability to structure meetings, follow an agenda and present her ideas in a more succinct and engaging manner. S. E. reported that there was a noticeable increase in input and enthusiasm from her colleagues.

2 Coaching for performance

Coaching, in a sense, is always about performance. Performance coaching specifically involves learning that improves the executive's effectiveness in a current job. It focuses on establishing and developing executive competencies in a current position. An executive might feel that he or she could be performing better in a particular area, such as leading a team more effectively. Goals in performance coaching may not be as clear cut as in skills coaching, and a considerable amount of time in the coaching sessions can be directed towards actually clarifying the executive's goals and specific areas to address.

Coaching for performance

L. C. is a senior executive of a large, rapidly expanding manufacturing company. He feels that he could be a better leader, but has neither the time nor the inclination to pursue any formal leadership training. Because L. C. was unsure of specific areas to work on, he and the coach first developed, and then prioritised, a list of leadership competencies. Clarifying the competencies and expectations of his role was particularly useful, as L. C. previously thought that leadership qualities were innate rather than skills that could be learned. During a period of weekly sessions over a six-month period, L. C. and the coach developed goals and action plans to enhance his performance of critical leadership competencies.

Both coaching for skills and coaching for performance are sometimes subsumed under the umbrella of 'remedial coaching'. We think this term should be used with caution. First, it tends to imply a 'deficit model' that is more akin to therapy than coaching, and second, it can suggest a 'quick fix' that is essentially inimical to the aims and process of coaching.

3 Coaching for development

As the name implies, coaching for development focuses on the executive's future career or a new leadership role. It entails assessing and clarifying expectations for future growth and developing the requisite competencies. Coaching for development frequently entails a review of the executive's purpose, values and vision. It can be a more confrontational form of coaching than coaching for skills or performance. The reason for this is that it involves a considerable degree of self-awareness and self-exploration in terms of strengths and weaknesses, particularly in relation to dealing with change and the unknown.

 Case Study

Coaching for development

B. D. is a 48-year-old regional CEO of a multinational advertising agency. He is being groomed to become the national director, a role that will involve being away from home for extended periods. The promotion has resulted in a crisis of confidence, and B. D. is questioning his purpose and ability to execute his new role. Part of the difficulty is a function of the organisation's weakness in the area of succession planning. The coaching sessions, which extended over a year, focused on two areas: establishing the competencies and roles for the future position, and assessing B. D.'s strengths and weaknesses in these areas. In some instances, it was impossible for B. D. to isolate potential competencies, as the organisation was undergoing some major structural changes. Consequently, many of the coaching sessions concentrated on exploring his attitude, fears and resistance to change and developing strategies to increase his flexibility and adaptability. Recognising and working through his own barriers to change prepared B. D. to assume the new role more confidently, despite its lack of definition.

4 Coaching for the executive's agenda

Coaching for the executive's agenda involves working with executives on any personal and/or business issues they choose to nominate. In the personal arena, it could entail balancing work and family life, while organisational issues could include leading organisational change, or developing strategic planning and long-term vision. At times, there is a crossover between agenda coaching and other types of executive coaching. Typically, agenda coaching occurs in the context of a long-term coaching relationship. Once a formal coaching relationship has been established, perhaps initially for skills coaching, the coachee sets the course and direction to move to the next level of success.

 Case Study

Coaching for the executive's agenda

A. J. is a 38-year-old partner in a highly successful and busy medical practice. Although she loves her work and is regarded as highly competent, she recognises that her life is out of balance. She has two children, aged six and ten, whom she sees only briefly each day. Even on weekends, she spends time writing reports and researching papers to present at conferences. Her husband and children are becoming resentful of her absence, and she in turn feels resentful of their demands and guilty that she spends too little time with them. These conflicts are impacting on her work performance and at home she is tense and irritable. The coach and A. J. together explored her values and purpose, particularly as they related to her family life, and collaboratively developed strategies to better balance her work and home life. As a result of these sessions, she decided not to bring work home on the weekends, and adopted time management techniques to use her work time more effectively. She committed to spending an extra hour each day with the children, and scheduled more regular holidays with the family. Once these changes were put in place, A. J. reported a remarkable change in her home life and stated that she was functioning more efficiently and effectively at work.

Other areas appropriate for executive coaching interventions include:

➤ coaching executives to be coaches rather than managers (see Chapter 11 for a detailed discussion and guidelines)

➤ providing ongoing support or upgrading support during or after a training or development program

➤ working with an executive after a 360-degree performance appraisal to establish goals and develop an action plan for continuing development

➤ coaching the executive through the pitfalls and challenges of a new position.

Executive derailment

It is perhaps not generally recognised that many executives today are undergoing a turbulent period of stress and change. They face enormous demands and some are even at risk of derailment. Frequently, our Global Business Coaching Resource Network is contacted by organisations seeking specialist coaches to work in this area.

Research suggests the following four reasons for executive derailment:

1   problems with interpersonal relationships

2   failure to meet business objectives

3   failure to build and lead a high-performing team

4   inability to change or adapt to change during a transition.

Other key issues among executives include:

1   leaders need many, but have very few, opportunities for continuing development

2   personal development seldom gets priority

3   senior executives are often isolated from feedback

4   there is a need for continuing support to encourage and sustain change and growth.

Some typical goals and benefits of executive coaching

Coaching clearly lends itself to the above-mentioned concerns. Rather than addressing each of these issues individually, we have grouped the major goals and benefits of executive coaching into three classes: interpersonal competencies, skill development, and organisational capabilities. These are outlined in Table 4.2.

Interpersonal competencies

➤ Gain knowledge and insight into themselves and the organisation, which allows executives to become more flexible and versatile

➤ Acknowledge and understand feelings and apply them more effectively in the workplace to improve and develop working relationships

➤ Work through blockages and resistance to change

➤ Recognise where previous strengths (e.g. an independent, autonomous style) have become a liability (e.g. in team work)

➤ Recognise and effectively manage stress

➤ Deal with conflict, both personal and with colleagues

➤ Modify interpersonal style, such as moving from a competitive to a more collaborative stance

➤ Develop trusting relationships with clients and colleagues

➤ Develop advanced communication skills
  ➤ maximise verbal and non-verbal interactions
  ➤ listen
  ➤ give feedback (especially praise)
  ➤ understand, predict and alter patterns of communication.

Skill development

➤ Learn and improve leadership skills—recognise and develop leadership competencies, for example increase awareness of diverse leadership styles

➤ Expand knowledge base of skills and competencies for career growth

➤ Clarify values, goals and choices and develop career satisfaction

➤ Develop better learning strategies

➤ Increase the learning curve in a new position

➤ Enhance entrepreneurial skills

➤ Improve presentation skills

➤ Maximise goal setting, and prioritise and manage time more efficiently

➤ Develop strategic planning skills such as how to plan and monitor projects more effectively

➤ Improve delegation skills.

Organisational capabilities

➤ Direct and support organisational change—a Harvard Review survey found that practising coaches rated 'dealing better with change' as the number one skills focus for future coaches

➤ Improve ability to manage an organisation, for instance strategic planning, negotiation and problem solving

➤ Lead re-engineering, restructuring or downsizing initiatives

➤ Increase productivity

➤ Strategically reposition the organisation in the marketplace.

Table 4.2   The major goals and benefits of executive coaching

Successful versus unsuccessful outcomes in coaching

To a certain extent, the success of a coaching intervention is a function of achieving the stated goals *via* the development and execution of an action plan. Yet the success of coaching is also related to the coaching process itself, and importantly, to what the coachee attributes success. Such attributions include:

➤ the degree to which the coach provides a supportive relationship

➤ the extent to which the coach stimulates the coachee to think, feel and explore new attitudes and behaviours

➤ the coach's skill in assisting the coachee to work through resistance to change

➤ the coach's capacity to deal with paradox and contradictions

➤ the coach's ability to provide resources and expertise from industry experience to broaden the coachee's knowledge base and options.

However, some coaching sessions can prove unhelpful and unproductive both from the coach's and the coachee's points of view. Some potential reasons for a negative outcome and some suggested guidelines to deal with these are discussed below.

➤ The coach may have a *tendency to prescribe simplistic solutions to complex organisational or life/balance issues*

What to do Particularly early on in a coaching relationship, coaches may have a tendency to try to prove their competency and feel compelled or trapped into offering advice on subjects beyond their knowledge. This pitfall can be avoided if the coach clearly delineates his or her role and expertise with the coachee and remembers that a coach is not necessarily an expert who provides answers, but a resource person whose function is to evoke answers from the coachee. The coach should freely admit to his or her limitations, however difficult that might be.

➤ *Coachees may have major interpersonal difficulties that impede the development of a trusting and satisfactory working relationship with the coach*

What to do It is important that the coach first determine whether the unproductive relationship is a function of his or her particular coaching style, gender or being assigned to a reluctant coachee. If the problem is more deep-seated and cannot be resolved in the coaching sessions, the coach should refer the person to a therapist with whom issues of trust and relatedness can be explored and worked through.

➤ *The coach and coachee may have unrealistic goals and expectations*

What to do   Similar to giving unqualified advice, a coach can sometimes respond to pressure from the coachee and his or her organisation and fail to establish realistic goals. One way for coaches to overcome this temptation (often the failing of an enthusiastic, novice coach) is to follow strict guidelines and a model for setting strategic and attainable goals. While a detailed discussion of goal setting is provided in Chapter 7, a simple model for the coach and coachee to follow is:

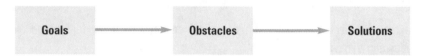

➤ *The coach may share his or her opinions too early*

What to do   Coaches should remember that coaching is 80 per cent listening and 20 per cent talking. Sharing their opinions prematurely may indicate to the coachee that they are not listening or that they have 'off-the-shelf' remedies and strategies for all occasions.

➤ *The coach may fail to follow through on monitoring and homework*

What to do   It is important to build a monitoring process into any coaching situation. Keeping records of what is agreed upon in each coaching session, holding the coachee to that commitment and reviewing each session keeps both parties on track.

➤ *The coach may respond to self-imposed pressure or perceived pressure from the coachee and his or her organisation to achieve quick results, and the outcome will be superficial rather than sustained behavioural change*

What to do   As coaching is a relatively young discipline, part of the coach's role is to educate coachees and organisations about the nature of coaching. Coaching is about change, and change can be slow, difficult and resisted. Many of our habits are deeply ingrained and changing them is often a time-consuming and gradual process.

➤ *The coach may work with a coachee to achieve organisational change in the absence of organisational support and resources*

What to do   Part of the coach's role may be to try to develop a culture of coaching in an organisation. In order to do this, it has to be established from the outset just what mandate and resources the coach has to involve other individuals and departments/sections in coaching. In their absence, the coach should inform the client of the likely negative repercussions on the coaching assignment.

➤ *The coach may fail to tie coaching, particularly if it is in the area of interpersonal skills, to work performance*

What to do   Many executives are dismissive of the so called 'soft skills'. The coach has to clearly relate coaching to job performance, or the executive will lack commitment.

➤ *The coach and/or coachee may be lacking in self-awareness*

What to do   Of all the above-mentioned possible pitfalls in executive coaching, the issue of self-awareness on the part of the coach and coachee is perhaps the most critical. The importance of self-awareness to the coaching alliance is discussed in the following section.

 Case Study

An unsuccessful coaching intervention

H. D. is a 50-year-old executive in a large government organisation. Despite her knowledge and technical experience, she is seriously lacking in assertiveness. Her voice is soft and tentative, her body language is defensive and closed and her general demeanour is one of uncertainty and apology. Part of her job description is to make presentations to international prospective and established clients. The company employed a coach to work with H. D. to improve her assertiveness, especially in the context of critical upcoming presentations. There was a certain urgency to the task, so the coach and H. D. hastily worked together to improve her presentation skills (voice exercises, videotaping, role-plays, etc.) and her general level of assertiveness. However, despite the coach's expertise, and H. D.'s seeming commitment, there was no measurable change in her behaviour even after nine coaching sessions. Senior management was frustrated and impatient, so the coach confronted H. D. about the lack of progress. In essence, H. D.'s behaviour was chiefly a function of a repressive, fearful upbringing. The coach, anxious to meet management's demands (this was the coach's first client in the organisation), had failed to establish the reasons behind H. D.'s behaviour and had set unrealistic goals and expectations. In turn, H. D., somewhat lacking in self-awareness and, in turn, eager to please the coach and management, had been reluctant to expose the depth of the problem and had complied with, rather than committed to, the 'agreed upon' goals and action plans. However, although the coaching intervention was unsuccessful in terms of its stated goals, H. D. gained some insights into herself and was considering seeing a therapist to work through some of her issues.

Self-awareness in executive coaching

The coach

As detailed in Chapter 2, self-awareness on the part of the coach is a major coaching competency. It is particularly salient when dealing with tough-minded executives. Powerful, smart executives can be confronting to both novice and experienced coaches. They can be intellectually challenging, even hostile, particularly in the first meeting. Feelings of inferiority, anger and envy could be triggered in the coach, who must be aware of his or her feelings towards people in power and authority. Not taking the perceived 'attack' personally, and responding without anxiety or anger, can offset hostility and begin the process of establishing mutual respect and rapport.

The executive

Executive coaching is about transformational change. It could be claimed that change pre-supposes a certain degree of self-awareness and self-understanding of a particular behaviour. As the self-awareness model in the flow chart below indicates, unless these are present, it is unlikely there will be any real sustained behavioural change.

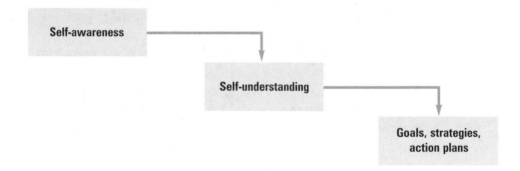

One of the most frequently asked questions in our seminars and workshops for psychologists and other professionals who wish to become coaches is: *To what degree should the coach pursue self-awareness and self-exploration with the executive?* Clearly, there is a continuum of self awareness, ranging from a cursory acknowledgment by the individual that his or her behaviour may be a source of concern to another (perhaps as a result of 360-degree feedback) to a recognition and acceptance of his or her behaviour and its impact on others.

The challenge for the coach is to obtain information and insights into historical patterns of behaviour without being seen as intrusive or threatening. The issue here is *how* the questions are asked as much as *what* is asked. In our experience, executives generally rise to an intellectual challenge. Rather than, for example, the coach exploring a theory he or she may have about the origins of the 'problem' or 'issue' by asking about childhood experiences or current feelings, it is often more effective to present the theory as a hypothesis and wait for the response. Of course, the coachee may dismiss the explanation, but it can also open up an avenue of discussion and possible insights. The exercise becomes one of problem solving rather than of personal psychological analysis. Finally, it is generally recognised that asking some individuals about their 'thoughts or reactions' is likely to elicit a less defensive response than asking about their 'feelings'.

Yet this approach to self-awareness and self-understanding is not necessarily adopted by all executive coaches. Some coaches, for instance, claim they are there to enhance work performance and have no mandate to investigate the psychological realm. Others work within a psychodynamic framework and suggest that unless they deal with intrapsychic conflict there can be no profound or lasting change. Perhaps it is a question of degree. For instance, Levinson notes that the coach may call attention to repetitive problems that the coachee has not recognised, but unless the coachee spontaneously makes some connection to early childhood experience, there is usually no need to interpret this.

There is, then, no general agreement on the *extent* of executive self-awareness necessary for a successful coaching outcome. The self-awareness model outlined above (self-awareness, self-understanding, goals, strategies and action planning) provides a helpful guide for coaches, and its use is illustrated in the following case study.

Case Study

The self-awareness model

N. W. is a 40-year-old executive in a large financial services organisation. He was assigned a coach because of frequent 'blow-ups' with colleagues. The interview and assessment procedure indicated that some form of relaxation and arousal control would be beneficial. N. W. was initially resistant to the intervention. The coach recognised that N. W. lacked *self-awareness*, in that he was unable to appreciate how his colleagues responded to his outbursts. To him, these flare-ups were brief, not personal, and he never held a grudge. Through feedback from colleagues and role-playing, he began to see how his behaviour might impact on others. Coaching conversations also revealed that N. W. considered it was his drive and forcefulness that got him to his current position. Tampering with this could make him 'lose his edge'.

Case Study

The process of developing some sense of *self-understanding* was rather protracted and occupied numerous coaching sessions. However, the coach realised that unless N. W. understood why he behaved the way he did, and that previous 'winning' behaviours were now liabilities, no real change would occur. Over 10 coaching sessions, N. W.'s self-awareness and self-understanding increased sufficiently to allow N. W. and the coach to develop *goals, strategies and an action plan* to deal with his anger outbursts.

Assessment in executive coaching

The question of assessment in executive coaching is a complex one. Certain assessment instruments are for use by registered psychologists only. Yet, obviously, many non-psychologists are coaches. While most of the assessment instruments listed below are for restricted use, there are generic assessment issues that apply to all executive coaches.

Why is assessment necessary?

Formal assessment is clearly an efficient manner of gathering data on the coachee. It can provide information on a person's intelligence, leadership style, emotional maturity, learning preferences, interpersonal and communication style. It can isolate weaknesses in particular areas, and highlight strengths the person may be unaware of, which can be capitalised on in the coaching sessions. Some instruments can be used as pre- and post-tests to measure progress in the coaching intervention. Assessments can provide a useful framework to open up discussion and clarify issues. Finally, they provide management with useful information about their staff.

While there is no denying the benefits of assessment, the question remains as to which assessments to use and how much assessment is necessary. To a certain degree, the type of coaching will determine the type of assessment instruments the coach employs. Yet the *extent* of the assessment remains a vexed question.

Some coaches suggest that the first step after being contacted by an organisation is an in-depth psychological assessment of the executive, which can involve up to three hours interviewing and a detailed personal history. We agree with others that this may be excessive. Some of the reasons for our disquiet include:

1   Many executives are competitive and defensive, and express concern about being compared to others on tests of ability and character.

2   Although coaches are bound by a code of ethics, once a report on the assessment leaves the coach's hands, there are no real controls on what happens to this information or how it is used.

3   A full-scale interview and assessment can be daunting and threatening to coachees, particularly if they are defensive about coaching anyway. It can jeopardise, or at least delay, establishing rapport and trust with the executive.

Some guidelines when doing assessments

Regardless of the assessment the coach employs, there are some guidelines that can offset some of the above-mentioned concerns. These are:

➤   The coach should reassure the coachee that the assessment allows insights into themselves and how others see them.

➤   The coach should highlight the value of assessments that inform the coachee of his or her interpersonal tendencies and inclinations, and how these can be positively exploited in the coaching relationship and the workplace.

➤   The coach should only use assessments directly related to what he or she can use or do in coaching sessions. All the reliability and validity in the world is irrelevant if the coachee cannot see the relevance of the assessment instrument.

Some common assessment instruments

1   **The Myers-Briggs Type Indicator (MBTI)** is one of the most frequently used assessment instruments in organisations. It examines eight personality dimensions (extraversion or introversion, sensing or intuition, thinking or feeling and judging or perceiving). It is a useful instrument for individuals and team members, and can be used for determining how an executive might relate to colleagues.

2   **Fundamental Interpersonal Relations Orientation-Behaviour (FIRO-B)** measures interpersonal orientation. It gives scores on expressed inclusion, control and openness (towards others) and wanted inclusion, control and openness (from others).

3   **The Milton Index of Personality Styles (MIPS)** is a measure of general personality. It correlates highly with the MBTI, but also measures motivating aims, interpersonal behaviour and response sets. It can be used as an aid in vocational or career selection.

4   **The 16PF** is a widely used personality measure designed for the selection, assessment and development of graduate, managerial, sales, professional and technical personnel.

5   **Wonderlic Personnel Test** is a reliable and brief measure of general cognitive ability. The test measures verbal, numerical and spatial abilities.

6   **The DISC Profile** measures core behavioural styles such as *d*ominant, *i*nfluencing, *s*teady and *c*ompliant.

7   **Type A Inventory** assesses individuals on the characteristics associated with a Type A personality—for example, extreme competitiveness, significant life imbalance (usually with high work involvement), strong feelings of hostility and anger, and an extreme sense of urgency and impatience.

Developing your own assessment instrument

Many coaches have chosen to develop their own assessment instrument, sometimes supplementing it with specific tests relevant to the issue(s) being addressed in the coaching sessions (e.g. an assertiveness questionnaire or conflict-resolution style inventory). Over the years, we have formulated, developed and tested our own *structured interview*—a one-hour pen and pencil, question and answer instrument that assesses a wide range of personal and executive competencies. There are no right or wrong answers, and there is no comparative data against which self-ratings are scored. The purpose of the structured interview is to gather information that can inform the coaching intervention.

Some of the areas covered in our structured interview include:

1   a rating on a brief emotions scale (state rather than trait)

2   self-ratings on 45 motivators: internal (e.g. fear of failure), external (e.g. challenge and competition) and universal (e.g. creativity)

3   a series of forced-choice and true/false questions that measure the following personal competencies: interpersonal and emotional skills (e.g. leading and influencing, sociability,

sensitivity, diplomacy), mental strengths (e.g. decisiveness, ability to focus, coping with pressure), opportunistic (e.g. risk taking, resourcefulness, initiative taking), potential (e.g. commitment and perseverance, resilience, achievement focus)

4 a self-rating on the importance of 48 personal competencies to position performance

5 a self-rating and 'ratings as others would see you' (e.g. peers, senior management, team members, etc.) on various leadership and management competencies.

The question and answer section is designed to obtain verbal information on coachees' major job functions, aspects of work they wish to or habitually avoid, personal strengths and weaknesses, and nominated areas they wish to improve on in the coaching sessions. Several of these latter questions are specifically designed to fit the relevant industry and the executive's position within that industry.

Some coaching tools, techniques and interventions

The following list outlines and briefly describes some of the more commonly used tools and techniques in executive coaching:

➤ assessment and feedback (intelligence, leadership styles, interpersonal styles, personality, locus of control, conflict resolution styles)

➤ active listening

➤ salient and purposeful questioning

➤ enhancing and developing learning styles

➤ creative problem solving

➤ brainstorming—testing hypotheses

➤ mind-mapping techniques—clarifying values and goals, ordering information, making oral and written presentations, organising time

➤ accelerated goal-setting strategies

➤ feedback

➤ modelling of desired behaviours

➤ video role-playing, simulations

➤ interpretation of behaviours

➤ clarifying emotions

➤ providing information—a resource person.

Some typical coaching interventions

Based on research and our experience as executive coaches, we have compiled the following list of the most frequently requested coaching interventions.

➤ leadership development—individual and group coaching workshops

➤ managers as coaches—individual and group coaching

➤ communication skills

  ➤ listening, reflecting, endorsing

  ➤ supportive communication skills

  ➤ giving feedback

➤ presentation skills (voice exercises, anxiety control, use of visual aids, mind-mapping)

➤ delegation (fostering personal mastery, principles of delegation, styles of delegation)

➤ negotiation—how to achieve a win–win rather than a win–lose settlement

➤ conflict management—styles of conflict resolution, how to deal with difficult people in the workplace

➤ managing stress—hypnosis, relaxation and meditation techniques

➤ burnout

➤ coaching for assertiveness

➤ time management

➤ managing multiple priorities

➤ influencing skills—enhancing power in the organisation, increasing visibility, relevance and flexibility of current job

➤ coaching for career development, succession planning, retirement

➤ coaching for a 'new position'.

Coaching intervention for leadership

Developing leaders' capabilities to their fullest potential is critical in any organisation. In fact, one of our most frequently requested coaching interventions is that of 'leadership development'. It is also a popular topic for our lectures and presentations.

There is a vast literature on leadership, including the desired personal attributes of a leader, styles of leadership and the competencies and skills of an effective leader. If coaching for leadership is to be effective, it has to traverse these domains. However, before discussing these issues, it is important to address the question of leadership and charisma. Are these qualities one and the same? Are leaders born, or does leadership involve skills and capabilities that can be learned?

Charisma has been defined as the ability of a leader to exercise broad and intense influence over the beliefs, values, behaviour and performance of others through his or her own beliefs, behaviour and personal example. It is generally considered that charisma is partly a function of the leader's personality and particularly a need for power. There is some evidence that charismatic individuals score high on intelligence, dominance, self-confidence, activity and task knowledge. However, what is critical to successful leadership is that these traits are expressed through the person's behaviour, and that different types of tasks require different leadership characteristics and behaviour. The coach and coachee therefore work together to translate these 'natural abilities' into action and to promote flexibility in leadership style.

While charisma is certainly an asset in any leadership role, it is neither necessary nor sufficient for good leadership. Leadership is less about personal charisma and more about visible commitment to action. It is about getting people committed to a course of action and to meet agreed upon goals.

With some notable exceptions perhaps, leaders are not born. At least to a certain extent, leadership capacity is something everyone can learn and improve on. According to Goleman, for instance, there is a strong genetic component to 'emotional intelligence', which he claims is a greater predictor of career and leadership success than raw intelligence. However, the amygdala, the part of the brain that processes and stores emotional stimuli and experiences, is also capable of learning through motivation, extended practice and feedback. Management and leadership skills can be trained into a person, whereas the passion and desire to lead an organisation may well be a set, unalterable predisposition.

Managers versus leaders

While it is not unequivocally accepted that there is a clear distinction between managers and leaders, some differences remain between the traditional manager and the manager or executive as leader. Some of these are shown in Table 4.3.

Yet, in many ways, a good manager is a good leader. Also, 'maintenance management' is still necessary to create and maintain standards of performance. What is required is that it be combined with leadership skills, such as providing a new sense of purpose, direction and motivation.

Coaching for leadership focuses on allowing leaders to recognise their strengths and weaknesses in these and other areas, and to develop new leadership skills, as well as enabling them to take effective action. It is only when leadership capabilities are translated into action that they have any true impact on individuals and organisations.

Managers	Leaders
➤ Administrate	➤ Innovate
➤ Imitate	➤ Originate
➤ Accept the status quo	➤ Challenge the status quo
➤ Focus on systems and structures	➤ People-focused
➤ Rely on control	➤ Inspire trust, empower others
➤ Emphasise short term and bottom line	➤ Visionary, look to the horizon

Table 4.3   The differences between managers and leaders

Types of leadership

One of the most commonly cited models of leadership is that of *transactional*, *laissez-faire* and *transformational types* of leadership. To some extent, an individual's style of leadership is partly a function of personality and partly a function of how they view employees and their beliefs about what motivates people. According to McGregor's Theory X and Theory Y, leaders and managers tend to view workers in one or two ways:

Theory X	Theory Y
➤ Dislike work, are self-centred	➤ Are self-motivated and responsible
➤ Need to be directed and controlled	➤ Committed to the organisation
➤ Respond to a reward and punishment style	➤ Responsible, respond to being treated well

Transactional leadership is essentially a behaviourist approach, based on rewarding employees only if they perform adequately or try sufficiently hard. As long as organisational goals are met, the leader does not seek to change workplace methods or structures.

Non-transactional or laissez-faire leadership tends to avoid confronting the issues, is non-interventionist and frequently resists taking a stand on important issues. It tends to be the least effective form of leadership.

Transformational leadership is about charisma that transmits pride, vision and mission. The transformational leader inspires and encourages free and creative thinking and always treats the individual on his or her own merits, seeking to develop the person's skills and capabilities. Although transactional and transformational leadership are not mutually exclusive, transformational leaders tend to be viewed more positively. They are better able to create a 'holding environment', whereby people can talk, discuss and prepare for change. They give direction and manage the rate of change and progress. The goal of coaching is to develop and enhance these transformational leadership skills.

Some of the qualities of a transformational leader include:

➤ *The ability to inspire commitment and align others*, which involves listening to and understanding the followers' values, goals and aspirations. Good leadership always entails a strong sense of personal values and a desire to transmit these through example.

➤ *Charisma* and the power to influence and persuade others, especially regarding change.

➤ *The ability to create structures and mechanisms* that inspire and encourage the desired actions and results. This can range from hiring the right person for the job to restructuring a department or business unit.

➤ *Accountability*—great leaders foster accountability and self-responsibility.

➤ *Interpersonal skills*—self-knowledge, the ability to engage in mutually productive interactions, appropriate self-disclosure as an element of establishing trust, being open to influence and maintaining emotional balance, particularly when things go wrong.

➤ *The ability to deal effectively with conflict*—does not suppress, ignore or deny its manifestations.

➤ *Flexibility*—being able to adapt and adjust a preferred style of management to suit the particular individual or situation.

➤ *Competence in the three domains of reality*—the 'I' (or individual) domain, which requires skills such as self-observation and self-knowledge; the 'we' (or collective, communal) domain, which involves skills such as listening, setting standards and innovating; and the 'it' (or external, objective world) domain, where skills such as analysing and model-building are necessary. These three domains of reality exist concurrently, hence leaders are required to be cognisant of, and have distinct qualities and skills in, each domain.

➤ *The ability to help the organisation develop skills and knowledge that enable it to perform and adapt to change*—a leader has to provide both the opportunity for learning and the resources to translate knowledge into action This role also involves developing future leaders.

Some questionnaires to measure leadership skills and styles

There are numerous categories of leadership styles, some empirically validated, others not. Many authors and organisations, for instance, use the Myers-Briggs Type Indicator as a guide to leadership styles. The following questionnaires can also prove useful to the coach wanting to establish the leader's capabilities and preferred style of leading. One of the aims of leadership coaching, though, is not only to assess and strengthen the leader's preferred style, but also to encourage versatility and enhance competence and confidence in using differing styles and methods to meet varying demands and circumstances.

The Leadership and Influencing Skills questionnaire measures skills such as creating vision, motivating and respecting others, setting performance expectations, conveying credibility, delegating and empowering, coaching, developing and guiding, controlling and monitoring performance and leading organisational change.

The Riso-Hudson Enneagram Type Indicator (RHETI) questionnaire identifies fundamental types and character traits. Types include the reformer, the motivator, the concerned helper, the committed, security-oriented loyalist, the artist, the spontaneous, busy generalist/dreamer, the decisive leader, the passive, reassuring peacemaker/preservationist and the thinker/observer.

The McPhee Andrewartha Influence Dimensions (ID) questionnaire assesses natural managerial skills and leadership style based on six dimensions including non-verbal behaviour and underlying perceptual systems. The four styles of leadership are planner, analyser, developer and creator. The instrument allows the individual to tailor his or her development needs and program according to strengths and weaknesses on the various dimensions.

Issues to address in coaching for leadership

When coaching executives for leadership development, either individually or in a group format, we find that the following issues are relevant to and productive of change and transformation and should be addressed by the coach:

1   Defining transformational leadership—authenticity, credibility, inspiration, intellectual stimulation, giving consideration to the individual.

2   Recognising leadership style—becoming a more versatile leader.

3   Inspiring vision—risk-taking, future orientation, articulating vision, gaining commitment to vision and demonstrating values.

4   Leading change—seeking opportunities for change, determining and guiding change, working with resistance, explaining and encouraging honest participation, defining and clarifying goals and strategies to achieve change.

5   Delegating—delegation as growth, development, empowerment and accountability; the stages of delegation.

6   Communication skills—especially giving praise and feedback.

7   Problem solving with staff and clients.

We should emphasise that the areas we address in leadership coaching are presented here as guidelines only. A good coach will match the coaching agenda or schedule with the specific needs of the executive and the organisation.

Case Study

Coaching for leadership

W. M. is a recently appointed CEO in a medium-sized services industry. He has no formal training in leadership. He employed a coach to assist him to develop his leadership competencies, particularly in the areas of 'motivating' staff and improving staff morale. W. M. was at a loss to understand why others in the company failed to share his enthusiasm and vision. Before working with the coach, he tended to attribute the general indifference and lack of commitment to personality factors such as laziness and lack of ambition. During the initial coaching sessions, it became obvious that although he could clearly articulate the company's vision, it was not being communicated in any meaningful way to others in the organisation. On the recommendation of the coach, W. M. began to talk to staff about their goals and how they fitted in with the company's future plans and direction. He was somewhat shocked to discover that many staff members, including senior personnel, felt the company was lacking in direction and vision. Together, the coach and W. M. devised strategies to better communicate the company's vision, to encourage participation in company policy initiatives and to conduct regular meetings where the goals of the various business units were analysed and discussed in relation to the overreaching goals of the company. Within three months, W. M. reported improved staff morale and commitment at all levels of the organisation.

Some competencies for executive coaches

This section discusses some specific core competencies of a successful executive coach. Executive coaches have skills that contribute to a culture where concern for people is matched with attaining the objectives of the company. They are experts in transition, in the process of change, decision making and problem solving. Executive coaches understand the skills and strategies of empowerment and how to assess and deal with interpersonal issues. Many coaches move from life skills coaching to executive coaching within organisations. There are some difficulties inherent in this transition, because executive coaching requires specific, additional skills and competencies. Research suggests the following competencies to guide those who choose to work in a corporate setting.

1 Understanding the organisational imperative

Regardless of whether executive coaches are working with an individual or groups of individuals in an organisation, it is essential that they position themselves within the organisation as a whole. To do this successfully entails understanding the organisation's culture, philosophy and requirements for success so that these can be aligned with the goals of executive coaching. Coaching within an organisational vacuum, unrelated to other development programs and not aligned with the goals and vision of the organisation, is unlikely to be successful or ongoing.

A coach is not expected to be an expert in the particular industry in which he or she may be working. However, the coach has to display some knowledge of the specific business world and its demands in order to demonstrate the unique benefits of coaching to the particular organisation. Such knowledge includes:

➤ the key challenges facing the organisation and the particular division for which the executive is responsible

➤ the stage of development of the organisation (is it in a growth period, downsizing, etc.?)

➤ the performance skills that the executive requires to be successful

➤ the personal skills and behaviours that will ensure executive competency and success (e.g. what is the most effective style of leadership in this particular situation, and which interpersonal issues are most likely to create barriers to success?)

➤ how to encourage a culture of coaching within a safe environment which fosters growth and development.

2 Comfort around top management

In order to be seen as credible and trustworthy, the executive coach has to be seen as being on the same wavelength as management and executives. Evidence suggests that it is rare for executives to hear objective and reliable feedback about their performance, particularly in the area of personal skills. Executives are highly successful, ambitious individuals who, for the most part, are unaccustomed to challenge and criticism. Their success can in fact be a barrier to change. A coach has to feel confident and knowledgeable in order to deal with any executive defensiveness or resistance to change. Some competencies in this area include:

➤ dealing comfortably with top executives, and recognising that the demands of their position can hinder self-reflection and make them vulnerable to perceived criticism

> understanding how executives think and how they view the world, and appreciating their drives and values

> being able to respond to executives' needs in a creative, appropriate and effective manner.

3 Political astuteness

In corporations there are always politics with which the coach has to contend. While the corporation may not be the hotbed of Machiavellian machinations portrayed in the movies, an unsuspecting coach can get caught in the crossfire. A successful coach is politically non-aligned, although aware of the political manoeuvring that is inevitable in any organisation.

The coaching process can suffer if there is disagreement or conflict among management regarding the introduction or process of coaching. It is therefore incumbent on the coach to educate and align all members of management with regard to the principles, process and benefits of coaching. Coaching works best within a culture of coaching, when it is incorporated into other development programs and where there is a consensus regarding its applicability and specific benefits. Some requisite competencies in this area include:

> being able to manoeuvre through political situations unobtrusively and sensitively

> accepting corporate politics as a reality and adjusting accordingly

> being seen as objective, non-partisan and truthful

> being able to deal with paradox and ambiguity

> maintaining confidentiality and trust.

4 Client focus

An effective coach is aware of the needs of customers, both within and outside the organisation. The coach functions as an active resource, exploring, building and maximising the individual's full potential. To do this it is critical to understand the coachees' relationships with their clients and their clients' demands and expectations. The coach can then help paint the big picture, with realistic descriptions of business goals, financial objectives, opportunities and directions. Some competencies involved in building and maintaining client focus include:

➤ having good client management skills—establishing and maintaining relationships with customers

➤ being able to relate to people at all levels, both within and outside the organisation

➤ being aware of the expectations of internal and external customers.

How to choose the right corporate coach

If you are hiring an executive coach for work-related issues, you can first review performance evaluation appraisals and ask: 'What are the performance or developmental needs that can be worked on to ensure further growth and success, for example technical skills or interpersonal skills?' Having identified, at least in broad terms, some areas where coaching would be useful, it might be helpful to consider the advantages of developing a network of coaches to meet your needs.

Develop a network of executive coaches

As in sports, where there are specialty team coaches, there are specialist executive coaches. Why? Simply because no one coach can be expected to know everything and be an expert in every area. An organisation should develop a network of coaches who have the experience, education and successful track records relevant to their arena. The panel of coaches should be able to provide total guidance to help the individual or organisation fulfil their goals and vision. For example, some of our associates specialise in short-term coaching interventions, others in group coaching, team coaching, crisis intervention or long-term coaching programs. Some organisations even have a supplementary list of trainee coaches they are nurturing for future specialist use. Locating a coach, least of all a panel of coaches, may not be easy. Check out local telephone directories and look on the Internet for coaching organisations, coaching resource centres and coaching networks.

Having located a source of potential coaches, it is important to remember that coaching is a relationship, a two-way interaction whose success depends largely on the 'goodness of fit' between the coach and the coachee. Furthermore, with the popularity of coaching increasing significantly each year, there will be a number of self-styled coaches attracted to the profession who, unfortunately, do not have the necessary training and experience. The following selection criteria are therefore offered as a guide to organisations and individuals to help them appraise a coach's suitability. Many of the questions a potential client should pose to an executive coach are covered in the section on 'What to look for in a business coach' in Chapter 3. However, a potential client should also investigate the coach's experience in the executive arena.

A checklist of some questions a potential client should ask an executive coach

☐ What is the coach's experience in your particular niche area?

☐ What is the coach's experience at your level of required intervention (e.g. senior management, executive, CEO levels)?

☐ What is the coach's experience with various types of coaching, for example:

  ☐ executive one-on-one coaching?

  ☐ group coaching?

  ☐ team coaching?

  ☐ life coaching?

☐ Can the coach work at the following levels:

  ☐ skills coaching (enhancing specific skills used in current job)?

  ☐ performance coaching (broadly improving a person's current job performance)?

  ☐ development coaching (focused on an individual's future job)?

  ☐ agenda coaching (broadly focused on the executive's agenda, for example leadership skills)?

A six-step model for executive coaching

This model for executive coaching provides a blueprint for coaches working in the corporate arena. The model offers guidelines for the coach from the first meeting with management, through to the weekly sessions and the final feedback session with management.

Step one Management meeting

Generally, an organisation has an individual or individuals in mind for coaching when it assigns an in-house coach or contracts an external executive coach. Frequently, due to an organisation's hesitancy about coaching or the low priority it gives to coaching, the coach's initial coaching assignment is in the context of 'remedial coaching' or coaching for skills.

Some guidelines for the executive coach when meeting with management:

1 Establish the role and status of coaching in the organisation—its successes and failures, and any future plans to 'roll it out'.

2 Determine the organisation's agenda and challenges in order to situate the coachee in a broader context. For example, what challenges does the organisation face? Why this particular individual, and what was the impetus for hiring a coach? What does the potential coachee know about coaching? Is coaching voluntary or was he or she simply assigned a coach?

3 Establish the personal, technical, and leadership competencies necessary for the executive's success.

4 Determine whether the organisation has the resources to support a coaching program.

Having established the context of the coaching role, it is essential for the coach to discuss and clarify the logistics of the intervention. For example, he or she should address the following questions:

1 Will the coach meet with the coachee prior to the first formal coaching session? Will all sessions be on site? What is the frequency of the sessions? What is the initial time frame for the coaching intervention? What is the period of review? What is the agreement regarding missed appointments?

2 What is the nature of the assessment process—how will progress be measured?

3 What are the feedback measures? What is the exact nature of the reports to management? Who will have access to these reports? Will they impact in any way on the executive's career, such as promotions and performance appraisals? What is the frequency of management feedback meetings? Will other members of the organisation (e.g. HR personnel) be involved? What are the limits of confidentiality?

4 What are the terms of payment? Does the organisation have any redress if it is dissatisfied with the coaching outcomes? Does the coach provide a guarantee?

Step two   Initial individual meeting with the coachee

Meeting individually with the coachee before the formal coaching sessions is critical for several reasons. First, it allows the coach to establish rapport in a casual, non-threatening situation. Second, providing information about the nature of coaching, what it entails and the coach and coachee's roles can serve to allay much of the executive's anxiety about coaching. Third, the coach can establish whether the executive is in agreement with management about the need for coaching and the areas or issues that should be addressed. Finally, a caution: despite management's claims to the contrary, our experience as executive coaches indicates that if an organisation does not have an existing culture of coaching, targeted coachees may be ill-informed about coaching and why it has been recommended for them. The individual meeting with the coachee provides the opportunity for the coach to highlight the 'performance enhancing' aspect of coaching so that the coachee does not simply view coaching as a 'remedial' intervention for a performance deficit.

Some guidelines for the coach include:

1   Provide a brief handout about coaching. The following checklist shows some of the information we include in our coach–client protocol.

Coach–client protocol checklist

✓ Explain the aims and goals of our organisation

✓ Outline some of the benefits of coaching

✓ Explain what is involved in a coaching session—what the coachee can expect, what the initial sessions involve, the nature of the assessment, what subsequent sessions entail

✓ Discuss the length and number of sessions, self-monitoring and homework

✓ Clarify what reports will be written and to whom

✓ Ensure the coachee is aware of, and in agreement with, any limits to confidentiality

2   Be prepared to answer the following questions that coachees frequently ask coaches:

➤ Why do I need a coach?

➤ Is there something wrong with my work?

➤ Are others in the organisation having coaching?

➤ How is it going to help me to do my job better?

➤ Have you had a lot of experience with this sort of thing?

Step three First coaching session

The first formal coaching session usually involves some form of assessment. Regardless of the type of assessment, it is not unusual for an executive to show some apprehension. Guidelines or a rationale for carrying out assessments are given in the section 'Assessment in executive coaching'. Our experience indicates that being assessed, regardless of the format, can arouse anxiety and hostility in some coachees. Some of the typical questions or rebuttals we have encountered in the first session are:

➤ I'm really not sure of the purpose of this assessment. If coaching is all about conversation, why can't I just tell you about myself?

➤ I've already done the Myers-Briggs and the DISC Profile and I didn't find them particularly useful.

➤ I hate being typecast.

Once these questions or rebuttals have been satisfactorily answered or dealt with, the remainder of the session is taken up with the assessment.

Step four Second coaching session

1   *Giving feedback*   The second coaching session begins with the coach providing feedback about the assessment. While there are general guidelines for giving feedback successfully (see the section 'How to provide effective feedback' in Chapter 5), some specific issues arise in the context of giving feedback to executives. Research suggests that people who rarely experience failure tend to become defensive and screen out criticism. Such an attitude, coupled with the tendency for many executives to score high on measures of dominance and control, highlights the importance of presenting feedback in a manner that will generate acceptance and commitment to change.

2   *The coaching agreement*   In our coaching work, we have found it useful to draw up a coaching agreement with our coachees. Such an agreement clarifies the coach and coachee's roles and also fosters the coachee's commitment to the success of the intervention. It can be used if the coachee falls behind, neglects to implement agreed upon strategies or fails to honour the coaching commitment. The coach then has the right to remind the coachee of the agreement. Areas addressed in the coaching agreement, which is signed by both coach and coachee, include:

➤ the coach's commitment and overall goals

➤ the coachee's commitment

> any specific limits on the confidentiality of the sessions

> cancellation procedures

> duration and termination conditions

> statements of record keeping and policy documents

3 *Obtain agreement on issue(s)* It is important in this session to obtain at the least a broad agreement on the issue or issues to be worked on in the subsequent sessions. This session is also a crucial time for the coach to examine any potential resistance from the coachee.

Step five Weekly coaching sessions

Depending on the agreed upon period for the coaching assignment, varying amounts of time can be spent on the following:

> *Recognising, examining and challenging any self-limiting beliefs (SLBs)* These SLBs may be impacting on the executive's current performance or could negatively affect the coaching outcome. During the assessment stage, we find it useful to ask coachees to self-rate themselves on a list of self-limiting beliefs (e.g. 'people aren't interested in getting to know me better', 'no one listens to me', etc.). These can be used to open up discussion on the way distorted thinking patterns can be self-fulfilling and self-sabotaging.

> *Examining values, vision and purpose* Clarifying values, vision and purpose is critical to setting achievable and strategic goals (see Chapter 7). To a certain extent, the type of coaching will dictate the degree to which these areas are emphasised and explored. Coaching for skills, for example, may involve less discussion of purpose and vision than coaching for development. What is important is that the goals established in the coaching sessions are in harmony with the values and vision of the executive, and that any conflict between the executive's personal goals and those of the organisation are isolated and discussed.

> *Establishing goals* Using the guidelines set out in Chapter 7, the coach and executive work together to establish what they wish to achieve in the coaching alliance. Although overall goals are frequently nominated very early during the coaching conversation (sometimes by management prior to this), these have to be operationalised in the following way: goals must be specific, challenging, time limited, measurable and include a feedback mechanism. The coach and the coachee then examine any potential obstacles to meeting these goals and brainstorm solutions to overcome or circumvent these hindrances.

➤ *Developing an action plan*   Having reached a consensus on goals and the strategies to deal with obstacles, the coach and the coachee then devise an action plan, or a blueprint, for achieving the goals (see Chapter 7 for a model for goal setting and developing an action plan).

➤ *Continuing regular coaching sessions*   The regularity of coaching sessions is, to some extent, a function of the type of coaching being conducted. Coaching for skills, for instance, tends to be more successful if the coaching sessions are scheduled on a weekly basis, particularly during the early phase. Initially the coachee requires support from the coach to develop new behaviours and then the coach provides feedback and reinforcement while these new skills are put into practice. We have found that, regardless of the type of coaching, in the early phase of the relationship, weekly sessions are more productive. Of course, this is subject to the coachee's availability, and the coach has to be flexible in terms of scheduling sessions. The first phase can extend over several weeks depending on the agreed goals and action plan. The coaching sessions can then be conducted on a fortnightly basis, moving onto a monthly basis once the new behaviours are firmly entrenched. As the coaching sessions become less frequent, the coach's role is to provide ongoing support and reinforcement and provide a platform for the coachee to discuss issues as they arise.

Step six   Management feedback

The logistics of giving feedback to management should be established during the first or second contact with the organisation. Some coaches choose to report only on generic issues among coachees and maintain strict confidentiality about the individual coaching sessions; some only report on the general progress of an assignment, such as whether or not the executive keeps appointments and is committed to the process; and others will submit reports to management only after these have been sighted by the coachee.

As executive coaches, we maintain that wherever there is 'double agency' (the client who pays the bill and the coachee), confidentiality will tend to present some ethical concerns. There are no hard and fast rules regarding the nature and the degree of feedback the coach should provide to management. Essentially, the coach has to balance the organisation's demands and the confidentiality rights of the coachee. In some respects, this can be a question of semantics. For example, rather than stating that an executive was 'lacking in leadership qualities', the coach could report that the coachee's goal was to 'develop and enhance leadership competencies'. See Chapter 6 for guidelines on writing reports to management.

Life issues in executive coaching

As mentioned previously, the question of dealing with life issues in executive coaching is somewhat controversial. While some coaches claim that personal issues lie outside the boundaries of executive coaching, others suggest that work and life issues are inextricably linked, and are therefore valid coaching topics. We accept that executive coaching should always be work related and performance driven, but we also believe that work and life issues are interrelated. Even though life issues typically are not the focus of executive coaching, to ignore them completely can hinder change and growth and undermine the coaching alliance.

The modern worker is increasingly concerned with quality of life issues, both work and personal. Work and personal concerns are not separate phenomena. We play different roles at work and at home, but we are the same person in each situation. Lack of satisfaction or imbalance in one area impacts on the other. Increasingly, we are devoting more time to our careers and 'keeping up' with the latest technological advances and influx of information. At the same time, more individuals are complaining that work is taking over their lives, that there is not enough time to enjoy family and friends and that they are on a treadmill over which they have little control. An American survey by *Business Week* and the Center on Work and Family at Boston University found that, of 8000 employees, more than two-fifths of workers claimed that work had a negative impact on their lives.

Changes in contemporary family structures have highlighted the interconnectedness between work and life issues. The modern family model is that of two working parents or a single working parent. More women are joining the workplace and 80 per cent will become pregnant and return to the workforce after a year. Men are increasingly sharing in more domestic responsibilities. These statistics highlight areas such as child care, decreased flexibility in available working hours and increased pressure, sometimes guilt, on the part of the parents. All these areas can affect how well an executive performs in his or her job. However, it should be acknowledged that research has found that women who juggle jobs and the demands of family are less depressed than those who stay at home.

Fortunately, the interrelationship between work and family life is being increasingly recognised. Yet until workplace policies that accommodate the demands of family and personal life are universally instituted, executives will continue to struggle with the frustration of performing successfully in their executive roles at the expense of other important roles, such as parent or spouse.

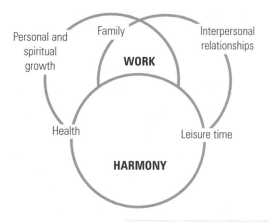

Work not only interacts with family and personal relationships; it also impacts on our health, our leisure time and our spiritual wellbeing. Transitions such as divorce, change in health status and retirement also affect how well executives perform their current tasks. These issues, then, are not extraneous to executive coaching. Figure 4.1 illustrates this interconnectedness.

The coach's role in seeking a work/life balance

To some extent, a well-adjusted life is a balanced one. We seek balance and satisfaction in all the areas mentioned above. Yet balance is not a static state; it is fluid and dynamic. The coach can work with the executive to move towards a state of balance, but both parties should realise that balance is an evolving, ongoing state rather than a set goal that can be achieved once and for all.

Balance implies choices. Life is not full of infinite possibilities and we cannot have everything we want in all spheres of our lives. There is usually a trade-off between the time we spend with our families, for example, and how much time we commit to work. The coach's role is not only to work with the executive to prioritise values and commitment, but also to recognise that balance involves choices that necessarily exclude something else, that is some loss. It can involve saying 'no' to extra work responsibilities. Interestingly, by far the greater majority of the executives we work with rate their ability to say 'no' to extra work (even when they already felt overburdened) as very low. At the same time, they want to spend more leisure time with family, partners and friends.

Health issues also can obviously impact on executive performance. Stress-related behaviours such as flare-ups in the office and fatigue could indicate to the coach that the executive's health might warrant intervention. Goals and action plans concerning diet and exercise can be the focus of the coaching alliance. Improvement in these areas impacts on personal and family relationships, interactions with colleagues and clients, and the executive's overall feelings of wellbeing and work performance.

Sometimes, especially during the so-called 'mid-life crisis' or when the executive is approaching retirement, spiritual issues can become a central facet of the coaching intervention. Spirituality does not necessarily involve formal religious beliefs. It can centre on the coachee's search for meaning and purpose in life, in a desire to feel more connected with others and with the universe. An underdeveloped spiritual life can result in an executive experiencing 'burn out' and a sense of futility despite apparent success in the workplace.

If these personal or life issues are not explored, or at least acknowledged, the coachee might consider coaching to be an added burden, another stress that can tip the scales in an already unstable or rocky life situation. The executive's agenda, and that of management, is typically work related. The executive may be reluctant to discuss personal issues, particularly in the early stages of coaching, and even more so if he or she is resistant to being coached and sees it as onerous. Yet the coach must remain vigilant of the executive's balance in various aspects of his or her life and be courageous enough to raise these matters, despite resistance and a limited mandate. Coaching is holistic: it concerns itself with all the interrelated aspects of the person's life (see Figure 4.2).

Figure 4.2   A model for working with life issues

The coach and the coachee work together to develop the coachee's self-awareness of imbalances in his or her life, or to strengthen and improve already existing balance and strategies. Together, they then identify the coachee's important needs, such as spending more time at home with family or 'agitating' for organisational reform to improve flexibility of working hours. The coachee learns about living with the reality that life is a series of trade-offs and choices which may involve saying 'no' and can entail a change in the belief that somehow all aspects of life could and should be in perfect balance. The coach and coachee then discuss strategies to integrate and balance life/work issues more successfully. An action plan is instituted and, when carried out effectively, results in personal growth, which leads to increased self-awareness in an ongoing cycle.

 Case Study

Life issues in executive coaching

T. J. is a 45-year-old executive in the financial services industry. He has agreed to undertake coaching to enhance his leadership skills. However, on the first and second meeting with T. J., it was clear to the coach that T. J. was experiencing significant difficulties in his home life. Although able to contain his stress levels at work, at home he would 'let loose', have temper outbursts, feel too tired to engage with his family and would retire to his study. Such behaviour was impacting negatively on his relationships with his wife and two children. The coach and T. J. agreed to institute an action plan that involved regular daily exercise, a simple relaxation (breathing) technique and time management strategies that would allow him to spend more 'quality' time with his family. It was only when T. J.'s stress levels decreased and his interactions with his family improved that he and the coach embarked on leadership coaching.

CHAPTER FIVE

The manager as coach

Key points

➤ The changing role of management

➤ Bringing about a culture of coaching

➤ The manager as coach

➤ How to provide effective feedback

➤ Some coaching skills for managers

➤ Career coaching in organisations

➤ Coaching managers to be coaches

The changing role of management

Over the past 15 years, management worldwide has undergone remarkable changes. There has been a flattening out of middle management, and the remaining managers are expected to be multiskilled and to have good 'people skills' and team building capabilities. Managers are expected to do more with fewer staff. Increased international competition in a global economy, greater consumer expectations of service and demands for efficiency in organisational structures require that managers continually develop their organisations and the people within them. The interpersonal skills and emotional competencies that facilitate a productive workplace are of the utmost importance. Managers have to understand their own emotional make-up as well as that of others in the workplace, and they have to be able to manage relationships and build networks.

Some evidence indicates that there has been a decrease in worker productivity compared to advances in technology over the past two decades. One explanation for this is that hierarchically based relationships between managers and employees breed fear and resentment, not creativity and empowerment. An important related issue is how we evaluate productivity. Increasingly, it is recognised that in modern business enterprises, capital is not as important as it once was. Some authors suggest that the performance of high-technology and service businesses, in particular, is influenced more by the quality of their management than by their assets. Technology itself is not productive, but well-managed, well-trained and motivated people can show measurable gains in output.

Historically, managers were selected on the basis of their technical skills and on their ability to 'get the job done'. People skills were low on the list of managerial competencies. Yet, research shows that the management of people has a greater effect on productivity and profitability than the combined effects of strategy, quality, manufacturing technology, and research and development. Goleman's concept of 'emotional intelligence', and an increased appreciation of the need for 'softer skills' and people-oriented skills in the workplace, highlight a shift in management and organisational priorities. Still, some authors suggest that many changes to the traditional style of controlling, coercive management are mostly cosmetic.

In our seminars and workshops that coach managers to be coaches, we find that managers are increasingly dissatisfied with the traditional 'boss' style of management and recognise the need to improve their interpersonal or people skills in order to be more effective and productive within their organisations.

Modern managers require excellent communication skills and the ability to deal with diverse employees, many of whom no longer respond to the traditional, hierarchical, top-down decision-making style of leadership. Often, the best employees seek self-development, self-responsibility and accountability rather than direction and control. They want to be coached rather than managed in the traditional style. Yet not everyone has naturally good interpersonal skills, and managers are rarely given any formal training in this critical area. However, such skills can be learned. Managers can learn a new, supportive, collaborative leadership style that builds trust and induces improved performance in the workplace. They can acquire the skills to become facilitators, empowerers and developers of other people.

Yet this is not to say that managers should become coaches rather than managers. Managers have to manage. While the role of a coach in executive coaching, for example, is typically non-directive, the manager as coach gives advice and instructions and may tell the coachee what to do or how to do something. The coaching model most appropriate to managers, therefore, is frequently a directive one, whereby the manager assesses the performance error, demonstrates the correct action and rewards the employee for the desired behaviour(s).

The role of the manager as coach is not limited to corrective or remedial coaching for performance deficits. Coaching, after all, is about performance enhancement. The manager's role also involves guiding, encouraging and enhancing top performers, as well as career coaching at all levels of the organisation.

Regardless of whether coaching is directive or non-directive, it offers managers a new way of relating. It entails a new process of managing that allows for their own personal growth and development, as well as the skill enhancement and development of their employees. Through becoming a coach, a manager can learn new styles of managing and communicating and will be engaged in a personal process of continuous learning.

As a coach, a manager will be able to recognise when a coaching opportunity arises. Coaching, as we have mentioned previously, is a conversation, a way of relating. Coaching can occur in formal settings, where the manager and staff sit together for an hour or so in weekly sessions and work together on goals and action plans for development. It can also occur in regular team coaching sessions. Importantly though, coaching can be informal and can occur on the spot whenever the manager sees the need, or indeed creates the opportunity for a coaching moment. As shown in Figure 5.1, the manager observes the situation, makes hypotheses as to the probable causes of a particular behaviour, gives feedback and chooses an appropriate response, such as rewarding and enhancing a skill or problem solving to build new skills.

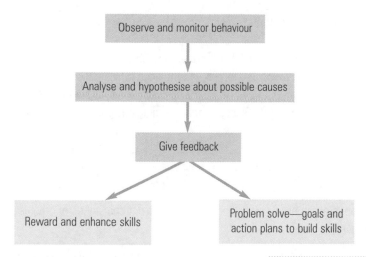

Figure 5.1   A coaching model for managers

Managers as coaches can occur at various levels of an organisation—senior managers may be required to coach middle managers and middle managers may be responsible for coaching line managers and supervisors, who in turn can adopt a coaching profile with individual employees. Coaching within organisations can occur in the absence of the manager. As more and more workplaces turn to self-managing teams, peer coaching or peer support is also becoming more critical. In this situation, peers observe, provide feedback and coach each other. Regardless of the level at which coaching occurs, it should be work-based, work-related and performance-oriented.

Bringing about a culture of coaching

While managers can be 'coached' to become coaches and adopt a coaching model, such a process cannot succeed within a vacuum. Our experience and that of other coaches has shown the importance of a culture of coaching to support the initiative. There is a need for commitment to coaching at all levels of an organisation. Unless there are individuals who will value, embrace, support and provide the resources for coaching, the interventions are unlikely to succeed or to permeate the organisation. Coaching is not an isolated phenomenon, but a viable, effective management performance improvement technique that can complement and enhance other improvement programs such as career planning and performance feedback.

Organisational alignment

The role of the coach (either external or in-house) may be to enlist support and enthusiasm for coaching within an organisation. Whether undertaking individual executive coaching, team coaching or coaching managers to be coaches, we have found that the process of organisational alignment is a good predictor of the success of a coaching assignment. This process follows the following steps:

1   *Step one* involves a meeting, or several meetings, with the person who initiated the contact regarding coaching. During these meetings, the coach gathers extensive information on:

> ➤ the needs of the organisation, including any current challenges or organisational change initiatives

> ➤ the history and status of coaching within the organisation, including its successes and failures

> ➤ the potential coachees and their specific needs

> ➤ how coaching will 'fit' with other development programs

> ➤ who will supervise the coaching assignment

> ➤ whether the organisation has the resources to support the intervention.

2   *Step two* involves a two-hour introductory seminar or workshop (depending on the number of participants) on coaching. This is usually attended by senior managers, line managers, supervisors, human resources personnel and potential coachees. Some of the topics covered include:

> ➤ what coaching is

> ➤ the history of coaching

> ➤ the differences between coaching, training and counselling

> ➤ how coaching can specifically benefit the organisation

> ➤ coaching as a critical leadership competency and responsibility

> ➤ who can be coached

> ➤ some typical coaching interventions.

3   *Step three* generally takes place in a group setting over a period of two to four hours. Essentially, organisational alignment involves ensuring that all those who will be affected by

the coaching intervention are informed and in agreement with the goals of coaching, and the specific rewards and benefits of coaching to the organisation. Any potential obstacles to the success of the coaching program are freely discussed, and an opportunity to brainstorm solutions is provided. Finally, methods and procedures for review and refinement of the program are also addressed.

Figure 5.2 illustrates the three steps involved in aligning management and others with the proposed coaching intervention.

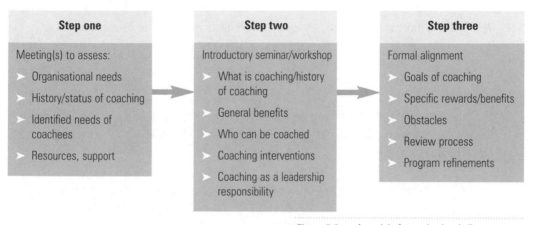

Step one	Step two	Step three
Meeting(s) to assess: ➤ Organisational needs ➤ History/status of coaching ➤ Identified needs of coachees ➤ Resources, support	Introductory seminar/workshop ➤ What is coaching/history of coaching ➤ General benefits ➤ Who can be coached ➤ Coaching interventions ➤ Coaching as a leadership responsibility	Formal alignment ➤ Goals of coaching ➤ Specific rewards/benefits ➤ Obstacles ➤ Review process ➤ Program refinements

Figure 5.2   A model of organisational alignment

The manager as coach

When managers adopt a coaching profile, the organisation benefits in numerous ways. Some general organisational benefits include:

➤ employees' commitments to the vision and goals of the organisation are clarified and enhanced—employees become committed rather than compliant

➤ commitment to training, learning and development is increased

➤ turnover is decreased because individuals feel ownership and investment in the company's success

➤ self-awareness is increased, and interpersonal skills are valued and developed

- workplace communication is improved, and a friendlier, more trusting environment is created

- employees become more self-directed, less dependent and more accountable

- new skills and competencies are learned and practised, and ongoing feedback is available to support new behaviours—this results in better skilled, more productive employees and measurable gains in output

- cooperation is increased, there is less competition and shared work objectives are accomplished

- employee conflict is reduced, which results in more attention to work issues

- staff are more motivated and enthusiastic and generate improved customer relations

- there is greater utilisation of human resources to address individual and team performance challenges.

The advantages and benefits of managers adopting a coaching profile are unequivocal. However, it is critical that the coach is aware of the potential obstacles to establishing a coaching program for managers to be coaches.

As noted above, one of the major drawbacks to managers adopting a coaching role is lack of organisational resources and support. Sponsorship and commitment at all levels of the organisation is crucial if coaching is to be anything other than a change of name in management practices. One reason that organisations may be reluctant to establish a coaching environment is that they feel they already have the competitive edge and do not really need coaching. While such an attitude is understandable, it is somewhat reactive and short-sighted. First, every company can improve its performance and employees can feel more satisfied and fulfilled in their working lives. Second, because a company may have cornered a niche market, this does not mean that its status will remain unchallenged or that it will never undergo major transformation and challenges. Some organisations may be too conservative, and not receptive to the new ideas and changes that coaching encompasses. Finally, while most companies recognise the need for excellence in technical skills, the need for personal development of staff can be a low priority.

While most managers recognise the benefits of coaching and the need to change their modus operandi, some fear they may lose their power base if they adopt a coaching style. Our egos can become invested in our roles, especially in the trappings of our authority. Coaching is a collaborative and more democratic relationship than the traditional 'command, control and coercion' model of management. If issues of control and a reluctance to renounce a hierarchical style are paramount, a manager may require individual coaching to gain insight into, and develop strategies to overcome, these obstacles to self-development as a coach.

Some managers fear that they do not have the requisite skills for successful coaching and will not know what to do and will fail. Such lack of confidence can manifest as a reluctance to confront staff and a fear of offending employees on whom they obviously depend. These insecurities are more easily overcome than some of the organisational blockages mentioned above. As managers acquire coaching skills such as goal setting, developing action plans, dealing with difficult employees and managing conflict, many of these anxieties dissolve. However, the issue of managers being resistant to coaching because they are uncomfortable with their skills highlights the importance of having trained, competent coaches, either in-house or externally, to train and coach managers and others in the organisation to be coaches.

Some managers insist they do not have the time to devote to coaching and development. Part of the coach's role is to present the benefits of coaching in such a way that it becomes recognised and positioned as an important leadership responsibility.

A manager as a coach

Case Study

W. J. is a senior manager in a medium-sized public service organisation. The organisation decided to introduce a coaching program in which W. J. would play a key role. W. J. has some reservations about coaching and an external coach was employed to work with him on an individual basis. Although many of W. J.'s objections to coaching were stated in terms of logistics and processes, the coach recognised that much of W. J.'s hesitation was due to some deep-seated beliefs he had about the role of the manager and how coaching might erode the manager's power base. W. J. tended to tell and direct others rather than asking, listening and requesting. He made decisions unilaterally rather than through collaborating and facilitating. The coach worked with W. J. to examine some of his beliefs and to appreciate that his model of the manager as 'boss' was limiting his own potential and that of his staff. Over a period of seven weeks, W. J. warmed to the concept of coaching, and he and the coach devoted the remainder of the coaching sessions to developing strategies to institute a coaching program for managers.

Some roles of the manager as coach

1 *Know your employees*

Employees perform better when they feel appreciated and valued. One way in which a manager can demonstrate interest in staff is by having a brief but comprehensive document of each employee's performance history. An example of such a document follows:

Checklist

Employee:... Position: Manager/Coach

Work role (major duties and responsibilities)...

....

Formal qualifications..

....

Training experiences...

....

Employee's greatest job strength..

Employee's greatest job weakness..

Emotional competencies..

....

Area to work on/performance deficit(s)..

Strategies and tools to assist in performance development..

....

2 *Foster and support a development and learning environment*

Although employees are responsible for their own professional development, managers have to develop a trusting, supporting and challenging learning environment. Learning, growing and changing are ongoing processes and should not be considered solely as isolated responses to problem situations. Many managers are unaware of the effectiveness of the learning programs in their organisations. A learning and development audit can assist them to recognise and enhance their learning processes.

3   *Work with employees to clarify values and vision*

As a coach, a manager will succeed only in so far as he or she can influence employees to commit to the company's vision. To do so, the coach first of all has to clarify this vision and determine whether the employee's values are in harmony with those of the organisation. A few simple questions can provide a wealth of data to the coach. For example: Do you enjoy your work? What motivates you? Do you enjoy working with your colleagues? What would you like to be different about your job?

4   *Ensure employees know what is expected of them*

One of the reasons for poor work performance is that staff may be unaware of their responsibilities. A good coach will know the necessary competencies for the individual's job position and can convey this information in a clear, straightforward fashion. During a coaching session it can then be determined whether the individual requires further skills training. While some authors suggest that managers should be responsible for all training, this is not always practical or time efficient. The coach's role may be to recommend further training, perhaps from an in-house source or from an external training supplier.

5   *Diagnose problems*

The coach observes, monitors, and diagnoses difficulties. Multi-rater performance assessments may be unnecessary, as the coach can gather adequate data on performance through direct observation, reports from supervisors or line managers, customer satisfaction data and from the individual's overall productivity. The manager can ask employees to evaluate themselves and disclose what they want and what they are getting from their work. Having established that there is a problem, and most employees recognise this even before the coaching session, the coach can attempt to determine its cause. Some reasons for poor performance include: inadequate skill levels, insufficient practice, poor interpersonal skills, lack of confidence in performing a task, disagreement about task priorities, insufficient performance feedback, organisational process weaknesses, inadequate resources and support, and a mismatch between the person and the task. Some writers caution that the coach should not 'psychologise' regarding motives and causes but rather focus on improving the performance.

6   *Find solutions*

Having diagnosed the difficulty and its probable cause, the coach and the employee work together to find new answers through a mutual problem-solving process. At times, depending on the nature of the problem, the coach may simply offer technical advice, demonstrate the skill or recommend further skills training. On other occasions, the manager's role may be to facilitate the problem-solving exercise and allow the coachee to make better choices and decisions. Different individuals have different needs, different styles of learning and varying levels of competence. The manager requires the insight and flexibility to adjust his or her coaching style to the particular employee.

7   *Establish clear performance goals*

An important part of gaining commitment to change and goals is for the coach to understand the individual's expectations and needs. If these are unrealistic, the coach has to confront the individual and discuss the reality of the situation. The coach and employee then work together to establish clear, attainable, measurable goals (see Chapter 7). Any possible obstacles should be discussed, and any resistance uncovered and confronted. Generally, most resistance is a function of the reason for the original performance deficit. For example, a lack of confidence in executing a task may not only cause a decrease in performance, but may also impact on the person's belief in their ability to achieve new goals and enhance their performance.

8   *Develop an action plan*

As with any form of coaching, it is critical to have an action plan to carry out the agreed upon strategies. Depending on the nature of the performance deficit, the plan may vary in complexity, performance measurement and time frame. There are some general guidelines for performance measurement that can be useful to the coach, such as:

➤   Why am I measuring a specific unit(s) of performance?

➤   What are the standards or criteria against which I measure performance?

➤   Which variables should be measured?

➤   Are existing measurement tools adequate and relevant?

➤   Who should measure performance?

➤   What time frame is adequate for the measurement process to be valid and reliable?

An example of a simple action plan is shown below.

Checklist

ACTION PLAN

Name: S. B.   **Position:** Customer service personnel   **Coach:** G. F.

Behaviour: Several (four) customer complaints about her rudeness during the past two weeks; peers and a supervisor report that she is difficult to work with.

Diagnosis: Insufficient on-the-job training which S. B. finds frustrating and stressful; inadequate time management skills resulting in disorganised, flurried behaviour with customers.

Goal(s): To reduce customer complaints to zero over the next four weeks; to reduce 'stress response' to levels acceptable to herself and her peers.

Action: Close, supportive peer supervision for two weeks.

Coaching in a simple mind-mapping exercise to establish priorities.

Two coaching sessions in stress-reduction techniques, e.g. abdominal breathing exercises, deep muscular relaxation.

Feedback and review: Two week time frame: self-report, peer/supervisor reports and the number of customer complaints.

How to provide effective feedback

The ability to give constructive feedback is crucial to the success of any coaching intervention and is one of the major roles of the manager as coach. However, in our workshops for coaching managers to be coaches, managers frequently report a lack of ease with giving feedback. We shall therefore discuss this issue in more detail.

Feedback is what we do when we offer our opinions or evaluations of someone else's behaviour or performance. It is any communication that gives another person information about how we perceive them and how their behaviour impacts on us.

Giving and receiving feedback is essential to ensure the goals of the individual and the organisation are met. It gives encouragement and direction. Many managers take it for granted that their employees know that they are doing a good job. Yet this is not necessarily so. Employees require reinforcement for their successes and information about areas that need improvement if they are to make gains and develop in their careers. Most individuals welcome feedback. Individuals high in achievement competence always seek feedback or ways to track their success. Even negative feedback is better than no feedback. Individuals soon lose motivation and enthusiasm if they believe that no one cares about their performance.

Feedback is a form of recognition that can motivate people. It shows employees that their manager cares enough about them to tell them the truth, and that their manager has sufficient trust in their capacity to accept the truth and in their desire for growth and self-development. As noted by Hill, the modern feedback process is led more by the employee. It emphasises counselling, self-appraisal and self-development. Feedback focuses on the important competencies required in a job and the outcomes required by the organisation, and it identifies key performance drivers required to achieve organisational success. Like coaching in general, good feedback emphasises goals and is forward looking.

Some benefits of timely and constructive feedback:

➤ It causes individuals to feel as though they belong and that their efforts and contributions are valued.

➤ Positive feedback acts as a reinforcer and strengthens the likelihood of the desired behaviour continuing, particularly if it is delivered intermittently. If feedback is negative (or critical), it can induce the individual to strive harder and improve and develop performance.

➤ It enhances the individual's strengths and contributions to the organisation.

➤ It can guide, offer and suggest ways to improve in the form of new ideas and new strategies.

➤ It builds a relationship between the manager and the employee by creating trust and an open two-way communication between the receiver and the sender.

➤ It builds self-esteem, confidence and accountability.

➤ It helps the employee unlearn unproductive or ineffectual habits.

➤ Feedback sessions save time. The manager can use the sessions to be pro-active and to nip problems in the bud.

➤ When feedback sessions are documented, they can serve as a progress report. This helps the manager keep track and prepare for the next session. Importantly, it shows employees that their manager takes them and their performance seriously.

While it may be true that many organisations get more feedback than they are willing or able to implement, feedback is at the heart of a coaching relationship. Yet many managers lack skill and confidence in providing feedback to employees. As a result, they avoid providing feedback or deliver it at inappropriate times and places in a rushed, abrupt, negative fashion or in such an oblique, vague manner that the employee does not understand the message. As already noted, one reason for this ill ease may be a fear of offending employees. Other managers may see feedback as a mere formality, and fail to recognise that individuals perform better when they are reinforced for their achievements. This is not to say, of course, that all feedback should be positive. At times, the coach has to be confronting and challenging. Yet even when feedback is negative, it can be delivered in a manner that is not likely to put the receiver off side or damage the relationship between the coach and employee.

Feedback should not be reserved for annual performance reviews or for when problems arise. Feedback should be built into the relationship between the manager and the employee. It is an unending process that allows for review and continuous growth.

Constructive feedback is more likely to occur in a friendly, supportive environment. It should be delivered in non-emotive language with the emphasis on the behaviour rather than the individual. It should never be given in anger or be judgmental. Feedback should be presented as an opportunity for learning and development rather than something threatening or intimidating.

Guidelines for giving feedback

As shown in Figure 5.3 below, it is essential that the coach be prepared for the session and does not simply recite a litany of complaints. Some ways the coach can prepare for the session include: pre-planning what to say; writing down a few key words to use; and writing down two or three questions to help the employee think about the situation and to encourage his or her involvement. Where relevant, the coach should acknowledge his or her possible contribution to the situation.

Feedback can be face-to-face or indirect, verbal or written, solicited or unsolicited. Face-to-face feedback is preferable. If the feedback is negative, it should always be given in private. Feedback should be given immediately after or as close as possible to the event, although if the manager is feeling frustrated or angry, it is wise to delay giving the feedback. Managers who dislike giving feedback tend to reserve it for correcting poor performance or behaviours. Feedback is about learning and is an ongoing process.

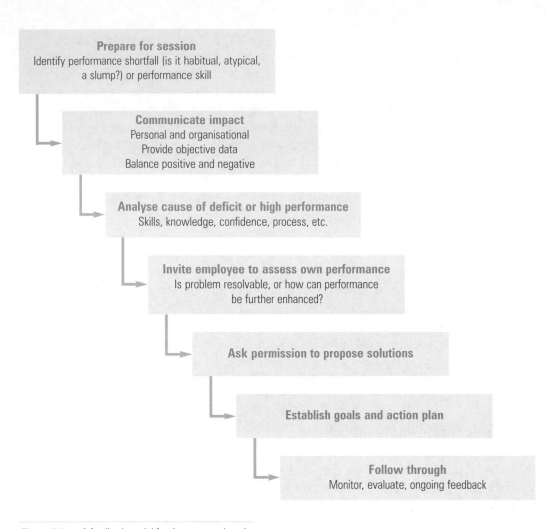

Prepare for session
Identify performance shortfall (is it habitual, atypical,
a slump?) or performance skill

Communicate impact
Personal and organisational
Provide objective data
Balance positive and negative

Analyse cause of deficit or high performance
Skills, knowledge, confidence, process, etc.

Invite employee to assess own performance
Is problem resolvable, or how can performance
be further enhanced?

Ask permission to propose solutions

Establish goals and action plan

Follow through
Monitor, evaluate, ongoing feedback

Figure 5.3   A feedback model for the manager/coach

The coach has to clearly identify the performance shortfall(s). The coach should consider whether the individual is performing erratically, whether the performance deficit is atypical, or whether the problem is a process or procedural one. Wherever possible, the coach should provide objective data to support his or her concerns (e.g. charts, statistics, reports and feedback from colleagues). Evidence suggests that subjective negative feedback is only accepted when it comes from a high-status, highly credible source. New or inexperienced managers, therefore, should provide objective data to support their observations.

The coach should communicate his or her response and the impact on the organisation. Comments should not be personalised, judgmental or evaluative and should always address the behaviour rather than the individual. If feedback is delivered in an emotive manner, the recipient responds emotionally and is unable to process the information the coach is giving them. It is essential that the coach is specific about the behaviour, whether it is positive or negative. The employee has to be clear about why the coach is praising or criticising him or her.

Together with the employee, the coach should analyse and determine the cause of the performance deficit. The coach should ask the individual for his or her explanation of the problem and listen carefully, particularly if he or she feels the individual is not being receptive to his or her comments. Can the person do anything about the problem? It is a waste of time giving personal feedback if the situation is not controllable by the employee.

The coach should clarify his or her expectations. This may involve reviewing job competencies or discussing the employee's particular strengths and weaknesses. The coach should communicate confidence, support and encouragement if the person is experiencing a slump, and should not be afraid of being confrontational if the behaviour is chronic or in need of urgent attention.

The coach should ask permission to discuss/propose solutions. As a manager, he or she has to be aware of what the individual needs to know in order to do the job correctly. The coach should have alternatives and solutions in mind before holding the feedback session.

The coach and coachee should agree on an action plan, and a timetable for improvement. The coach should clearly establish simple monitoring procedures and agree to a follow-up session to review progress. Effective questioning will establish the quality of the planning and the improved performance. Some questions to clarify this process include: What obstacles might stand in your way? How confident are you that you will be able to institute these changes?

Figure 5.3 illustrates a feedback model for the manager/coach. It provided guidelines for giving feedback, from preparing for the session through to establishing goals and an action plan.

Giving praise can present as much difficulty for some managers as does a confronting style of feedback. Yet praise can be a powerful form of reward. We find that some managers are personally reluctant to give praise because they themselves have never received it or appeared to need it. They claim a 'job well done' is sufficient reward for them. Others suspect that employees will become complacent and lose motivation if praised too much. However, honest, sincere and appropriate praise can prove as great an incentive to most employees as monetary and other rewards. Individuals welcome praise for who they are as much as for what they do.

Some methods of reward include thanking employees for a job well done, smiling, describing the individual's successful efforts, showing a personal interest in an individual's career after a special achievement or featuring an employee of the month.

Giving feedback

K. G. is a 52-year-old senior partner in a law firm who is undertaking annual performance appraisals on his junior partners. He is particularly apprehensive about giving feedback to I. H., who colleagues and some clients describe as dominating, abrasive and lacking in interpersonal skills. K. G. himself is intimidated by I. H. The coach and K. G. worked together on applying the feedback model shown in Figure 5.3 to I. H.'s situation. Once he had a structure and general guidelines for giving feedback, K. G. claimed he felt more confident and less defensive. After the feedback session with I. H., he reported to the coach that the approach had been particularly effective. Inviting I. H. to assess her own performance allowed her to comment freely on her behaviour and to present her side of the story, including some of the difficulties inherent in working in a male-dominated environment and the lack of ongoing feedback from senior partners. K. G. also remarked that asking I. H.'s permission to present solutions encouraged collaboration and offset any resentment on her part.

Some coaching skills for managers

Research suggests the 10 most frequently cited skills for successful managers are the ability to: (1) develop self-awareness; (2) communicate verbally; (3) set goals and articulate a vision; (4) manage individual decisions; (5) motivate and influence others; (6) build teams; (7) define and solve problems; (8) delegate; (9) manage time and stress; and (10) manage conflict. Interestingly, these also constitute many of the skills of a successful coach. It would appear, then, that any concerns a manager might have about coaching detracting from managing should be allayed. Coaching is a *style* of managing. The model of coaching skills shown in Figure 5.4 incorporates and expands on the 10 competencies listed here.

Develop self-awareness in self and others

Communicate verbally and effectively
  ➤ know your employees
  ➤ clarify your expectations

Set goals and articulate a vision
  ➤ conduct individual coaching sessions
  ➤ establish performance plans
  ➤ develop action plans
  ➤ provide ongoing support and feedback

Manage individual decisions

Motivate and influence

Build teams
  ➤ conduct team coaching sessions
  ➤ encourage collective responsibility

Solve problems

Delegate

Manage time and stress

Manage conflict

Figure 5.4   Coaching skills for managers

The purpose of this section of the book is to assist managers to adopt a coaching style to develop these managerial skills. Of the 10 listed competencies, several are covered in other sections of this book: managing individual decisions and motivating and influencing others (Chapter 4), verbal communication (Chapter 8), setting goals and vision (Chapter 7), self-awareness (Chapters 1 and 4) and team building (Chapter 6), while problem solving is discussed in several chapters. Therefore, the following section will concentrate on coaching skills for managing time and stress, and dealing with conflict and delegation. We then discuss the critical role of the manager as career coach.

Managing time and stress

While a detailed account of time and stress management is beyond the scope of this book, the topic raises two issues for the manager as a coach. These are: (1) how the manager effectively manages his or her own time and stress and thereby provides a role model for employees; and (2) how the manager can recognise and coach employees who are having difficulties in these areas.

Research indicates four main sources of stress in the workplace:

1   *Time stressors*   Essentially, this type of stress results from employees having too much to do in too little time. Time stressors can include impossible deadlines, insufficient staffing and poor communication of expectations and expected schedules.

    The coach's role: First, the manager has to recognise the signs and symptoms of time stress. These are usually obvious and manifest themselves in incomplete work assignments, poorly executed tasks and lack of enthusiasm in assuming further responsibilities. Psychologically, employees might experience and exhibit anxiety, frustration, anger and even depression if the situation is longstanding, seemingly impossible to resolve or beyond their control. The coach should:

    ➤ Determine with the employee whether any duties can be delegated or performed more efficiently.

    ➤ Help the coachee prioritise urgent tasks that require immediate attention and important tasks that are non-urgent. Attending to important, non-urgent tasks can frequently offset or reduce urgent problems.

    ➤ Use simple mind-mapping techniques to plot out tasks and number them in order of priority.

    ➤ Determine whether as a manager he or she can provide the resources to reduce the stress.

2   *Encounter stressors*   Interpersonal interactions are at the centre of many organisational problems. Some evidence shows that lack of trust among individuals affects communication, the sharing of information and decision making. A study by Northwest National Life of the 10 most significant stressors associated with burnout found that seven dealt with encounter stress.

    The coach's role: The manager should develop and encourage a supportive work environment where employees experience trust and feel valued and free to express opinions. Findings from the Northwest National Life survey show that employees who rate their managers as supportive have lower rates of burnout, lower stress levels, fewer stress-related incidences and increased productivity, loyalty and efficiency than employees with non-supportive and interpersonally incompetent managers.

3   *Situational stressors*   These stressors usually relate to work design situations or how the individual does his or her job.

The coach's role: Our experience working with managers suggests that difficulties within this area can frequently be prevented or ameliorated by establishing clear and open lines of communication between employees, line managers and senior managers. The coach should ensure that there is a forum for discussion or complaints where problems can be addressed at an early stage. Additional responsibility or an increased role in decision making could alleviate stress, or conversely, less responsibility or more accountability from management may provide solutions. The critical factor in dealing with situational stressors seems to be that the manager as coach should be pro-active rather than allowing crisis situations to develop.

4   *Anticipatory stressors*   The degree to which we experience stress is related to what we fear will happen as much as it is a reaction to what is happening. Some individuals are more prone to anticipatory anxiety than others. While this is partly a function of personality characteristics or physiological 'hard-wiring', the coach can work with employees to develop strategies to deal with and lessen anticipatory stress.

The coach's role: Anxiety can actually motivate and encourage the individual to meet deadlines, solve problems and develop new strategies to enhance current work performance. On the other hand, anxiety can be overwhelming and can leave the individual immobilised and incapacitated. In the latter case, the manager would be wise to refer the person out for therapy, whether that involves hypnosis, cognitive-behavioural therapy or counselling.

Usually though, much anticipatory anxiety can be dealt with by building up resilience to stress. The manager can encourage and teach deep relaxation techniques, as well as encourage and provide opportunities for individuals to exercise, do yoga or meditate, either on-site or out of office hours. Role-playing or rehearsals of upcoming situations that are engendering anxiety can also prove beneficial.

Managers are expected to function as a role model for their employees. A reasonable level of physical fitness, some commitment to exercise and good diet is therefore desirable. It is also crucial that a coach has, to some degree, come to terms with his or her own anxiety levels and is seen to be able to contain them. As with all coaches, being able to recognise their own anxieties leads to more patience with, and empathy for, the coachee/individual, rather than a defensive minimising of the other's concerns.

Managing conflict

In our workshops for coaching the coach, we have found conflict to be the most disliked and avoided topic. While it is generally accepted that conflict is an inevitable facet of the human condition, and hence a normal part of personal and organisational life, most managers would prefer not to have to deal with it.

One way for managers to come to terms with the inevitability of conflict is to actually review some of the benefits associated with it. If there is little disagreement or total consensus on issues, there is a tendency to stagnation; conflict can provide an opportunity for growth and learning. Conflict can also stimulate creative problem solving. Of course, too much conflict can be as detrimental to organisations and individuals as too little.

Managers as coaches need to assess the source of conflict within the workplace. It is generally wise for managers not to rely on a 'personality' explanation for all conflict. It is true that some individuals are difficult to work with and seem to be involved in more conflict and disagreement than most. The manager has to be able to decide whether the conflict is genuinely a result of the individual's personality and, if so, what to do about it. However, sources of conflict can result from several factors, including:

1   *Personal differences*   Conflict can be a function of differences in age, gender, culture and education. As a coach, a manager's responsibility is to open up channels of communication and facilitate discussion about differences among employees. While the manager's role is not necessarily that of peacemaker, conflict can be assuaged if individuals can freely discuss and attempt to understand their differences and how these impact on working together.

2   *Poor information processes*   If communication channels are unclear or are cluttered, employees may be unsure of what is expected of them, procedures may seem unnecessarily complicated and frustrating, and performance benchmarking may seem vague or inconsistent. The manager is responsible for addressing these weaknesses, for clarifying roles and expectations and, importantly, for reinforcing or rewarding the individual for a job well done.

3   *Role incompatibility*   Conflict can arise when there are different priorities between departments or conflicting demands between different sections within the same department. Each party may consider the other to be obstructionist. The manager's task again is to mediate, to facilitate a form of meaningful exchange between the disagreeing parties and to encourage problem solving and changes to processes that will decrease conflict.

4   *Environmental stressors*   As mentioned above, environmental stressors generally relate to features of the actual working environment that engender distress and conflict. These can include lack of budgets for training, poor safety conditions and stress associated with downsizing and other major organisational change.

The manager has first to determine the cause of the conflict and then obtain commitment from the parties involved to resolve it. While there are various models of conflict resolution (e.g. collaborative, forcing and accommodating), these are perhaps more relevant, say, for the executive who is engaged in conflict with a colleague or client. For the manager as coach, conflict management involves a variety of coaching skills rather than a particular model that can be applied to every situation. These skills can be summarised as the ability to:

➤ identify the cause of the conflict

➤ ask for suggested solutions

➤ offer win–win solutions

➤ give feedback

➤ use corrective coaching where necessary

➤ be directive in a non-threatening manner.

Case Study

Resolving conflict

G. B. is a 45-year-old manager of a medium-sized IT company. He is a self-described 'nice guy' who is having difficulty with two recently employed key personnel who are causing dissension among staff. G. B. avoids conflict whenever possible. The situation has reached the stage where productivity is being affected and staff morale is very low. G. B. employed a coach, and during the coaching sessions he came to recognise that he had always entertained the 'distorted' belief that if one is nice to others, they should be nice in return. In fact, he sometimes used his 'niceness' as a means of control to get others to behave as he desired. The coach and G. B. also discussed the potential benefits of conflict and the impossibility and undesirability of denying or avoiding it. G. B. and the coach continued to develop a model of conflict resolution that G. B. found relatively easy to put into practice once he had gained some insights into his self-limiting beliefs about conflict.

Delegating

Another area that presents difficulties for some managers wishing to adopt a coaching style is delegating. Delegating involves coaching. It offers the opportunity for employees to learn new skills, develop a sense of self-worth and develop a greater sense of autonomy and accountability. Delegating, as long as it is not seen as 'simply off-loading responsibility', can engender greater commitment and loyalty in employees. It is generally accepted that individuals who feel trusted by their managers work more effectively and productively than those who do not. Delegating also gives managers more time to manage.

Delegating can also be seen as a form of empowerment. Some authors object to the notion of empowerment, suggesting that it is a hierarchical, power-driven notion that should be dismissed from the management lexicon. Others suggest that empowerment is not what the manager does for his or her staff, but what impediments the manager takes away to leave space for individuals to empower themselves. There are five dimensions of empowerment that the manager as a coach should instil. These are:

1 *A sense of self-efficacy*, or the feeling that the individual has the capability and competence to carry out a task without being hindered by external obstacles.

2 *A sense of self-determination*, or the feeling that the individual's choice determines his or her actions.

3 *Personal control*, or the belief that the individual has an impact on the outcome of events.

4 *A sense of meaning*, or a sense of purpose and value, in what the employee is doing.

5 *Trust*, or the belief that the manager will treat the individual fairly and will be consistent and reliable.

A manager's willingness or unwillingness to empower or delegate is a function of: (a) his or her belief and trust in the competence of others; (b) interest in his or her employees; (c) a fear that he or she may lose power and position or be manipulated; and (d) a need for control. Individuals with a high need for control tend to believe that delegation will result in chaos. In fact, often, when such individuals do delegate, it tends to be seen as just another attempt to dominate and control.

The following checklist offers a guide for managers when delegating to their staff.

GUIDELINES FOR DELEGATING

✓ *Choose what task(s) to delegate*

Is there time to delegate?

What does the task(s) involve?

Is the task appropriate for the individual?

Has the person the capacity/skills/information/interest to execute the task?

Will the task enhance the individual's work skills?

✓ *Assign the task to the individual(s)*

Allocate the necessary resources

Begin with an easy task

Reward the correct performance

Increase the task difficulty

✓ *Model the desired behaviours*

Provide guidance

Offer support and encouragement

Supervise the task

✓ *Give feedback*

Career coaching in organisations

One of the key roles of the manager as a coach is to provide career coaching for employees. The primary purpose of career coaching is to help employees consider alternatives and make decisions regarding their careers. In return, the organisation gains the benefit of knowing about employees' career perspectives and can therefore plan and provide opportunities for them to fulfil their career goals. Of course, human resource personnel also provide career coaching services.

Some advantages of in-house coaching

The qualities and skills of a successful coach are common to both external and in-house coaches. However, there are several advantages to having an in-house coach. These include:

➤ Managers and HR personnel are more familiar with the company's culture and climate than external coaches. They are integrated into the organisation and are more aware of future directions and the projected required skills and competencies.

➤ Managers can assess the need for career development programs in the organisation and can design them. Having designed a program to meet the specific needs of the company, the in-house coach can then promote the program. As a result, the company can realise its full investment in human resources and attract quality, committed employees who take responsibility for their own careers.

➤ In-house coaches can use performance evaluations on which to base practical and realistic suggestions about career planning. They can identify employee strengths and weaknesses and recommend appropriate training and coaching activities to enhance employee performance.

➤ Careers are stagnating and plateauing at increasingly early stages. If the likelihood of further promotion is low, many people retire or seek work with another organisation. Rather than costly recruiting, the manager can encourage lateral moves, rotate responsibilities and lower the rate of job progression. The in-house coach is acutely aware of areas where growth in individual skills and competencies is required and employees who have plateaued can be offered further training and development to become more multiskilled and generalist. These strategies can result in renewed enthusiasm and commitment on the part of the employees.

The manager as coach can assist individuals to assume and develop different roles within the organisation, such as coaching new recruits, mentoring likely successors and chairing various committees. In this way, individuals can adopt a useful, nurturing and 'giving back' role in the company, thereby fulfilling the task of 'generativity' described by Erikson.

As noted by Bardwick, one of the difficulties involved in career plateauing and lateral moves is that recognition and status are usually tied to job level, title, promotion and compensation levels rather than performance, expertise, entrepreneurialism and teamwork. A redefinition of prestige and status would likely encourage individuals to remain within the organisation, rather than seeking a higher job level or title elsewhere.

Some advantages of external coaches

Although the above benefits are indisputable, there are also advantages to employing an external coach in organisations, such as:

➤ An outside coach allows staff to be more open and candid about their goals and concerns. Some employees may feel misgivings and mistrust about revealing dissatisfaction about their careers to managers. External coaches may be perceived as being less biased and more empathic.

➤ Individuals may be reluctant to reveal any weaknesses to someone within the organisation.

➤ Individuals, particularly those in top positions, frequently have no one with whom they can discuss their ideas or concerns. An external coach can provide an objective, confidential and professional 'ear'.

➤ Importantly, managers and HR personnel require training in coaching skills. Usually, external coaches are called on to provide this critical service.

Some specific roles for the manager as a career coach

Managers frequently offer career advice as part of their general managerial duties. However, there are specific coaching roles that the manager as coach can adopt. These include:

➤ *Designing and implementing appraisal systems and standards* The manager and HR personnel are in an ideal position to give feedback and help employees clarify the opportunities and limits that exist within the company. Future options and directions can be discussed so that individuals can prepare for and adapt to these demands.

➤ *Conducting a review of current and future career plans.*

➤ *Setting goals* While the process of goal setting is essentially similar for all types of coaching, the manager as a career coach is in a unique position to assess and discuss the employee's level of commitment to his or her career goals. The manager can guide employees in assessing their career motivations and career options and can participate actively in goal setting and action planning.

➤ *Providing ongoing support and encouragement during the implementation of the agreed upon career strategies.*

➤ *Working with employees who may be stressed or dissatisfied with their job* Interpersonal issues at work, such as conflict with colleagues or team members, may adversely affect performance. Coaching to improve communication skills and to look at ways to resolve conflict can enhance performance and keep the individual focused on his or her career path trajectory.

A guideline for career coaching

The following guidelines provide a blueprint for managers in their role as career coach.

1	Clarify values, interests and beliefs.	9	Prepare individuals for future assignments.
2	Clarify work styles and preferences.	10	Recommend new skills and training.
3	Act as a sounding board.	11	Encourage self-control over career.
4	Review previous experience.	12	Deal with fears—failure, success, etc.
5	Assess strengths and weaknesses.	13	Consider long-term career plans.
6	Review options/choices.	14	Develop and establish goals.
7	Uncover alternatives.	15	Develop an action plan.
8	Establish specific needs for improving job performance.		

Coaching managers to be coaches

So, how does a manager become a coach? Ideally, each manager who desires to adopt a coaching profile should receive individual, one-on-one coaching from an experienced coach, either in-house or external to the organisation. Individual coaching allows for greater self-awareness, and leads the manager to become more cognisant of, and more accepting of, his or her strengths and weaknesses, prejudices and preferences. Individual coaching provides a private, confidential environment for these issues to be discussed freely and honestly. Furthermore, a manager who has benefited from personal coaching is more likely to 'spread the word' and enthusiastically enlist others in a coaching program.

However, individual coaching for managers is not always a viable proposition. Particularly in large organisations, it can be costly and time-consuming compared to group coaching. Most coaching therefore tends to be done in a group workshop setting, usually on a weekly basis for approximately two hours over a period of eight to twelve weeks. Again, this time schedule is ideal and may not be appropriate for all situations. Sometimes, for instance, because of time constraints and managers' schedules, our workshops are held over an intensive three- or four-day period. Although there are follow-up workshops to these intensive coaching sessions, the time frame does not allow for the extensive monitoring, practising of new skills and feedback processes that contribute to sustained behavioural change.

The following outline is a summary of the workshops that we conduct with managers who wish to adopt a coaching style.

Workshop: coaching managers to be coaches

Purpose

1 To develop managers/coaches who are able to facilitate the development, learning and performance of individuals and teams.

2 To provide the foundation for managers to develop their own ability as coaches.

3 To help managers understand what coaching is and how it can offer new possibilities for more effective interactions in the workplace.

4 To help managers understand the practical value of coaching as a performance enhancement technique.

5 To help managers develop self-awareness and recognise their own strengths and weaknesses as a manager and leader.

6 To help managers to develop an understanding of the process of coaching as well as coaching skills and techniques.

Who attends

Workshops are typically attended by senior managers, middle managers, human resources personnel, line managers and supervisors. The number of workshop participants varies from six (with one facilitative coach) to twelve (with two facilitative coaches).

Course content

➤ The qualities of a successful coach—for example, self-awareness, openness, patience and listening skills.

➤ Managerial self-awareness—how to reflect on and assess own attitudes, behaviours and skills as they manifest in the workplace; self-evaluation and feedback about performance.

➤ What is coaching? How is it different from counselling and mentoring? Types of coaching, for example directive versus non-directive, career coaching, performance enhancement and corrective coaching. When to apply different types of coaching.

continued...

- How to establish and encourage a culture of learning and development—coaching as a style of relating.
- The role of the manager as a coach—recognising and creating opportunities for coaching.
- Coaching as a conversation—how to develop trust and rapport; enhancing communication skills, for example practising attending, inquiring and reflecting.
- How to assess and diagnose performance deficits—defining the problem; analysing possible causes; generating alternative solutions; establishing clear performance objectives.
- How to set goals and develop action plans.
- Developing effective monitoring strategies, giving feedback, benchmarking and following-through on agreed upon strategies.
- How employees learn on the job—styles of learning; supervision and feedback.
- Creative problem solving—how to engage employees in finding solutions; working more creatively and more effectively as a team.
- Some specific coaching skills—giving feedback; delegating; dealing with conflict; dealing with difficult employees; managing workplace stress; career coaching; and leadership skills.

 Case Study

Coaching managers to be coaches

G. P. is the manager of a medium-sized retail company. Although formally trained in management, he lacks the ability to translate some of this knowledge into practical, everyday management skills. He tends to avoid delegation and is constantly overburdened with work. When he does delegate, it is because he is simply unable to execute the task. He off-loads the task(s) without any consideration for the individual(s) involved and, consequently, the delegated tasks are resented and poorly executed by employees. During a workshop on coaching managers to be coaches, G. P. recognised that his behaviour was determined partly by his need for control and partly by his lack of confidence in employees' skills and commitment. Through developing his self-awareness and accepting that delegation presents an opportunity for employee growth and development, which in turn can engender commitment and loyalty, G. P. experienced a major turnaround. A follow-up coaching session two months later revealed (from self-reports and appraisals by employees) that G. P. was more willing to delegate, and more effective in supervising and giving feedback.

Team coaching

Key points

➤ The growth of team coaching

➤ What constitutes a good team?

➤ When are teams appropriate?

➤ Types of team coaching

➤ Some characteristics of good teams

➤ Stages of team formation

➤ Some obstacles to team coaching and what to do about them

➤ Some qualities of a successful team coach

➤ A six-step model of team coaching

➤ Coaching virtual teams

The growth of team coaching

While a substantial part of our work involves one-on-one executive coaching, increasingly there is a need for team coaching. One of the chief reasons for this development is that, as mentioned in Chapter 5, the management model of 'managers as coaches' is fast taking hold in many organisations. Second, the growth in the popularity of 'self-managing', cross-functional and multiskilled teams presents an avenue for coaches to guide and support the development and skilling of team members. Finally, team coaching can be more cost-effective and time-effective than individual coaching.

High-performing teams in a high-performing culture is an imperative in the current marketplace. Team coaching can benefit everyone involved—the business, customers, managers and individual team members. Building effective teams within businesses and organisations can differentiate one company from its competitors. As team members become more self-directing and goal-oriented, companies improve quality and productivity and build stronger and more lasting relationships with customers.

What constitutes a good team?

A group of individuals working together on a project does not necessarily constitute a team. Maddux lists some of the major differences between groups and teams. These are shown in Table 6.1.

Groups	Teams
➤ Individuals work independently	➤ Members are interdependent
➤ Self focused, hidden agendas ownership	➤ Mutual goals, purpose, mission, sense of unity,
➤ Distrust and disagreement	➤ Openness, trust; disagreements seen as positive
➤ Unclear communications	➤ Open, honest communication
➤ Conflict avoided or escalates	➤ Recognise value of conflict; conflict resolution strategies in place
➤ Conformity	➤ Free expression

Table 6.1   Differences between groups and teams

Of these variables, two have been highlighted as the best discriminators of groups and teams. These are (a) the heightened level of dependency among team members and (b) the degree of commonality, or the degree to which the goals of the team override the goals of individual members. In *The Wisdom of Teams*, Smith and Katzenbach (1993) offer the following definition of a team:

> a small number of people with complementary skills who are committed to a common purpose, performance goals and approach for which they are mutually accountable.

When are teams appropriate?

In the same way that not all groups are teams, not every situation requires a team effort. We are frequently asked to design customised team seminars and workshops for our international clients. One of the issues we have encountered is that of the appropriateness of the team model to address certain issues. On occasions, we have advised against using a team model and instead recommended one-on-one coaching for one or two individuals working on a specified project.

A coach who has been employed to work with a team must be aware of the appropriateness of the team format for specific issues. While abundant evidence indicates the benefits and successes of teams, it would be unwise to assume that teams always offer the best solution. Indeed, there is a growing literature that suggests otherwise. Some authors suggest that team participation is stressful and non-productive, with ongoing power struggles that are rarely resolved. Self-managing teams are particularly notorious for their inability to reach consensus and make decisions. Finally, even in top organisations, teams often exist in name only, and there is conflict between the disciplines of strong executive leadership and that of performance teams. However, despite the cautions against presuming that all tasks require teamwork, team coaching can be challenging, effective and performance enhancing.

Types of team coaching

The following list summarises the types of team coaching that we most frequently conduct.

1   Coaching managers to be coaches (discussed in detail in Chapter 5).

2   Team building—coaching a team to perform as an effective unit, for example members of a brand team in an advertising agency.

3   Coaching team leaders—developing the team building skills of team leaders, for example a team of state managers responsible for leading their own departments.

4   Coaching individuals who do not belong to one team but who have issues in common, for example how to deal with conflict among employees or how to give effective feedback.

Some characteristics of good teams

While each team has its own unique characteristics, there are several features common to all successful, high-performing teams. These include:

➤ *Common purpose*—a clear course and a sense of direction provide context and guide the team's actions.

➤ *Clear and specific goals*—have an action plan in place and strategies to achieve the goals.

➤ *Each member understands and is competent at his or her position*—members have complementary skills such as technical expertise, decision-making skills and good inter-personal skills.

➤ *Open communication channels*—information and learning is shared among team members. Communication is timely, clear and focused on the strategic goals of the organisation.

➤ *Members encourage and support each other.*

➤ *Flexibility*—able to rotate members to other positions; a sharing or shifting of leadership roles.

➤ *Know and utilise each member's strengths and know their weaknesses.*

➤ *Mutual trust*—share knowledge, experience and ideas on how the team can function more effectively. Individuals collaborate rather than compete.

➤ *Mutual accountability for team results*—share the glory; do not apportion blame when things go wrong. Team members can also work as a team while apart, and can contribute to a sequence of activities rather than a common task that requires their presence in one place at the one time.

➤ *Consistency*—members can work and perform to their potential on a consistent basis.

 Case Study

Team coaching

V. A. is an executive coach who specialises in team coaching. She was employed by a large national retail company to work with a group of senior executives. They were state departmental managers who were part of a national strategic planning team. The team existed in name only. Communication channels were ineffective, team members had hidden agendas and there was little sense of cohesion or unity among them. During the initial team coaching sessions, it appeared that individual differences and 'personality clashes' were at the basis of the team's inability to perform successfully. However, it became apparent to V. A. that the team lacked leadership from 'above'. The vision, mission, goals and priorities of the organisation were vague and the team had never clearly established its own goals and responsibilities. V. A. worked with the team members to first examine the values and strategic vision of the organisation. It was only when the team was able to situate its purpose and overall goals within a broad organisational context that the members felt competent and enthusiastic about dealing with the interpersonal and procedural issues that were blocking the team's development and effectiveness.

Stages of team formation

A team can be seen as an 'organism' that goes through various stages of formation and growth. Although each team has its own unique characteristics, it is generally accepted that most teams undergo five stages of development. These are: (1) forming; (2) storming; (3) norming; (4) performing; and (5) adjourning. Table 6.2 describes these five stages in relation to the behaviour of team members, as well as the coach's role during each stage.

Stage	Team members	Coach's role
Forming	Need to feel included	Develop a sense of belonging/cohesion
		Encourage commitment
	Feel pressure to conform	Encourage role differentiation
	Uncertain about the rules	More directive than facilitative, clarify rules and expectations
	Depend on the coach	Clarify roles, model expected behaviours
	Anxious about purpose and goals	Clarify purpose, task, goals, action plans
		Establish performance measures
		Establish feedback mechanisms
		Set short-term, achievable goals
Storming	Challenge authority/competence of coach	Give non-defensive, fair, firm guidance
	Assert individual will versus team	Acknowledge individual differences
		Encourage interdependence
	Engage in conflicts	Use conflict resolution skills
	Defensive about feedback	Use positive, corrective feedback
	Test limits	Maintain balance between harmony and productive disagreements/dissent
	Resist discussions	Encourage team members to recognise and develop team processes
Norming	Group norms emerge	Encourage team cohesion, repair any damage from storming phase
	Focus on goals/results, welcome feedback	Focus, feedback, set more challenging goals
	Share, trust, develop harmony	Do not hold back for fear of reverting to previous storming/conflict stage
Performing	Team functions in terms of common task(s)	Acknowledge individual contributions
	Possibly engage in group thinking and exclude non-team contributors	Challenge group thinking
		Encourage creative problem-solving
	Possibly become demotivated	Maintain focus
		Set and achieve more challenging goals
Adjourning	Complete task(s), disband team	Encourage individual growth and transfer of skills to other situations
	Experience feelings of separation and loss	Acknowledge and discuss emotional issues
		Phase out team meetings rather than ending abruptly

Table 6.2   Five stages of team formation

Some obstacles to team coaching and what to do about them

Every team is different. The individual characteristics of the team members alone ensure that team dynamics will differ markedly from one team to another. While it is clearly impossible to attempt to cover all the variables that can impact negatively on a team's process and performance, it is possible to isolate and alert the coach to several potential obstacles. These centre on:

1 goals and expectations

2 roles

3 systems and procedures

4 interpersonal issues.

1 *Goals and expectations*   The purpose and goals of the team coaching exercise may not be clarified. Goals may not be realistic and, importantly, they may not be synchronised with the individual team members' values.

What to do: One of the major roles of the team coach is to ensure that sufficient individual and/or team time is allocated to establishing the individuals' commitments to team goals and dealing with any resistance. Focusing on and encouraging team commitment is an ongoing part of the coaching process. The overall goal(s) should be re-visited and reviewed on a regular basis, while goals for each session should be established at the commencement of each team meeting and reviewed at the following session. Such procedures not only keep the coach and team members on track, but they also provide regular reinforcement for successes and allow the development of alternative strategies for failures.

2 *Roles*   The roles of the individual team members may not be clearly delineated within the organisation. Roles may be overlapping, inappropriate or unrelated to the individual's ability. Some specific issues arise for the coach working with self-managing teams. Working within such teams, the leader's role changes from one of leading and directing to one of coaching or facilitating. Leaders may believe members are incapable of managing themselves or fear that their supervisory role may be threatened. Workers' identities may also be threatened and they may not be willing to assume greater responsibility.

What to do: A coach may believe that a particular team is performing poorly because individuals are misplaced within the organisation, or they perceive themselves to be so. Such a situation can lead to a conflict of interests. While it is imperative that the coach establishes and reassures team members of the confidentiality of the coaching sessions, management may need to be involved if structural changes are warranted within the organisation. One method to resolve this potential dilemma is to reach a consensus to invite management to a team session where the matters can be aired. Obviously, this tactic is more likely to succeed where there is an existing culture of coaching and where management has been aligned and visibly supports coaching. Leaders of self-managing teams may require individual coaching along the lines of a manager as a coach. The coach has to assess the reality of fears regarding self-management. It is possible that the team members do not have the requisite technical skills and the coach could recommend further training and development. Again, the appropriateness of teams should be evaluated against the benefits of a single leader group.

3   *Systems and procedures*   Our experience suggests that frequently there is a lack of consensus about how to proceed to achieve goals. Organisational systems may be archaic or too complex, or the procedures may be poorly documented.

What to do: Brainstorming sessions, problem-solving exercises and mind-mapping are some techniques a coach can employ to define and redefine procedures and systems. As noted above, feedback to senior management may be necessary if major structural changes are required.

4   *Interpersonal issues*   These can impact on top performing teams. Some of these include:

(a) *Fear of change*   Some individuals may fear that change will result in a loss of their power and status. (See Chapter 10 for a detailed discussion on change.)

(b) *Internal competition*   While competition is the sine qua non of business, and spurs us on to greater and greater achievements, it can, if excessive, lead to win–lose attitudes and struggles for power, status and resources.

What to do: Competition between teams working on a similar project, for example, should be discouraged. Internal politics and conflict inhibit creative problem solving.

(c) *Hidden agendas, territorial struggles and mistrusting other team members.*

What to do: The coach's role is to create a safe environment where openness and honesty are the norm. Hidden agendas are to be examined and confronted by establishing what the individual team members want, what they fear and what they wish to avoid. While team sessions are not group therapy, and the coach is not a therapist or confessor, genuine self-disclosure is critical for team members to move beyond their individual concerns towards mutuality and goal achievement.

(d) *Group dynamics* While an in-depth knowledge and experience of group psycho-dynamics is patently not warranted, the team coach should be conversant with at least some group dynamics.

What to do: Perhaps a major issue to be tackled in a team situation is that of a strong positive transference towards the coach. It may manifest as a team member wanting to be the 'favourite child'. The coach has to respond sensitively and neither favour nor reject the individual (countertransference). Countertransference can also involve the coach's own need to be liked, to be in control and to be 'the expert'. The coach's personal way of dealing with conflict also impacts on the team. One of the coach's roles is to deal with and relieve tension. If there is an unconscious or conscious wish to avoid conflict, for example, the coach may tend to smooth over dissent or reach a superficial consensus. Conversely, unconscious hostility can result in prolonged and ultimately unresolved conflict in the team sessions.

Some other common defence mechanisms of team members include:

Flight	Fight	Pairing
Withdrawing	Projection	Subgroups
Intellectualising	Interrogation	Scapegoating
Generalising	Competing/blaming	

What to do: Some of these defence mechanisms are unconscious and, consequently, individuals are frequently unaware of the patterns or reasons for their behaviour. A sensitively attuned coach can bring these behaviours into the open in an objective, non-judgmental way, and is able to situate them in the context of the group's processes rather than attributing them to individual 'pathology'. Uncovering these defences offers individuals the opportunity to formalise and openly discuss fears and anxieties. The master coach functions as a 'container' in the sense of 'holding' anxieties and giving them back in a more manageable form, and in the real sense of a container in which people can engage in ' genuine, quality dialogue.

(e) *Emotional problems of team members* A team member may manifest emotional problems above and beyond any issues discussed above.

What to do: If the coach judges the behaviour to be 'clinical', then management has to be involved, and the person referred out to a clinician. If the individual has problems functioning in a team unit, due for instance to team pressures, concurrent individual coaching may be indicated. The person may lack interpersonal skills and may be unpopular with other team members who exclude him or her. It is likely that other team members would resent the coach seeing the 'disaffiliated' team member on an individual basis, so it would be wise to refer the person to another coach.

Caveat: While possessing a knowledge of, and the skills to deal with, group dynamics and group processes will contribute to successful team coaching, it is important that the coach heeds Katzenbach's warning that team sessions are about enhancing work performance.

Some qualities of a successful team coach

As well as the qualities of a successful coach discussed in Chapter 2, team coaching also demands additional competencies. A successful team coach:

1   Has an understanding and appreciation of team dynamics.

2   Recognises and assesses his or her own and the team members' strengths and weaknesses.

3   Is able to develop commitment to a shared purpose and vision.

4   Focuses on achieving, performing, stretching, demanding and challenging tasks.

5   Has good communication skills—listens, questions and tests all assumptions.

6   Has the flexibility to facilitate or be directive as the situation demands.

7   Is prepared for free discussions and encourages individual differences and disagreements.

8   Always moves from conflict to consensual decisions.

9   Provides learning opportunities—encourages self-directed learning with the emphasis on the process of learning rather than knowing.

10 Provides ongoing feedback—appraises, rewards achievements and focuses the team on goals and vision.

A six-step model of team coaching

The following six-step model of team coaching (see also Figure 6.1) is a version of the guidelines provided in our training workshops for professionals who want to be coaches.

Step one   Management meeting(s)

It is critical that the team coach situates the coaching intervention in the context of the organisation's agenda, needs and resources. The composition of the team has to be discussed, and the logistics of the coaching sessions has to be clarified with management. The three stages in this process are:

1   The coach should determine the following:

> Is team coaching the most appropriate format for the targeted intervention? Could the desired change be achieved more effectively by individual coaching?

> What does the organisation need? Are there targeted interventions, or are the organisation's aims vague and unfocused? Is the coach provided with adequate access to people and information to understand the system? Does the coach have the opportunity to establish communication channels within the team and with other groups and departments within the organisation? Is coaching a secret?

> Does the organisation have the resources to support coaching? Can the organisation support change? Will it countenance and support changes to procedures and systems and provide the team with resources to achieve its aims? Are non-team members aligned with and visibly supportive of the purpose and goals of the team?

2   The coach should then assess the suitability of individuals for the team.

The coach rarely has the luxury of being involved in the selection of team members. Frequently, there is an existing team, or team membership is a function of the organisational structure. Yet the success of team coaching is dependent, to a certain extent, on the make-up of the individual members. While there probably is no such person as 'a perfect team player', certain characteristics tend to mitigate against effective team membership. These include: an inability to subordinate the ego; a disruptive, hostile attitude; and being too individualistic and a 'loner'.

In addition to the personality types of individual team members, the size of the team also impacts on its effectiveness. In our work with teams in small and corporate organisations, we find that smaller teams tend to work better together, get more things done and are easier to facilitate. Five to eight members are recommended. Again, the size of the team may be beyond the control of the coach, but management should be cognisant of the barriers to success presented by larger team numbers.

3   The coach should establish assessment, benchmarking, feedback and reporting procedures, considering, for example:

> Will team members be met with individually or as a group prior to the commencement of the team coaching sessions?

> Will there be concurrent or follow-up individual coaching? If so, by whom?

> Will team members be assessed individually? What form will this assessment take? Who will have access to the data? Will written reports be produced on the team and/or individuals? What are the parameters of confidentiality?

> Where will the team sessions be held? How frequently? For what time period? Are there any processes in place to ensure attendance?

Step two   Individual meetings with each team member

This step is *crucial* to the success of any team coaching intervention. Despite organisations' assurances that all members have been briefed on the purpose, process and benefits of coaching, it is not uncommon for a coach to be met with an anxious, hostile 'team' with little knowledge of coaching and the belief that they have been singled out because of performance deficits. Much valuable time can be wasted on educating the team and assuaging their fears and uncertainties.

An individual briefing session of approximately 20 to 30 minutes with each member can circumvent these problems. A handout on coaching (what it involves, what is expected of coachees, assessment procedures, the coach's role and an outline of the agenda for the sessions) should be given to each individual. Any individual concerns can be discussed and, as well as establishing rapport and aligning individuals to the coaching experience, the coach can gather valuable data on issues that can be addressed in team sessions.

Step three First meeting with the team

1 The coach should acknowledge everyone's uncertainty, encourage open expression of differences and exhibit a willingness to listen and learn. Whether or not team members have worked together previously, there is generally some initial unease at the beginning of the first coaching session. We have found the following exercise to be extremely effective in breaking down barriers and establishing rapport among team members.

Exercise

An introductory icebreaker exercise

Team members are to form into pairs and ask each other the following questions. They are to take notes and use the information to introduce their partner to the team.

What is your name? ....

What position do you hold? ....

What are your chief duties? ....

....

What are your hobbies and outside interests? ....

....

What is your greatest strength? ....

What is your greatest weakness? ....

Relate the time you felt most successful. ....

....

....

How do you differ from other people? ....

....

What would you consider to be a successful team intervention in the present setting?

....

....

2   The coach should then define his or her role as a coach:

Facilitate	Monitor	Coordinate
Problem-solving	Goals	Team activities
Conflict management	Obstacles	Liaise with management
Interpersonal relations	Achievements	

A useful definition to place on a flip chart is:

> The coach's primary role is to intervene in the discussion with the intention of improving how the group thinks and interacts. The coach is not there to tell or give the team answers (or technical advice), but to invoke your own answers through collaborative dialogue (Hargrove 1995).

3   The coach should establish the parameters of confidentiality. For example, he or she should:

➤ establish which reports (if any) will be given to senior management

➤ establish the information that these reports will contain

➤ obtain consensus that what is said in sessions will be confined to meetings and not discussed with non-team members.

4   The coach should clarify his or her expectations and discuss expectations for the performance of the team during the coaching sessions with regard to:

➤ the rules of attendance

➤ what happens if a team member's performance fails to meet expectations

➤ personal accusations not being permitted in group sessions

➤ all ideas being given a fair hearing

➤ whether he or she will attend the team's regular team meetings or presentations

➤ whether there will there be homework

➤ the structure of the sessions—interactive, non-didactic, workshop and exercise format.

5   The coach then gains agreement on objectives for the coaching sessions. For instance, the following items could be written on a flip chart:

Individuals' needs and wants	Why are we here?
The team's rationale	What are our goals?

Step one	Step two	Step three
Management meeting	Individual meetings with each team member	First meeting with the team
➤ appropriateness of teams ➤ establish organisation's needs/resources ➤ target individuals for teams ➤ establish assessment, benchmarking, reporting procedures.	➤ establish rapport ➤ explain coaching (roles, agenda) ➤ gather data.	➤ acknowledge uncertainties ➤ clarify roles/expectations ➤ establish boundaries of confidentiality ➤ agree on objectives (aims, purpose) ➤ distribute assessments.

Step four	Step five	Step six
Second meeting with the team	Formal coaching sessions	Management feedback
➤ give feedback from assessments ➤ encourage commitment to goals and vision ➤ examine resistance to goals.	➤ establish goals and action plan for session(s) ➤ group exercises/ discussions, etc. ➤ review, give feedback ➤ continue on with weekly coaching cycle ➤ final meeting.	➤ give regular feedback on team's progress ➤ make recommendations for future individual/team coaching.

Figure 6.1   A six-step model of team coaching

The coach can then establish consensus on the team's purpose and goals and on the team coaching process.

6   Having discussed assessment procedures individually, the coach then distributes questionnaires. Some useful questionnaires include:

➤ the Team Development Questionnaire (gives individuals an indication of their current level of functioning as a team member)

➤ Attitudes of an Effective Team Builder (identifies strengths and weaknesses regarding attitudes that support team building)

➤ the Myers-Briggs Type Indicator (MBTI) (measures how individuals prefer to receive information, make decisions and orient their lives)

➤ the Fundamental Interpersonal Relations Orientation (FIRO) (measures inclusion, control and openness and is useful for assessment of team members and coaches).

Step four   Second meeting with the team

At the second meeting with the team the coach should:

1   Give feedback from assessments.

2   Review and encourage commitment to vision and goals.

3   Examine resistance to proposed goals.

Exercise 1 is a simple method for collaborative goal setting and problem solving to achieve the team's agreed upon goals. As we discuss in Chapter 10, it is useful for a coach to devote a coaching session to examining any distorted beliefs that may be self-limiting and self-sabotaging for the coachees. Distorted thinking can also hamper the development and performance of a team. We have found Exercise 2 to be useful in promoting self-awareness and minimising resistance to coaching and team participation.

 On a whiteboard, the coach writes the following terms:

GOALS   OBSTACLE(S)   SOLUTIONS

Each team member is encouraged to write his or her ideas on the board. The team members then engage in a brainstorming session until consensus is reached.

 On a flip chart the coach lists eight common cognitive errors (e.g. 'No one asks for my advice' 'If I delegate, I'll lose control' 'I must have love and approval from all the significant people in my life' 'If you want something done, do it yourself'). Each team member nominates one self-limiting belief (SLB) from the list and gives it a rating from 1 (very much) to 6 (not at all) on the extent of its influence on his or her life. The team then engages in discussing/challenging these self-limiting beliefs.

Step five   Commence formal coaching sessions

The most effective team coaching occurs in a workshop format with groups of six to eight (one coach) or 10 to 12 (two coaches). If numbers are larger, and particularly if there is only one coach, the sessions tend to be didactic, inflexible and constitute training rather than coaching.

Some common team coaching topics include:

➤ How to give feedback.

➤ How to improve people skills in the workplace.

➤ How to be an effective leader.

➤ How to deal with difficult people.

➤ How to build high-performing teams.

1   First, the coach should establish a goal and action plan for the coaching session. For example, the goal may be to understand the principles of giving effective feedback. The action plan would involve (a) completing a designated workshop exercise on giving feedback and (b) during the following week, each team member giving feedback to a staff member based on the principles learned in the workshop. Each individual would then write a brief report on the feedback session and discuss this with the team at the next coaching session.

2   The following exercise was designed for the purpose of familiarising team members with the feedback model introduced in Chapter 5.

 Exercise   **Giving feedback**

The team forms into pairs. Each individual is given a copy of the feedback model described in Chapter 5 (see Figure 5.3) as well as the following case scenario about Sidney S.

Reading time = 15 minutes.

Case scenario: Sidney S. is the manager of a large department in a medium-sized retail organisation. Performance appraisals have been introduced this year, and it is time for Sidney to give feedback to 20 staff members. Sidney has had little management training, avoids confrontation and has been procrastinating for more than a month.

Based on the material supplied, each pair is to discuss the following questions:

✍ What might be some reasons for Sidney's reluctance?

✍ What can be done to overcome them?

✍ What resources might Sidney need?

✍ What essential principles of giving feedback does Sidney need to put into place?

Each pair then gives feedback to the group. On a flip chart the coach lists the responses of each pair and the team discusses and attempts to reach consensus on them.

3   The coach reviews what has been assimilated and learned.

4   The coach obtains an agreement on and commitment to the 'homework' exercise, which is that each team member gives feedback to a staff member during the ensuing week using the feedback model and other information gained in the coaching session.

5   The regular weekly coaching sessions are continued. Team coaching sessions can be conducted either on a weekly basis (one-and-a-half to two hours per week for six to eight weeks, depending on the agenda) or over an intensive two-day program. While the latter is obviously more time-effective for the coach, an organisation may not be able to 'spare' all team members for two full days. Second, weekly sessions allow for ongoing monitoring and feedback. The coach and other team members can thereby support and encourage each member as they go about the sometimes difficult process of change and introducing new behaviours.

6   The time frame of the coaching sessions is established prior to its commencement. Yet the final meeting can be fraught with difficulties if the coach has not worked through the adjournment stage. Team members can experience uncertainty, separation anxiety and feelings of abandonment. The coach can offset these issues by:

➤   Providing a forum for, and acknowledging, these feelings as a normal part of bonding in the team process.

➤   Reviewing and evaluating the team's performance based on expectations and goals—for example: What results were achieved? How were they achieved? What strategies were successful and why? Are there any unmet goals and expectations? Do team members feel responsible for their successes?

➤   Demonstrating (using examples from the team's feedback, homework assignments, etc.) how the transfer of skills within the coaching sessions has equipped members to deal individually and competently with other issues that will arise.

Step six   Management feedback

Management feedback, in terms of who to report to, about what, when, and how frequently, is established before the coaching sessions begin. The coach regularly reviews the progress of the team, gives management feedback as agreed (e.g. twice during a 12-week coaching intervention) and, where necessary, makes recommendations for individual coaching or further team coaching. The first management reports should include:

➤   the background to the team coaching project

- the assessment measures used and the generic issues raised
- action plan 1
- the results—what has been covered/achieved thus far
- a summary and recommendations
- proposed action plan 2—for remaining team coaching sessions

The second management report should include:

- action plan 2
- the results
- a summary and recommendations
- planned 'follow-up' team coaching and/or individual coaching.

Coaching virtual teams

Information technology (IT) is reshaping the fundamentals of business rules. It has contributed to new ways of managing, communicating and working. Information technology currently accounts for half of all business capital investment. However, many senior managers, particularly those over 45 years of age, have little formal or informal training in leading in the computer age. Today, understanding, managing and driving technology is an essential component of the manager's job. As well as recognising and maintaining the competitive advantage that IT can bring, managers and organisations have to manage the human side of IT and adapt aspects of jobs, skills, competencies and careers to it. Personal relationships, not ownership or technology, may be the key mechanism for coordinating complex business processes. It is in the realm of personal and interpersonal skills and communication techniques that coaching has its widest application.

Virtual teams

Although the term 'virtual organisation' appears to have no consistent or agreed upon definition, the concept of virtual teams seems to imply permeable interfaces and boundaries where project teams rapidly form, reorganise and dissolve as the marketplace changes. Virtual teams work across geographical, cultural, personal and organisational boundaries with technologies ranging from e-mail to sophisticated software systems designed specifically for virtual team working. A discussion of the benefits of remote workers, virtual offices and virtual teams is well beyond the scope of this book. The purpose of this brief section is simply to explore some of the personal and interpersonal issues that can impact on virtual team members, as well as discussing some coaching skills for the virtual team manager.

Some issues impacting on virtual team members

Virtual teams are subject to the potential drawbacks of all teams (e.g. loss of individuality), as well as communication barriers and isolation. These points are discussed in more detail below.

➤ Networking technology is heavily reliant on language. However, IT language differs from face-to-face language, which is a multidimensional experience. Technology does not allow for nuances, tone of voice or gestures and facial expressions, much of which is left to the imagination and fantasy. It has been questioned whether virtual teams can ever function effectively in the absence of face-to-face interaction.

➤ Virtual interactions, like any large group dynamics, can result in loss of individuality and a loss of a sense of self through becoming anonymous and being generalised and labelled into a group without being recognised for individual differences.

➤ Even though one of the frequently cited advantages of virtual workers is increased productivity because members are freed from non-essential meetings, office socialising/ gossip and office politics, these events also create bonds and fellowship. Without these, virtual workers can become isolated and alienated.

Coaching skills for managers of virtual teams

Coaching virtual team members demands many of the qualities and skills a manager needs to coach in a face-to-face situation. The essential principles of coaching as discussed above and throughout the book apply equally to virtual coaching. However, there are additional challenges the manager/coach has to face when working with virtual teams.

Before discussing guidelines for working with virtual teams, we would like to note that despite the above-mentioned personal and interpersonal issues that can impact on virtual team members, virtual teams are not intrinsically alienating or doomed to communication breakdown. Indeed, some computer-mediated communication groups actually involve more social discussion, depth and intimacy than face-to-face groups, even when participants are geographically and culturally diverse.

Coaching is about recognising the factors that contribute to the success of virtual teams and developing and enhancing these qualities and competencies in team members. A critical variable in the success of virtual teams is that of trust. Studies have found that trust between team members can be engendered and maintained by some of the following factors:

➤ social communication and predictable communication

➤ the communication of enthusiasm

➤ coping effectively with technological uncertainty

➤ good leadership

➤ individual initiative.

We shall briefly discuss some recommendations for the manager/coach in working with team members to enhance their competencies in these five areas.

1   *Social communication and predictable communication*

The manager/coach's role: As a coach, the manager's role is to guide team members with regard to what and how to communicate. In particular, the skill of communicating regularly, explicitly and on a timely basis is essential for virtual team members. For instance, failure to respond to an e-mail can leave the sender wondering whether it has been received, whether the receiver has been offended in some way by the contents or whether the receiver is not fully engaged and committed to the project. Coaching for communication skills can offset many of these potential concerns and anxieties.

2   *The communication of enthusiasm*

The manager/coach's role: The coach's role is to ensure a sense of complementary objectives so that all team members participate willingly and enthusiastically. Through his or her own enthusiastic transmitting of the organisation's vision and goals, the manager can enhance organisational identification as a means of linking virtual workers and teams.

3   *Coping effectively with technical uncertainty*

The manager/coach's role: As a coach, the manager should possess excellent conflict prevention and conflict resolution skills and be adept at coaching team members to recognise, avoid and handle conflict. Potential conflict can often be offset by recognising the seeds of conflict early in the process. If there is conflict between two individuals, for instance, it is preferable for the coach to address those concerned, rather than involving the entire team. Importantly, the coach functions as a role model. The manager should handle crises and uncertainties with a calm, rational, problem-solving approach that will inspire team members to act accordingly.

4   *Good leadership*

The manager/coach's role: Although the manager assumes leadership of the entire virtual team, natural leaders tend to emerge within the team depending on the situation and the expertise required at any given time. The manager should coach individuals to develop their leadership skills. Ideally, team members should be flexible and able to adapt to the demands of rotating leadership. Some individuals, for example, may have issues with control and may be unable to accept leadership from others. Yet again, the responsibility of leadership can intimidate certain people. The coach has to recognise and work with the individuals' styles of leadership and attitudes to assuming or relegating the role of leader.

5   *Individual initiative*

The manager/coach's role: One of the manager's roles is to choose individuals who are best suited for virtual teamwork. Not everyone is suited for the role, despite having the technical skills and competencies. Some characteristics of successful virtual team members include responsibility, dependability, independence and self-sufficiency.

Self-efficacy, the coach and the virtual team

Self-efficacy is the judgment an individual makes about his or her ability to carry out a particular behaviour. How an individual assesses his or her self-efficacy plays an important role in influencing remote worker effectiveness, perceived productivity, job satisfaction and the ability to cope. Self-efficacy is consistently related to work performance across organisations and industries.

Self-efficacy is determined by several factors. One of these is past accomplishments. The coach, always working from a model of strengths rather than one of deficits, highlights past successes, particularly if the individual is floundering or feeling uncertain about his or her capabilities. Self-efficacy is also influenced by vicarious experiences or observing the desired behaviours by others. Again, the coach functions as a role model. Social persuasion also affects self-efficacy. The coach provides guidelines for behaviour, models these behaviours and offers useful and constructive feedback when the individual puts these new behaviours into action. Listening empathically, allowing the team members to voice their doubts and concerns, and guiding and supporting them in the adoption of new behaviours and skills can increase self-efficacy. The coach's role may be to provide further or advanced IT training, as well as using the existing IT to creatively coach virtual team members.

PART THREE
Coaching skills and issues

Strategic goal setting and developing an action plan

Key points

➤ Some elements to consider when setting goals

➤ Purpose and coaching

➤ Values and coaching

➤ Vision and coaching

➤ Goals and coaching

➤ Establishing an action plan

Some elements to consider when setting goals

This chapter addresses strategies to establish attainable goals and to develop an action plan to achieve these goals. However, our goals, and indeed our attempts to achieve them, do not exist in a vacuum. Goals are closely interconnected with our purpose, values and vision. Therefore, any coaching program must address these issues. Purpose, values and vision tend to be examined in more depth in life skills coaching and frequently constitute the core of the coaching sessions. Yet, as discussed in Chapter 4, their place in business and executive coaching is not to be underestimated. Unless goals are in harmony with our desires, beliefs and values, we are unlikely to achieve them. Understanding and developing purpose, values and vision are crucial to any coaching process. The chapter is therefore intended as a guide for coaches who are working in business, executive and life skills coaching.

Purpose and coaching

Purpose provides the foundation for our values, vision and goals. Our purpose defines our uniqueness in the world. The centrality of purpose in our lives is best illustrated by existentialist philosophy. A basic tenet of existentialism is that meaning is not automatically bestowed on us but is a product of our searching, discovering and creating a unique purpose. It is this purpose that then gives meaning to life and to everything we do.

Purpose can be expressed in all areas of life, such as career, health, personal and intimate relationships, family, personal development, finances, retirement and spirituality. Yet not all of us recognise our purpose or can articulate it. In order to facilitate the discovery or uncovering of a coachee's purpose, the coach might ask questions similar to those posed by existentialist therapists, such as: Do you like the direction in which your life is going? Are you pleased with what you are now and what you are becoming? Are you moving closer to your ideal self? Such questions grapple with the core of our being in the world. They may, however, appear too abstract for more pragmatic coaches and clients. The following questions are also useful to unearth the client's passions and purpose in life:

➤ What are the real loves in your life? What frees you to feel most fully alive? What are the things that lift you and give you the most joy in your life?

➤ What have you done that has left you feeling deeply satisfied or proud?

➤ What emotions were you experiencing?

➤ What do you feel good about in your life right now, e.g. family, relationships, career?

When the coach and coachee are exploring purpose, it can be useful to approach the topic from three descriptive levels:

Level 1 *The source level*, where we seek out and define the wellspring from which our purpose is derived, for example: What is my meaning in life? Why do I get up in the morning?

Level 2 *The service level*, where we ask: How shall I live? How shall I express my purpose every day? How shall I live according to my higher values?

Level 3 *The vocation level*, where the coach and coachee discuss issues such as: What are my talents and abilities? How can I best use them? In what occupation can I use them?

Developing a purpose statement

Having established our purpose, it can be useful to develop a purpose statement. Such a statement can serve as a frame of reference, can help in decision making and can provide a basis for creating a vision and goals that are truly meaningful.

Unearthing our purpose in life can be a protracted process for some individuals. Some coachees may consider the topic of purpose to be too abstract, too 'new age' or simply irrelevant to what they want to achieve in the coaching sessions. In the corporate arena, for instance, we have found that, occasionally, questions about purpose initially are met with dismissive humour, self-parody or even a mild degree of annoyance. Yet as coaches, we must persist in encouraging and supporting clients to discover and reawaken their life purpose. Such knowledge and surety can prove invaluable to the individual, particularly during times of transition, stress and change.

Finally, the experience of discovering our purpose can be psychologically and emotionally profound. Belf lists several common reactions from clients she has worked with:

➤ disconnection—some clients cannot readily identify with the purpose statement because of the discrepancy between current reality and their purpose

➤ fear of change

➤ grief over lost opportunities

➤ healing

➤ empowerment.

Values and coaching

Our purpose in life is closely interwoven with our value system. Personal values are the core of our personality and play a large part in unifying our behaviours. They are something we instinctively move towards prompted from within. Our values influence the way we respond to people and events, direct and motivate us towards certain goals and even influence our choice of career and partners.

Motivation can be extrinsic (coming from external sources) or intrinsic (coming from within). Abraham Maslow, for example, suggests that internal psychological factors such as self-esteem and personal competency determine the level of effort we make. Behaviourist theories, on the other hand, claim that our behaviour is motivated more by external rewards and punishment. While evidence seems to indicate that intrinsic motivation is more likely to lead to a successful, fulfilled life, it is not always easy to ascertain. What motivates one person may leave another unmoved. There is an almost infinite list of potential values to explore in the coaching relationship. For instance, some of the core values addressed in life skills coaching include:

➤ a comfortable life

➤ family security

➤ happiness

➤ mature love

➤ wisdom

➤ equality

➤ freedom

➤ inner harmony

➤ friendship

➤ a sense of accomplishment

Other values include: leadership, expertness, prestige, independence, duty, power, adventure, loyalty, success, knowledge, beauty, self-determination, confidence, fun, financial freedom and intimacy.

We have found it useful in our work with executives to ask them about the extent to which they value and are motivated by factors in the following values checklist.

Checklist

Values checklist

From the following list, *place a tick next to five statements* that you personally believe in, are passionate about and, taken as a group, most accurately describe your concerns. *Rate each of these five statements* in order of importance from 1 (low) to 5 (high).

☐ Knowledge	....
☐ Leadership	....
☐ Power	....
☐ Self-development, personal growth	....
☐ Fear of failure	....
☐ Recognition—advancement	....
☐ Financial security—material possessions	....
☐ Challenge	....
☐ Competitiveness	....
☐ Career fulfilment	....
☐ Task accomplishment	....
☐ Enjoyable work—fun at work, getting a piece of the action	....
☐ Deadlines	....
☐ Client satisfaction	....
☐ Business growth	....
☐ Respect	....
☐ Team spirit—support, helping others, friendships	....
☐ Creativity/imagination—inspiration	....

As with purpose, some of us may not have clarified our values. Consequently, we may feel conflict in our work, our interpersonal relationships and our lifestyles. We may even be engaged in activities and relationships that are incongruent with our values.

If behavioural change is the ultimate goal of the coaching program, coaches must know what motivates coachees and what they truly value. Coaches can work with coachees to discover, unearth and clarify their core values. Once these values have been established, vision and goals can be developed.

Establishing values

There are several methods whereby coaches can work with their coachees to determine core values. For instance, neurolinguistic programming (NLP) has isolated two elements of motivation and values called the motivation direction. According to this notion, we *move towards* what we want and *move away from* what causes us pain and discomfort. Our values determine what we will move towards or away from. Coaches can discuss the following questions with coachees to discover or clarify their values:

1 Name three values that are important to you and that you move towards, e.g. security, freedom.

2 Name three feeling states that you wish to avoid, e.g. shame, rejection.

3 What values or feeling states do you need in order to create your ultimate destiny, to be the best you can possibly be, e.g. self-discipline, self-determination?

Another strategy that coaches might employ to encourage and support their clients in the search for values involves asking them questions about people and events that have had significant impact on their beliefs and actions. The following exercise by Leider is useful to unearth these influences.

Exercise

1 Identify three people who have had the greatest impact on your life. What specific advice or value has remained with you?

    ✍ Name .... Value ....

    ✍ Name .... Value ....

    ✍ Name .... Value ....

2 List three books, tapes, movies, poems or sayings that have contributed to your values. What insight has stuck with you?

    ✍ Resource .... Insight ....

    ✍ Resource .... Insight ....

    ✍ Resource .... Insight ....

Exercise

3 List five peak experiences that have profoundly shaped your life/career direction.

✎ Experience.. Value ....

✎ Experience.. Value ....

✎ Experience.. Value ....

✎ Experience.. Value ....

✎ Experience.. Value ....

Values in the workplace

Having discovered and clarified our personal values, it is important that these are in harmony with those of our workplace. People want to make a difference in their work environment and peak performance is more likely to occur if there is a match between their personal values and those of the organisation. Self-employed individuals and those who work in a family business are more likely to view the values of the business as an extension of their own values. However, there are several aspects of the larger organisation or corporation where value conflict could occur. These include:

➤ What is the organisation's commitment to diversity, such as their track record on promoting women and minorities?

➤ Is the organisation 'family friendly'? Does it provide child-care facilities? Are there flexible working hours and adequate leave conditions for single parents?

➤ Does the organisation offer learning and development programs that truly foster your career growth and advancement?

➤ Does the organisation value personal growth?

Vision and coaching

Goals begin with a vision of how the future should be. Each of us has a personal vision that can serve to unify our identity, beliefs, values and actions. Vision is a picture of our way of life, anticipating that which may or will eventuate. Vision also affects how successful we will be in life and work. For example, Farber and Wycoff found that highly successful sales people always have a vision that their product or service actually improves the quality of people's lives. Our vision reflects our deepest values and desires: it gives us direction and defines us. Yet we cannot simply acquire a vision. It is an ongoing process that evolves along with self-development and growth.

How a coach can help create and develop vision

If our goals are to be attainable, they have to be congruent with our vision. Before establishing the coachee's goals, the coach and coachee develop a vision and articulate this in a vision statement. Some useful questions for them to discuss include:

➤ What do you see yourself doing in the future?

➤ What are your interests and talents?

➤ Do you have a role model?

➤ How does your vision relate to your current life circumstances in the following spheres: your career, your personal relationships, your family, your personal self-development?

➤ What do you want to change about your current situation?

Mind-mapping techniques can also be employed to facilitate the development and expression of vision.

Some strategies for maintaining a vision

Once the coachee, with the support, questioning and encouragement of the coach, has developed a personal vision, certain strategies can be invoked in order to maintain the vision. The coach and coachee can work together on the following tactics.

➤ Focus on what you want—become focused and pursue your vision with determination, patience and persistence.

➤ Believe in the attainability of your vision—be accountable to yourself for results. Acknowledge you really want them and 'go for it'.

➤ Take it one day at a time.

➤ Commit psychologically and emotionally to your vision.

➤ Eliminate excuses for not moving ahead.

➤ You can define 'success' any way you choose.

➤ Be able to energise yourself.

➤ Plan ahead, be prepared and be persistent.

Vision in the workplace

Personal vision motivates work performance if it is synchronic with the vision of the workplace. Vision in the workplace or organisation produces a link between the day-to-day routine of the smallest task and the overall objectives and values of the organisation. The vision must be shared by all, and constructed from the core values expressed by all members of the organisation.

Coaches frequently work with teams in organisations. A team vision helps clarify and illuminate the core values and principles that will guide and drive the team. While team coaching is discussed in detail in Chapter 6, it is relevant here to discuss the importance of the coach working with the team to develop a vision statement. Research indicates that a viable and compelling vision statement should:

1   *contain left-brain and right-brain components*—the vision statement should contain objective targets, goals and action plans (left brain) and metaphors, colourful images and emotions (right brain)

2   *be interesting*—the statement should contain information that contradicts weakly held assumptions and challenges the status quo

3   *contain passions and principles*—a vision statement has be grounded in the core values of the team and what they feel passionate about.

Furthermore, the authors draw from research to suggest three principles underlying team commitment to a vision statement. These are:

1   People who publicly espouse their commitments are more likely to behave consistently with their declarations.

2   Team members should be involved in reaching consensus about various aspects of the vision.

3   The vision should be communicated frequently.

Exploring vision frequently involves change and growth. It is therefore possible that the coach will encounter some resistance or hindrance from the coachee. Our experience suggests the following common causes of resistance to working with vision:

➤ lack of clarity of vision

➤ fear of change (what does the coachee have to lose?)

➤ perceived potential conflict with significant others

➤ lack of motivation

➤ self-doubt

➤ fear of failure

➤ fear of success.

Obviously, these issues have to be worked around if the coachee is to develop a vision, write a vision statement and link these to strategic goals and an action plan. The majority of these obstacles can be dealt with in the coaching sessions. Our observations suggest that some forms of resistance involve the coachee's lack of confidence and perceived lack of support, while others are a function of self-limiting beliefs and cognitive distortions. If the problems are deep-seated, the coach may decide to refer the individual to a therapist.

Goals and coaching

Alfred Adler (1870–1937) believed that life goals were the source of human motivation. We set goals for ourselves and our behaviour becomes unified in the context of these goals.

Goal setting is a powerful technique that allows us to choose who we want to be and where we want to go. In coaching, strategic goal setting derives many of its principles from sports psychology. As in the sports arena, goal setting in life skills, business and executive coaching provides coachees with a long-term vision and short-term motivation. Setting and achieving goals highlights our capabilities and it engenders confidence and motivation to set even higher and more difficult goals. Goal setting allows individuals to expand their horizon, stretch their limits and realise their true unlimited potential.

Benefits of goal setting

The benefits of goal setting are numerous. For instance, Damon-Burton found that individuals who set effective goals:

➤ suffer less stress and anxiety

➤ have better concentration

➤ show increased self confidence

➤ perform better

➤ are happier with their performances.

Some further benefits of goal setting include:

➤ It keeps the individual focused—unifies efforts and energy.

➤ It provides clarity and direction.

➤ It increases determination, patience and persistence.

➤ It builds self-esteem when goals are met.

➤ It increases the individual's ownership of his or her life—the individual becomes pro-active rather than reactive.

➤ It increases existential meaning.

Goals in life skills coaching

A life skills coach, or a business or executive coach working with personal life issues, supports and encourages the coachee to translate personal dreams and aspirations into specific, attainable goals. Together they orchestrate the coachee's future. While the list of possible goals is limitless, with much individual variability, it can be useful to categorise life goals into the following four classes:

1 *Personal goals*, e.g. health, security, self-development, independence and self-determination

2 *Career goals*, e.g. career path, income, education and training, new skills and retirement options

3   *Relationship goals*, e.g intimacy, partnerships and friendships

4   *Financial goals*, e.g. financial security, budgets, children's education, owning a home, establishing a business and retirement plans.

Other goals in life skills coaching may centre on spiritual development and personal success, as well as managing transitions such as divorce, parenthood and bereavement.

Our goals change throughout our life span. Erik Erikson described 'Eight Stages of Man' and their attendant aspirations, which he called *tasks*. These tasks are psychosocial in nature and, if we manage each of the stages well, we carry away various strengths that help us navigate the remainder of life's passages. Stages Six, Seven and Eight pertain to ages 18 to old age and are therefore particularly relevant to coaching adults. Coaches can enhance their own insights and coaching skills by being aware of some of the issues associated with each of these stages.

➤ During Stage Six (early adulthood, 18–30 years), our task is to *achieve intimacy* and *avoid isolation*. Some specific goals a coach can explore with coachees during this stage include: being closer to others; developing and maintaining loving relationships with partners, lovers and friends; and participating in community life.

➤ During Stage Seven (middle adulthood, 30–60 years) our task is to *overcome self-absorption* in favour of *generativity*, or concern for the future and future generations. Some examples of generativity include raising children, teaching, writing, inventing and engaging in social activism. A life skills coach can explore, support and encourage the coachee to establish goals around issues such as: engaging in worthwhile past times and hobbies; career changes, for example working in an area of service that contributes to the wellbeing of others; and participating in mentoring programs.

➤ During Stage Eight (late adulthood, 60+ years) our task is to aim for *integrity* rather than *despair*. Some goals at this stage may be: planning for retirement; coming to terms with our life; spiritual development; and attaining wisdom in the face of death.

Setting effective goals

Before discussing some of the critical features of goal setting for coaches, a few caveats are in order. While coaching is about goals, action plans and achievement, a successful and empathic coach always operates from the following principles:

1   Regardless of whether the goal is achieved, the individual's self-worth and self-acceptance are paramount.

2 Some goals are not achieved.

3 People do not intentionally try to fail.

4 A true measure of an individual's worth is what he or she tries.

5 Achieving goals is a way of travelling, not a specific journey.

6 Striving for self-acceptance after loss or failure provides an opportunity to learn and grow.

As noted earlier, goals have to be aligned with the individual's purpose, vision and values, otherwise there may be lack of commitment and conflict. Goals may be assigned by others or by the workplace. Research has shown that, in sports, assigned goals affect performance through their impact on personal goals. It is therefore imperative that the coach establishes whether externally assigned goals are congruent with the coachee's personal goals.

Having clarified purpose, vision and values, sometimes over several coaching sessions, the coach and coachee then proceed to establish a goal or goals. There are three basic steps to goal setting and these are outlined below.

Step one Establish a history of goals that have and have not been achieved

A good coach will investigate, through strategic questioning or through a more formal assessment (e.g. Rotter's Locus of Control Scale), the extent to which coachees believe they are in control of their own destinies. Some individuals (externalisers) tend to attribute success or failure to events beyond their control, for example luck, fate or chance. Internalisers, on the other hand, view results or reinforcement as contingent on their own actions. Individuals with an internal locus of control tend to set more effective goals and are more likely to achieve them.

Step two List possible goals, even those with low attainability

The coach and coachee then work together to prioritise goals in terms of urgency and importance, and, where appropriate, establish a goal hierarchy.

Step three   Analyse the goals

There is a vast literature on the characteristics of attainable goals. Several critical features of goals include:

1   *Goals must be clear and specific.* If they are vague, global, unsystematic or too numerous, they are unlikely to be met. It should also be established how they are to be operationalised. As an example, a business person may have as a goal to better balance his or her work and home life. One way to achieve a more balanced life could be to spend more time with family. The coachee should specify in detail how this goal is to be achieved. For example, the actual goal might be to have dinner with the family three nights during a working week and to take the children to the movies every second Sunday afternoon. Another example of goal specificity would be to aim to exercise three times a week for 30 minutes rather than simply to 'get fit'.

   Having established the specific goal(s), the goal statement should be worded positively rather than negatively. For instance, a coachee working on anger control could define the goal as 'maintaining calm and control in staff meetings' rather than 'not getting angry during staff meetings'. Littrell, though, cautions that goals are not always the opposite of what the person does not want. He also makes the important point that goal setting and goals should be fun, interesting and exciting.

2   *Goals should be appropriately difficult and challenging.* According to 'achievement motivation theory', a goal must be attainable, but achieving a goal is not rewarding if anyone can do it. Too high a goal can result in frustration and demoralisation, while too low a goal can be demotivating and can lead to lower levels of performance. It is important that the coach establishes the individual's degree of self-efficacy. Stretch goals move individuals beyond their comfort zone and force them to re-appraise their situations and break away from old behaviours and habits. A good coach inspires coachees to raise the bar of excellence. Hargrove claims that by coaching individuals to stretch, the coach creates a gap between aspirations and knowledge and resources. Such a gap results in creative tension, which the individual or group then seeks to resolve. Yet goals should be realistic.

3   *Specifying the time span involved in achieving goals is critical.* If the time frame for achieving goals is open-ended, there is no sense of urgency, and the coachee is likely to procrastinate and put the goal on the backburner. While very long-term goals can provide standards

against which shorter-term goals can be evaluated, they tend not to affect relatively immediate tasks. Immediate goals, however, direct and focus attention and behaviour and increase motivation because they provide more opportunity for task mastery. Long-term goals should be broken down into achievable segments within a specified time frame.

4   *It should be clear how goal achievement will be measured.* Goals should be performance-oriented rather than outcome-oriented. When outcomes are the measure of success, it is difficult to tease out the individual's contribution to goal success or failure. Performance outcome measures also ensure that goal achievement is under the individual's control. The coach and coachee work together to determine how achievement will be measured and how frequently. Together, they then develop a plan to track and reward success.

5   *Feedback should be built into the goal setting process.* While feedback is discussed in detail in Chapter 5, it is relevant here to mention the importance of building feedback into the goal setting process. Positive feedback helps the individual improve, achieve and develop. It increases self-esteem, confidence and job ownership. Through feedback, the coach lets the coachee know whether the level of effort is adequate or needs to be increased. The following issues have to be clarified by the coach and coachee: How will the desired behaviours be monitored? What is the procedure for reporting feedback? How frequently? Will it be done formally or as part of the ongoing dialogue in coaching sessions? Are the measures of success, or performance benchmarks, clearly understood? Ideally, coachees should 'own' the goal, self-monitor their progress and provide their own feedback. Research suggests that, generally, feedback should be:

➤   closely linked to accomplishments

➤   immediate

➤   a mix of positive indicators of successfully performed behaviours as well as further indications of what could be achieved.

Establishing an action plan

Having established a goal or goals that meet the requirements listed above, it is imperative that the coach and coachee develop an action plan together, which they both sign and keep a copy of. Action plans address *how* and *when* goal-achieving strategies are carried out. We believe that, regardless of the coachees' commitment and determination, goals are rarely achieved without an action plan being in place. From our first-hand observations, it is not uncommon for coaching sessions to 'drift', with both coach and coachee losing focus. Alternatively, some coaches may respond to perceived pressure from management, the coachee or indeed themselves for a 'quick fix'. As a result, coaching in the chosen areas can become superficial or there may be a tendency to try to achieve too many goals too quickly. Having an action plan to guide the coaching process keeps both coach and coachee on track, and provides a structure for monitoring, feedback and performance benchmarking. It also serves to 'hold' the coachee to his or her goals and commitments.

Case Study

Coaching for 'life purpose'

R. W. is a 30-year-old librarian who is dissatisfied with her life direction. Although competent, respected and financially secure, she feels she is wasting her time, and is burnt out and unmotivated. She has always harboured a desire to study art and become a painter. Her friends and family have always discouraged her from taking such a risk. Feeling increasingly frustrated and unfulfilled, R. W. employed a coach to support and encourage her to clarify her purpose in life and to establish goals, strategies and an action plan to achieve her life purpose of developing her creative talents and becoming an artist.

The steps in the following action plan are a useful guide not only for coaching interventions, but also for any individual intent on achieving goals. The contents of this action plan were devised collaboratively by R. W. and her coach in the two sessions following her initial assessment.

Checklist

ACTION PLAN FOR LIFE SKILLS COACHING

✓ State your purpose: *to develop as a creative individual*

✓ State your values: *creativity, beauty, individuality*

✓ State your goal(s):   *to enrol part-time in art college*

                                to move from full to part-time work as a librarian

✓ What potential obstacles stand in your way? *disapproval from friends and family, financial insecurity, fear of failure*

✓ How will you deal with these obstacles? *enlist help of significant others, work one day every weekend, examine self-limiting beliefs with coach*

Checklist

✓ What do you wish to achieve:

    ✓ in weeks? *align friends and family with new plan, apply to art college*

    ✓ in months? *working part-time and attending art college*

    ✓ in years? *complete art degree, exhibit own work*

✓ What is the first action you will take? *talk to partner about the economic feasibility of the plan and possibility of bank loan*

    ✓ How will you do it? *talk to partner over dinner*

    ✓ When will you do it? *tonight*

    ✓ What other people or resources do you need to assist you? *colleague to job share at library*

    ✓ How will you obtain this support? *discuss with colleague and supervisor*

✓ What is the measure of your success? *partner's agreement to bank loan, and finding a colleague to job share*

✓ What is the deadline for getting these results? *two weeks*

✓ What is the next step (etc.)? *enrolling in art college*

Action planning in a business or executive setting

The essential steps of action planning are equally relevant to life skills, business and executive coaching. As discussed in Chapter 4, the executive coach and coachee work together to establish goals and an action plan. In some instances, the CEO or senior management may request an overall action plan for the coaching sessions. Such a plan should include areas or skills to be worked on, objectives, strategies and performance benchmarks. The coachee should sign off on the plan before it is shown to management.

Case Study

Executive coaching

J. F. is a 42-year-old executive in the banking industry. He has been promoted recently to a position involving a high degree of client contact. Previously, J. F. spent most of his time working with two colleagues and a computer. Although extremely knowledgeable in his particular area, J. F. is not able to successfully convey his expertise and enthusiasm to prospective clients. While presenting to clients he becomes anxious, somewhat defensive and frequently appears unprepared. Senior management expressed concerns about whether J. F. is suited to his new role and recommended that he undertake coaching to explore his career path and to improve his presentation skills. The coach and J. F. together devised the following overall action plan (see page 170), which was then presented to senior management. Having established the overall action plan, the coach and J. F. then collaboratively employed the steps in the life skills coaching action plan (as described above) to develop specific strategies to achieve each of the stated goals.

Figure 7.1 shows the steps involved in establishing effective goals and developing a workable action plan.

Step one	Step two	Step three
1 Discover purpose	1 Establish a history of goals/ achievements/failures and determine the coachee's locus of control	Develop an action plan
2 Establish values	2 List possible goals and prioritise goals	➤ nominate goal(s)
3 Develop vision	3 Analyse the goals	➤ determine obstacles
	➤ challenging	➤ set deadlines
	➤ time limited	➤ establish reporting procedures
	➤ measurable	➤ establish performance benchmarks
	➤ provide feedback	➤ determine resources and support needed
		➤ plan first step/action

Figure 7.1   A summary model for goal setting and action planning

Checklist

ACTION PLAN FOR EXECUTIVE COACHING

Prepared by:.........................

Name: J. F.

Purpose: to provide support and role model for children by being successful in career

Values: career fulfilment, respect, task accomplishment, client satisfaction, self-development and personal growth

Goals: increase self-confidence, improve presentation skills and thereby improve job competency

Areas to be worked on/ skill dimensions	Objectives	Strategies	Performance ratings			
			Date	Self	Others	Target
Communication skills in the context of presenting	To increase self-confidence based on achievement/ability rather than competitiveness	Cognitive restructuring ✓ self-defeating beliefs ✓ fear of negative evaluation	—	4/10	5/10	8/10
	To increase fluidity of communication	Presentation skills ✓ role playing ✓ deflecting ✓ rephrasing ✓ relaxing				
	To control arousal levels	Video critiques of presentations ✓ video of presentations ✓ self-monitoring ✓ feedback				

CHAPTER EIGHT

Communication skills

Key points

➤ The coach as communicator

➤ The art of listening

➤ Non-verbal communication

➤ Asking questions

The coach as communicator

Coaching involves communication. It is a two-way relationship, whereby the coach communicates interest, curiosity, enthusiasm and support, and the coachee communicates his or her values, needs, aspirations, problems and solutions. A successful coach, then, has to be adept at listening attentively and empathically and communicating ideas clearly and persuasively. While a detailed discussion of communication skills is beyond the scope of this book, two features of the communication process are critical to good coaching. These are *listening* and *questioning* skills.

Effective communication skills are a function of our interpersonal effectiveness. These interpersonal skills or qualities, many of which were discussed in Chapter 2, include openness, empathy, supportiveness and positiveness. Communication skills such as effective listening and questioning can only occur within an atmosphere that encourages openness, trust, equality and disclosure. The coach has to establish a climate whereby the coachee feels free to voice opinions, feelings, ideas and doubts. It is all very well for the coach to possess listening skills, but they are not especially useful if the coach fails to set the stage for truthful, empathic and sincere communication. The coachee has to trust the coach and believe that the coach is genuinely concerned with his or her progress, is supportive and is 'onside'.

The coach also has to reassure the coachee that he or she will adhere to the agreed upon conditions of confidentiality. When the coach is also the manager, employees may fear that what is said in the coaching sessions could be 'used against them'. In our experience, such a situation is more likely to occur when coaching is employed only on a remedial basis and not considered as a part of ongoing learning and development. In these situations, coaching is quite likely to be perceived as a threat, with coachees being wary of disclosure.

Communication skills are also related to self-awareness. Coaches have to be cognisant of their style of communication and of any particular biases and prejudices that can interfere with the communication process. They should also have a clear idea of how others perceive them and, if unsure, may need to seek feedback from coachees either formally or informally. The manager as coach should be particularly mindful of this aspect of communication, as the literature suggests that one specific manager skill deficiency is managerial self-awareness.

More importantly, coaches have to be aware of their tendency to disown and project their own negative qualities onto the coachee. A coach who has unconscious hostility towards a coachee, for example, might attribute lack of progress to the coachee's hostility and resistance, when the blockages in growth are really due to organisational barriers. Transference, as mentioned previously, can also occur within the coaching relationship. For instance, the coachee might have an unconscious fear or awe of authority and transfer these feelings onto the coach. If the coach in turn has unconscious needs to be autocratic and admired, this countertransference can result in dependency and lack of growth on the part of the coachee. While it is true that these processes of projection, transference and countertransference are unconscious, the coach can act to lessen their impact by consciously recognising that the goal of coaching is self-responsibility, self-growth and self-development. Coaches can productively use the knowledge of their own strengths and weaknesses to guide, encourage and support the coachee.

Elements of communication in coaching include:

➤ establishing a trusting climate

➤ listening

➤ questioning

➤ empathising

➤ communicating ideas clearly

➤ ensuring confidentiality

➤ fostering self-awareness.

The art of listening

It is generally suggested that 60 to 80 per cent of a coaching session involves listening. Most of us consider ourselves to be good listeners, yet some authors claim that poor listening skills are often listed as the number one cause of conflict between managers and employees. Listening does not simply entail hearing. It involves using our critical skills, recalling related issues and themes, asking relevant and stimulating questions and reaching some conclusions. The primary purpose of listening, however, is to truly understand the other person's point of view, how they think and feel and how they 'move through the world'.

Some barriers to listening

The following list discusses some of the major impediments to hearing and understanding what the other person is saying.

➤ *We may have preconceptions about what the person might say*. Sometimes, we believe that we can anticipate what the other person will say. It may be we do not find it particularly interesting or it may be repetitious. Whatever the reason, we fail to really hear the message.

➤ *Our attention is selective* and can lead to bias in what we hear, that is we hear what will reinforce our prejudices and fixed beliefs.

➤ *We think faster than people can talk,* and our attention can wander. If the coach is a rapid processor of information, and the coachee is not especially articulate, there is a danger that the coach will grow impatient, become distracted and not fully attend to what the coachee has to say.

➤ *We may be unable to tune out irrelevant information*. Active listening involves focusing on the coachee and deciphering the central messages and patterns in relation to the current issue and the overall goals of the coaching enterprise.

➤ *The physical environments can contribute to poor listening*. Telephones ringing, other people's conversations and any background distractions can impede listening.

➤ *We may lack concentration* because we are daydreaming, planning what we will say next or thinking about another matter entirely and this will affect our ability to listen. Listening requires effort and concentration.

 Case Study

Coaching for communication skills

T. P. is a 33-year-old account director for a large international organisation. Senior management employed a coach to work with T. P. on his team leadership skills. Colleagues complained that he was brusque, impatient and arrogant. T. P. was very amenable to coaching and willing to modify his communication style. He was unusually intelligent and processed information very rapidly. He did not appreciate that others might process information more gradually than he did, and he attributed their 'slowness' to lack of enthusiasm and commitment. He and the coach worked on active listening skills that enabled T. P. to become more attuned to what his colleagues were saying, to ask questions and seek feedback rather than presuming that his message was clear, and to adapt his verbal communications to their pace. When talking to others, T. P. tended to drum his fingers on the desk and look around. Together he and the coach developed simple strategies to ensure that T. P.'s non-verbal signals were congruent with his newly developed verbal communication skills.

Some benefits of effective listening

When the coach displays good listening skills, the coaching alliance is enhanced in the following ways:

➤ The individual feels understood and valued and hence is more likely to be genuinely disclosing and open.

➤ The coach obtains useful, valid data that can only enhance the coaching process.

➤ Individuals are offered an opportunity to state their thoughts and feelings more clearly. This can lead to increased insight and open the door to creative thinking and problem solving.

Some inappropriate listening behaviours

In addition to not concentrating and attending to what the individual is saying, a coach can also disrupt the listening process by engaging in certain behaviours. These include:

➤ *Interrupting* while the person is talking—it indicates impatience and lack of respect.

➤ *Giving advice* or offering solutions while the coachee is talking.

➤ *Reassuring or consoling*, thereby preventing the coachee from fully describing his or her situation or feelings.

➤ *Using emotionally laden language*—emotive language from the coach tends to generate a similar response in the coachee. Emotional states impact on our ability to process information, so anything useful that may be said is lost or misinterpreted.

➤ *Using humour or changing the subject*—humour is essential to coaching and when used appropriately can generate pleasure and a sense of fun in what might otherwise become a too serious endeavour. However, humour that is used inappropriately can signal lack of empathy and flippancy. Occasionally, the coach might feel the need to change the subject if the coachee appears 'stuck'. If this is necessary, the coach should signal the change in direction and provide a rationale for it.

Some guidelines for listening

The following guidelines can assist coaches to make sure that the channels of communication between themselves and their coachees are clear and open.

➤ *Look interested and alert.* Concentrate all your energies on listening. The more interested and focused you are, the more animated and interesting the speaker will become.

➤ *Minimise distractions.*

➤ *Be patient and do not interrupt.*

➤ *Keep up with the speaker's flow of ideas.* Try not to get sidetracked or stuck on one idea.

➤ *Provide clear feedback to show that you are listening.* This is done through non-verbal signals (discussed below) as well as nodding, agreeing (e.g. 'I see', 'Uh-huh') and encouraging (e.g. 'go on', 'tell me a bit more about that', etc.).

➤ *Identify the central issue.* Isolate the main points to yourself, summarise and build up a portrait of the person and what is being said.

➤ *Avoid labelling, judgment or evaluation until you have heard the whole story.*

➤ *Take notes in such a way that it is not intrusive or distracting to the speaker.* The person will feel you are taking them seriously if you do take notes and the notes provide a memory aid for you for this and future coaching sessions.

➤ *Analyse and reflect back what you have heard.* You can paraphrase or restate what the person said, clarify your understanding by asking questions, or simply state your interpretation of what you have heard.

➤ *Always summarise the key points of the conversation at the end and ask the coachee whether he or she agrees.* Sometimes it can be useful to ask the coachee to summarise what has been said.

Matching the communicator's style

Neurolinguistic programming (NLP) practitioners claim that we express ourselves in terms of how we perceive the world and according to which senses affect us most strongly. They suggest there are four ways or channels in which we can respond: (1) *visual*—people who tend to respond to the world in a primarily visual way tend to respond with 'I see your point', 'That looks good' or 'I see what you mean'; (2) *auditory*—some auditory responses include 'Sounds good', 'I hear you' or 'It comes through loud and clear'; (3) *intellectual*—these type of responses tend to emphasise the rational or logical aspects of a situation, such as, 'Sounds reasonable', 'That makes sense' and 'It doesn't add up'; and (4) *kinaesthetic*—some typical responses include 'That feels good', 'I've got a good feeling about that' and 'That feels okay to me'.

According to NLP theory, excellent communication depends on using the system preferred by the person to whom you are speaking. Thus, coaches should try to *match* their style of communication with that of the coachee. This matching has to be done subtly. If the coach is not skilled in this technique and it is glaringly obvious to the coachee what is happening, the coachee may feel that he or she is being ridiculed.

Non-verbal communication

Listening not only involves hearing, interpreting and giving feedback on what we have heard. It also involves using and interpreting the non-verbal aspects of communication. We transmit messages using words, gestures, voice and body language. It is generally accepted that the impact we make on people in the first few minutes of contact is based 60 per cent on visual messages, 33 per cent on vocal messages and only 7 per cent on content. Although in time content increases in importance, it is never more than 50 per cent of the impact. This rather startling information indicates the importance of non-verbal signals. Non-verbal communication modifies, changes or complements what is being said. Many of us, however, remain unaware of the non-verbal messages we are sending to others. Furthermore, when there is a discrepancy between verbal and non-verbal signals, people pay more attention to the latter.

Many books suggest that non-verbal signals can be understood in isolation and that a certain signal, such as folded arms, always signifies resistance or lack of receptivity. Such a claim is misleading. Non-verbal communication always exists within a context and is part of a pattern. Some non-verbal signals include:

➤ *Vocal factors*—the pitch, tone, rhythm and inflection of our voice is very revealing. High-pitched, rapid speech, for instance, signifies enthusiasm and excitement. A slow, monotonous voice can indicate a lack of enthusiasm, ponderousness or even depression. Frequently, it is not what is said, but how it is said that has the greatest impact.

➤ *Eye contact*—the importance of eye contact in communication cannot be overestimated. There are, of course, cultural factors that determine the appropriate degree and frequency with which we should engage in eye contact and this may vary according to the status of the individuals involved. Generally, though, eye contact expresses interest and a desire to listen. It allows the person to gauge your receptivity and friendliness. While lack of eye contact usually demonstrates nervousness, insecurity or indifference, excessive eye contact can be seen as hostile and intimidating. A general rule is to maintain eye contact for a few seconds, then look away or at the person's body gestures, then resume eye contact, and so on.

> *Facial expressions*—Some authors claim that many emotions are accompanied by unique facial characteristics that are recognised cross-culturally. Facial expressions signifying anger, joy and disgust, for example, are easily recognised. In a coaching situation, smiling can defuse a potentially heated situation, and can show encouragement and support.

> *Hand, arm and leg postures*—how we sit, the position of our arms and whether we cross our legs facing the other person or away from them, can indicate our intentions. If our bodies are turned away from the speaker, we are expressing lack of interest, dislike or an unwillingness to continue the conversation. Uncertainty can be signified by a hand covering the mouth or by touching or playing with our hair. The coach has to be aware of his or her own gestures as well as those of the coachee. They speak volumes about what is taking place.

> *Silence*—for many of us, silence is a source of discomfort. It can make us uncertain and anxious. Yet silence can signify that we are reflecting on what the other has said, that we are allowing them space to continue and that we are patient. During a coaching session, the coach can use silence to attend to the coachee by means of body posture and can observe the other's eyes, gestures and expressions. A good coach is comfortable with silence, while being aware at the same time that prolonged periods of silence can make the coachee uncomfortable.

Asking questions

Skilful questioning is one of the coach's most important tools. It allows coachees to express doubts, fears, ideas and agreement, and it elicits information that can constructively direct the coaching dialogue. Asking questions allows the coach to monitor the coachee's understanding and intentions. Coaching is about creating awareness and this is better raised by questioning than telling.

Types of questions

Knowing what types of questions to ask and when to ask them is an invaluable coaching skill. The major types of questions include:

> *Closed questions*   Questions that require a 'yes' or 'no' answer are generally not considered particularly useful in coaching. However, sometimes they are necessary to get the conversation back on track if the coachee is being circumstantial or seems stuck. Examples of closed questions are: 'Don't you agree with the strategy we discussed?' or 'Is there something we can do to change the situation?'

➤ *Open or non-directive questions*   These questions encourage the individual to elaborate and reveal their true thoughts, feelings and ideas. They also serve to stimulate creative thinking and problem solving. Coachees feel that the coach is interested in their point of view, that the coaching process is democratic and that they have some control. An example of an open question is: 'What is it about this strategy that makes you uncomfortable?'

➤ *Directive questions*   Sometimes, the coach may wish to focus the discussion or explore areas of agreement and disagreement. Directive questions ask the individual to expand on or explain their position in more detail. An example of a directive question is: 'Which colleague are you having problems communicating with?'

➤ *Feelings questions*   Questions that ask for an emotional response can provide useful information to the coach as well as allowing the coachee to ventilate any feelings that may be impacting on the coaching relationship. Simply being asked 'How do you feel about that?' can be liberating to some coachees. Of course, some individuals will answer in an intellectual style (e.g. 'I think...'), but the coach should persist and ask what the coachee actually *feels* about a particular situation.

➤ *Visionary questions*   Coaches frequently ask questions that tap into an individual's visions and dreams, or enquire about past successes. These questions provide a forum for the coachee and coach to talk about coaching, learning and change.

Many coaches consider that the most effective questions are: What? When? Who? How much? How many? Questions beginning with 'why' are discouraged as they can imply criticism and arouse defensiveness. If the coach requires a reason or explanation for the coachee's behaviour, it is more useful to ask 'What were the reasons?' Otherwise, 'why' questions should be qualified by non-verbal messages such as a friendly, enquiring tone that does not signal disbelief or disapproval.

Some useful questions

At the beginning of a coaching session, it is useful to ask:

➤ What would you like to get out of this session?

➤ What would you like to take away from the session?

➤ How do you feel about coaching?

➤ What do you want to be thinking, doing and feeling?

➤ When do you feel at your best?

➤ What would you like to change?

➤ How would you like things to be?

➤ What barriers stand in the way of achieving what you want?

➤ How do you best learn?

➤ Do you have a particular problem-solving strategy?

➤ What would you like to accomplish?

➤ What is your overall goal?

➤ What situations challenge you?

Coaching, as we have emphasised, is a collaborative process. While the above questions can serve as a guide for the coach, questioning should always occur in the context of what the coachee is saying. The coachee sets the agenda and the coach uses his or her listening and questioning skills to move the dialogue forward to achieve the coachee's goals. The following model (see Figure 8.1) summarises for the coach the key aspects of effective communication as discussed throughout this chapter.

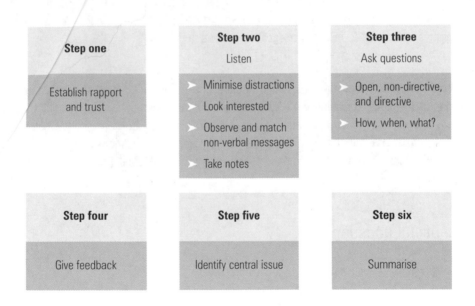

Step one

Establish rapport and trust

Step two

Listen

➤ Minimise distractions

➤ Look interested

➤ Observe and match non-verbal messages

➤ Take notes

Step three

Ask questions

➤ Open, non-directive, and directive

➤ How, when, what?

Step four

Give feedback

Step five

Identify central issue

Step six

Summarise

Figure 8.1   A coaching communication model

Learning

Key points

➤ What is learning?

➤ Coaching and learning

➤ Some facts about learning

➤ Coaching and adult learning principles

➤ Some obstacles to learning

➤ Emotions and learning

➤ Models of learning

➤ Learning styles

➤ Organisations and learning

What is learning?

Coaching is about change, and change involves learning. So, what is learning? A commonly accepted definition is that learning is a relatively persistent change in an individual's possible behaviour due to experience.

The laws of learning or how we learn is central to psychology. What follows is a very brief and simplified account of some of the major learning theories. Historically, behaviourist learning models have focused on associative (or classical) and instrumental (or operant) learning. According to classical conditioning theory (e.g. Pavlov), we learn because we associate certain behaviours with certain stimuli. For instance, after presenting the sound of a metronome together with food on numerous occasions, Pavlov found that dogs would salivate at the sound of the metronome even in the absence of food. They were *conditioned* to respond to the metronome.

Instrumental or operant learning theories (e.g. Skinner 1971) proposed that we learn by trial and error and that our behaviour is shaped through reward or punishment. Rats will continue to press a lever if they are rewarded with food pellets and will desist if given an electric shock. Social learning theorists such as Albert Bandura emphasised internal mental states such as expectancies, and considered vicarious learning and modelling to be important to the learning process.

Currently, learning theories emphasise the central role of *cognitive processes* in learning. Our behaviour and how we learn is not only a function of the environment, but also involves mental events, mental representations, our beliefs, expectations, emotions and intentions. As coaches, we cannot take it for granted that coachees will learn simply because new information, ideas or strategies will enhance their performance. We need to investigate beliefs, past successes and failures at learning, how the individual learns best and potential obstacles to learning, both personal and organisational.

Coaching and learning

One of the essential premises of coaching is that life is a learning opportunity. We have to become lifelong learners to make ourselves marketable in a knowledge-based economy and, hence, have to commit ourselves to continuous learning throughout our careers. Apart from our work life, our personal growth and development is also dependent on our curiosity and willingness to learn.

Learning is a personal experience. Each of us tends to have a preferred method of learning. Some individuals prefer to learn by listening to a lecture or a seminar given by an expert. Others prefer watching videos or reading books and journal articles. Group discussions and feedback can provide some people with the best learning opportunity. The coach has to consider the coachee's preferred method of learning. For instance, recommending a particular book to a client who has neither the time nor inclination to read books can be a futile endeavour. Furthermore, the coach has to establish the degree to which the client perceives the learning task to be appropriate and how much the task is seen as a priority.

It is vitally important that the coach be aware of the coachee's level of confidence and fears about embarking on new learning challenges. Challenges that seem too great can instil anxiety and resistance, while underchallenging an individual can result in lack of interest and motivation. Individuals only learn if they believe they have the potential ability to learn the required skill. In part, this is a function of the coachee's past successes and failures in learning.

It takes courage to learn and to put ourselves in a position where we might fail. Most of us do not like failure. We view it as something to be ashamed of rather than a valuable way to learn what went wrong and what we can do to change future outcomes. Some useful questions coaches might ask if they were trying to find out about the coachee's failures at learning include:

➤ What happened?

➤ What do you think are the reasons why you did not succeed?

➤ How did you feel about it?

➤ What did the experience teach you?

➤ Can you relate the experience to other similar incidences?

➤ What would you do differently next time?

➤ What do you need to learn in order to be able to behave differently next time?

The coach can also ask the coachee to think about some incidences that were successful. Typical questions the coach can then ask include:

➤ What happened?

➤ What did you do?

➤ What or whom did you learn it from?

➤ How did you learn? (e.g. watching others, asking advice, figuring it out for yourself?) Was it something visual, auditory or emotional that triggered the learning experience?

These questions about learning generate the coachee's self-awareness about how he or she learns. Generally, most of us do not spend a lot of time thinking about how we think or how we learn. As coachees become more aware of their learning experiences, they are likely to become more curious about the entire process of learning. Rather than viewing learning as simply acquiring new skills and strategies, they will begin to see learning as a process of attempting personal change and growth, that is transformational learning.

Some facts about learning

It is useful for the coach to bear in mind the following salient facts about the learning process:

➤ Current learning models are learner-focused and emphasise learner ownership.

➤ We tend to learn best through more active, problem-based learning and immediate feedback through discussion with peers and instructors.

➤ We learn the most through experiences that are challenging but not overwhelming.

➤ We learn best when we employ a variety of tactics and involve the five senses.

➤ We learn the most when we have strategies that coordinate what we have learned with challenges likely to teach those lessons.

➤ We are more likely to engage in active learning when we believe our efforts, rather than external factors, determine our success.

➤ Learning is more likely to occur when we have a need to seek knowledge and understanding.

➤ Coachees have different levels of commitment and willingness to participate in coaching— this affects the level of learning that will occur.

Coaching and adult learning principles

Coaching derives many of its principles from the fields of psychology and education. Coaching methods are informed by adult learning principles, particularly those espoused by Malcolm Knowles. He distinguished between helping adults learn (andragogy) and how children learn (pedagogy). Knowles focused on the importance of learner choice and emphasised the centrality of the adult learner's motivation. According to his view, discovery and curiosity lie at the heart of adult learning. He made four assumptions about adult learning. These are that, as people mature:

1   their self-concept is no longer dependent on others but becomes more self-directed

2   their accumulated knowledge becomes a resource for learning

3   they have a greater need and become more willing to learn when it will help them deal with real life issues

4   they want to be able to apply the knowledge and skills they learn now so that they can live more effectively in the future.

If coaches truly are to help individuals learn, they need to build these assumptions into their coaching models. The following is a brief description of how coaches can address each of the four assumptions:

1   Adults with a positive self-concept (or descriptions about themselves) learn better and are less threatened by a learning situation. By establishing a trusting, mutually respectful climate with honest feedback and a genuine commitment to the coachee's agenda and needs, the coach can encourage and support learning.

2   Coaching is about developing and enhancing strengths. The coach uses techniques that build on and enhance the resources that the coachee brings to the alliance. Past experiences, past successes and failures, and preferred methods of learning are all part of the resources and experience of the coachee.

3   Sometimes the coachee may not be able to articulate his or her specific needs, whether in a life skills coaching or an executive or business coaching context. Part of the coach's role is to provide the opportunity for coachees to assess and clarify their needs in the present circumstances. Ways in which this can be done include looking at values, dissatisfactions and aspirations, as well as examining blocks to change, or doing a formal needs analysis within a specific life or work situation.

4   Although part of the coaching process may involve hypothesis testing, coaching never remains in the hypothetical sphere. It is always about real life and practical issues. Part of the coach's role is to ensure that the coachee has opportunities to apply what is discussed and learned in the coaching sessions to real life situations and to monitor and give (and receive) feedback on the practical application of new or enhanced skills and capabilities.

Some characteristics of the adult learner

In coaching the adult learner, it is imperative for the coach to be cognisant of some of the following factors:

➤ *Self-concept*   Self-concept and self-esteem are based on past experiences, which influence how we learn. Positive self-concept and high self-esteem are more likely to be associated with a positive response to learning situations. An individual with poor self-concept and low self-esteem may view the learning situation as threatening and may feel unable to institute or cope with change.

➤ *Stress and anxiety*   If the individual feels threatened in any way, energy is diverted into defensive behaviours that detract from the learning process. The coach has to be aware of the coachee's stress levels and provide conditions for optimum arousal. A brief relaxation or meditation exercise at the beginning of the coaching sessions can lower anxiety levels and facilitate learning.

➤ *Past experience*   Our past experience, meanings and values impact on how we receive new information. It is useful for each person to be aware of his or her past experiences and how these impact on the present. Past experience and knowledge have to be valued by the coach, yet, at the same time, if these are preventing the coachee from learning, the coach may have to challenge him or her and point out the limitations of current knowledge and skills.

➤ *Motivation*   Most adult learners are generally concerned with changes they experience in the direction they have chosen. They tend to focus on the problems and concerns relevant to their current life situation. Coaching is always about the individual's needs and goals and focuses on developing and enhancing skills that can increase life satisfaction and personal growth.

Some obstacles to learning

Learning is a complex experience, and there are several features of the learning process that can make learning difficult for us. First, learning reaches a plateau after a while. The learning curve, which indicates the rate of assimilation of learning, rises then levels off. Coaches and managers have to be aware of this phenomenon and set goals and objectives that encourage and support the coachee to continue on to the next stage of learning.

Second, as humans we need to make sense of the world. As five-year-olds we develop ideas about how the world works. These ideas get hard-wired into the brain and it can be very difficult to shift them. Prior beliefs, then, can be a serious impediment to subsequent learning and can block openness to new ideas and new experiences. Finally, new ways of learning can be provocative and often create stress and anxiety because they challenge the individual's old frames of reference.

Emotions and learning

Our emotions impact on our learning. Everyone is familiar with the experience of being in an emotionally overwrought state and being unable to think or process information efficiently. Any kind of learning, therefore, is more likely to occur in a secure, non-threatening environment, otherwise the limbic system in our brains takes over and interferes with our higher cognitive processing. Of course, there has to be an optimum level of challenge and stimulation, otherwise the process becomes boring and, again, information is not assimilated.

It is excessive emotional states that hinder learning rather than feeling emotions as such. For instance, emotion guides effective effort. How much we learn depends on our persistence and confidence in the face of setbacks. It has also been suggested that feeling tactics can be an effective way of learning. Individuals who can manage the anxiety and uncertainty associated with new challenges can acknowledge and confront themselves when they recognise that their emotions are causing them to avoid the challenge of learning. Individuals who are not in touch with their feelings may continue to avoid or deny the need for new learning situations.

Our motivation to get better and better at something is spurred on by the experience of 'flow'—of being at one with what we are doing. The concept of being in the flow zone is frequently found in the sports psychology literature. Playing tennis, for example, we are in the flow zone when we are at one with the ball, when we are not thinking about how we will hit it but rather are inseparable from our performance. Being in this state frees us to excel at our performance and our life. We become more able to 'live life as life lives itself'. When we are in this state of flow, genuinely absorbed and at one with what we are doing, the levels of alertness in our brains are raised.

Models of learning

Recent managerial practices and the coaching literature emphasise the experiential learning model of David Kolb. Developed in the early 1980s, the model postulates the learning process as shown in Figure 9.1.

Figure 9.1   Kolb's model of learning

According to this model, the single learning loop is recurring and never-ending. More recent models have included Argyris's notions of 'double loop learning' and 'triple loop learning', which are necessary for the restructuring of mental models and personal transformation. Briefly, single-loop-learning involves helping the coachee embody a new skill through incremental learning, such as developing more effective customer relation skills. Double-loop-learning occurs when the purpose of the coaching alliance is to reshape and restructure the coachee's underlying beliefs so that they are capable of doing different things. Such learning could involve being able to view a problem differently so that the coachee, for example, could not only improve his or her skills in chairing meetings but could also consider alternatives to holding meetings.

Finally, triple-loop-learning is a transformational experience, whereby there is a shift in a coachee's point of view about him or herself. An executive who has always felt inadequate and resentful about having to give presentations might, for example, experience a 'breakthrough' which transforms his or her fear into a sense of seeing presentations as a way of contributing, of giving others the gift of his or her knowledge and experience. Learning in this instance involves a personal transformation.

One current experiential coaching learning model builds on the work of Kolb and Argyris. It sees learning as being involved in an activity, looking back critically, determining what is useful to remember and using this to perform another action. A summary of this model is:

(E) experience the activity (the new skills)

(S) share the activity (by describing it)

(P) process the activity (identify common themes)

(F) generalise the experience (form principles and guidelines for real life situations)

(A) apply what is learned to another situation.

The above model is clearly useful for coaches, particularly managers as coaches, to work through the learning process with the coachee. The coach, in effect, is acting as an experiential educator.

While these models can guide the learning process, they assume that the behaviour to be improved or enhanced has already been identified. Another useful model for learning a new skill or ability in a coaching situation involves identifying the elements in the specific behaviour to be improved or enhanced. The five steps of this model are as follows:

Step one   Recognise the inadequacies in the present way you do things.

Step two   Identify the behaviours involved in the new skill or ability.

Step three Practise these behaviours.

Step four   Seek and give feedback on your performance.

Step five   Integrate the behaviours into your repertoire of skills and abilities.

One of the aims of this chapter is to explore various models of learning that have proved, or could prove, useful to the coach and coachee. There is no definitive model and we do not suggest that the learning models discussed here are in any way mandatory. We employ the following model, shown in Figure 9.2, which borrows from and expands on the models we have discussed above.

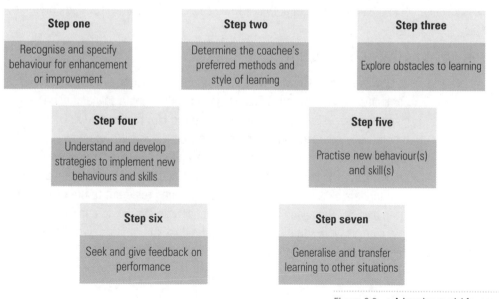

Figure 9.2   A learning model for coaches

Learning styles

As well as preferred methods of learning, some authors suggest we have preferred styles of learning. For instance, Honey and Mumford have developed four basic learning styles based on Kolb's learning cycle. These can be assessed by their learning styles questionnaire (LSQ), which they claim explains why some people learn and others do not. While such a claim is not accepted unequivocally, the LSQ has high face value and many of our coaching colleagues attest to the usefulness of the instrument. It can help the coachee understand his or her own learning style preferences as well as weaknesses. The four identified learning styles are: activists, reflectors, theorists and pragmatists. We briefly describe each of the four styles below, along with some coaching strategies for those coachees who score low on each of the preferred styles.

1   *Activists* are individuals who like to become involved in experiencing situations. They like new opportunities, feel comfortable in the limelight and tend to maintain high profiles. They learn best:

> ➤ in the present

> ➤ when there is an element of risk

> ➤ when they can 'bounce off' and become energised by others.

Coaching strategies: for coachees who score low on the activist style, the coach and coachee could target a number of activities to be carried out within a specified time.

Case Study

Low-activist learner

K. D. was a highly knowledgeable, competent manager of a large IT company. He was having difficulties doing annual appraisals and especially giving feedback. Senior management referred him to a coach. K. D. was theoretically oriented and had read widely on the subject. He was conversant with the theories of feedback and communication, spoke expertly on the dynamics involved in the feedback process and even developed his own models of feedback. However, he remained reluctant to put his theories into practice. The coach 'directed' and encouraged K. D. to apply his model to a current work situation and to give feedback to at least two individuals per week as a homework exercise.

2   *Reflectors* prefer to think things through. They like to listen, watch and gather data before committing themselves to a decision or conclusion. They tend to be cautious and conservative in the face of new knowledge and experience. They learn best:

➤ when given time to think or mull things over

➤ when they are given access to all available information to guide their decisions

➤ when they are not pressured by deadlines or hasty decision-making processes.

Coaching strategies: coachees who score low on the reflector style can be encouraged to keep a learning journal or diary and aim at adding several learning experiences per week, or one per day.

Case Study

Low-reflector learner

M. T. is a successful real estate manager. She is very energetic and active and claims she learns best by doing rather than contemplating. However, recently she has made a number of unwise decisions, chiefly because of her impulsiveness and failure to think the situations through. As part of the coaching homework, the coach devised several hypothetical work situations and encouraged M. T. to develop strategies/answers based on her own thinking and reflecting about the problems.

3   *Theorists* are interested in ideas for their own sake. They like to assimilate and synthesise new information and fit it into their theories and explanations of how the world works. They learn best:

➤ when they can use models and systems that make sense to them

➤ when they can understand and explore links and connections between facts and ideas

➤ when the subject matter is objective and based on rational principles.

Coaching strategies: for coachees who score low on the theorist style, the coach and coachee can target a certain amount of time to be spent on reading books and journals containing new information. Part of the coachee's homework may be to prepare a brief synopsis of this new information and how he or she has incorporated it into their existing ideas.

Low-theorist learner

Case Study

F. W. is the owner of a medium-sized manufacturing company. Because of market demands he had to introduce considerable changes to the company. F. W. was somewhat contemptuous of theorists and felt a lot of time was wasted reading about rather than dealing with issues. He was attempting to introduce change within a theoretical vacuum, which included not knowing about the effects of change on his employees. Each week, during the initial phase of coaching for change, the coach chose a brief but succinct article on theories and impact of change and requested that F. W. read the material and write a brief summary on how it applied to his company and the changes it was undergoing.

4   *Pragmatists* are interested in ideas to see if they work. Ideas in the abstract have little meaning for them. They like to solve problems, are practical and want to put new knowledge to use. They learn best:

➤   when they can link ideas to real life situations

➤   when they can try out strategies and ideas

➤   when they can deal with practical situations.

Coaching strategies: individuals who score low on the pragmatist style should be encouraged to develop and set out a practical plan based on certain ideas and in a certain format.

Low-pragmatist learner

Case Study

C. M. is a 40-year-old marketing manager who is constantly generating new and exciting ideas for business. Previously, the company had a niche market and C. M.'s ideas were usually adopted without hesitation. However, recently the company has faced increasing opposition and different strategies were called for. C. M. tended to generate ideas without developing them or looking at their practical implications. The coach and C. M. worked together on C. M.'s ability to develop his ideas in a more pragmatic way. For instance, when C. M. came up with a new marketing technique the coach would ask him to develop a brief practical outline of how it would be implemented and its impact in the current, competitive business climate.

Organisations and learning

Throughout this book we have emphasised the importance of the organisation and its approach to learning and development. Coaching individuals occurs in the context of their workplace and problems in organisations are inseparable from people and how they think and behave.

When lecturing or giving presentations on organisations and learning we are frequently asked, 'What constitutes a learning organisation?' Some CEOs and managers, for instance, believe that their organisation promotes learning because it provides structured training and development programs. Yet organisational learning is more than that. It includes the capacity or processes within an organisation to maintain or improve performance based on experience. Organisations learn as they produce, and production systems should be viewed as learning systems. Learning is intrinsic to work performance, not something that occurs externally in a classroom or workshop setting.

Organisations need to be aware of how their learning and development programs and processes operate. Because of the increasing awareness of the critical impact of learning on productivity and growth, more and more larger organisations are approaching us to conduct a learning and development audit. Essentially, the learning and development audit has four aspects:

1   assessing the strengths and weaknesses in organisational learning and development structures

2   establishing a profile of the organisation's ability to learn, both formally and informally

3   assessing the successes of current learning and development systems and how these may be enhanced

4   benchmarking (best practice, best in class, world class) the organisation's learning capacities compared to other companies of similar type and structure.

Today, organisations need transformational learning rather than just incremental learning. Transformational learning involves challenging basic assumptions about business and the organisation itself. Creating an environment for transformational learning involves a long-term commitment to continuous growth and learning. An environment that is supportive of learning is one that encourages individuals to be self-aware, to recognise their strengths and weaknesses and to develop action plans to enhance their performance.

Many organisations, however, focus only on the intellect and tend to ignore the emotional needs of individuals. Coaches can assist organisations to develop safe, constructive learning environments where CEOs and management teams incorporate the emotional aspects of learning and development into their business strategies and processes.

Trusting, supportive
climate

Goals and action
plans to enhance
performance

Commitment to
continuous growth and
development

**Transformational
learning**

Self-directed
learning

Awareness of individual and
organisational strengths and
weaknesses

Emotional needs
incorporated

Figure 9.3   Transformational learning in organisations

It is commitment rather than compliance that will bring about learning and sustained behavioural change in organisations. Commitment is a function of how individuals value and own their learning experiences. The best learning is self-directed. A healthy organisation and a good coach provide opportunities for individuals to learn rather than telling them what to do. The features of an organisation that are critical for transformational learning to occur are shown in Figure 9.3.

The learning culture

Every organisation has a unique learning character or culture. For instance, some organisations provide in-house training and coaching for all staff at particular levels, for example senior managers. These programs are either individually tailored or delivered in a group setting. Other organisations prefer to hire external coaches and service providers. Sometimes this is on a remedial basis, at other times it is part of the overall training and development strategy. However, some organisations encourage individuals to be responsible for their own self-development and provide little in the way of formal, structured learning opportunities.

The coach has to be aware of how each organisation approaches learning and must be sufficiently flexible in order to adapt his or her services to the learning profile of the specific organisation. Coaching has to fit with the philosophy and direction of the company and should be seen as a vital and integral part of the learning environment, otherwise coaching will remain out on a limb with limited opportunity to expand or show its true value and benefits.

Coaching should always he seen as part of the ongoing learning and development goals and strategies of an organisation. If it is seen as an isolated event, the chances of its success are minimised. For instance, an organisation may carry out a coaching intervention such as leadership development, but research suggests that coaching to modify leadership style is a necessary but not sufficient condition for organisational improvement. It must be accompanied by coaching in how to communicate the leadership style to the employees. In addition, the same study found that employees need specific training or coaching to recognise and respond to differing styles of leadership. Coaching within an organisational vacuum limits its potential for achieving sustained personal and organisational growth and development.

The coach also has to be cognisant of the politics of learning in any organisation. Some human resources personnel, for instance, may be worried that their position will be undermined by external program deliverers such as coaches. Yet human resources individuals can play a significant role in coaching interventions. They themselves can become coaches and, indeed, many are adopting a coaching profile. Their role may be that of in-house process consultants facilitating the coaching program, aligning others in the organisation and playing a key role in evaluation. The coach and human resources personnel can work together to identify future development needs and design coaching interventions and processes to meet these requirements.

Finally, we learn from difference. It broadens our perspective and opens up new avenues and possibilities. A learning organisation appreciates differing points of view and encourages new and different ways of improving performance. Some individuals learn best by accessing others, so the organisation should provide a climate whereby individuals feel safe and comfortable seeking advice or support from others who have met similar challenges. Most of us need to become better and more versatile learners, but this will only occur in an organisation that truly values and resources new and exciting learning opportunities such as coaching.

A model for organisational learning

Three learning-related factors have been found to be connected with business success. These are:

1   Well-developed core competencies that serve as launch points for new products and services.

2   An attitude of always supporting continuous improvement in all facets of the business.

3   The ability to fundamentally renew or revitalise.

The coach can work with a business or organisation to choose the most effective way of enhancing learning. For instance, it could be more effective for a company to continue to embrace existing styles, such as being an imitator rather than an innovator in the marketplace. The coach and manager could discuss ways to improve on those factors that already facilitate success. Another general direction the coach and manager could pursue would be to change the learning orientation of the organisation. For example, a company may wish to become more innovative and develop new and creative products.

Finally, learning in organisations can be viewed as a three-step process, which the coach can also use as a model when assisting businesses and organisations to establish a culture of learning and development. These three steps are shown in Figure 9.4.

Step one	**Step two**	**Step three**
Knowledge acquisition	Knowledge sharing	Knowledge utilisation
➤ skills	➤ disseminate information throughout organisation	➤ integrate
➤ insights		➤ generalise
➤ relationships		➤ transfer skills

Figure 9.4   Steps in organisational learning

CHAPTER TEN

Coaching as change

Key points

➤ The nature of change

➤ The coach's role in change

➤ Resistance to coaching

➤ Self-limiting beliefs

The nature of change

Change can be wonderful and exciting, but it can also instil fear and anxiety. We fear what the future may bring. In the workplace, we fear that new technologies and new procedures might make us redundant, or at the least appear incompetent. We employ much of our energy coping with what is already happening to us and around us, sometimes to the extent where we feel we're just 'keeping it together'. We fear that change will destabilise us because we do not have the energy or strategies to cope with new demands.

Of course, some of us welcome change for its own sake, regardless of the costs and benefits. Generally, though, change is difficult for most of us. It can challenge our values, our beliefs and even our very notion of who we are.

There are several techniques or strategies for dealing with change and our resistance to it and we shall discuss these later in the chapter. At this point, it is perhaps relevant to discuss how our resistance to change is partly a function of our beliefs about the nature of time and existence. We have a tendency to view time as something concrete, to divide it into units and to fear its passing. Time in a sense is the enemy. Yet some philosophers place time in a different context. Aristotle, for example, argued that time does not exist, except for change. Wittgenstein talked of eternity as timelessness and claimed that the eternal life belongs to those who live in the present where there is no interval between two events.

We cling to certainty and permanence, yet live in a universe where death is the only certainty and impermanence underscores all of existence. Everything and everyone is constantly undergoing change. To recognise the impermanence of existence and the futility of living in the past or the future may be a lifetime's work. Understanding impermanence on an intellectual level may not be too demanding, but *living it* is extremely difficult.

Yet, even some recognition of life's impermanence can impact on our behaviour—we can begin to live more fully in the present, be less conditioned by the past and less fearful of the future. Coaching is about moving forward and, to that extent, can be said to be future-oriented. Yet again we emphasise that coaching is a process—a process of change and self-awareness that is firmly grounded in the present. The *changing* and development are as important as the end result.

Coaches work with their clients to enhance their life situations—their work, home, interpersonal, social and spiritual lives. While goals, action plans and forwarding action are always crucial to a successful coaching intervention, the coach and coachee should be situated in the *now* of the coaching relationship. Both need to be aware of its shifting, changing landscape and be able to move freely within it, accepting and embracing change as a fundamental truth of existence.

Why change is difficult

Change means an alteration in our world, an interruption of how we usually cope with the world, with ourselves and with others. Change is a beginning and signifies the end of something. It is the most common situation causing anxiety and feelings of helplessness because it always means some disruption of ties or relationships.

Change is difficult because it takes time and effort and because it is a gradual process and not a 'quick fix'. It requires patience and tolerance for our failure to change and develop as quickly as we expect or sometimes demand of ourselves. Change is uneven and it is easy to become discouraged when everything seems static and our efforts appear to be in vain. In such instances, there is a tendency to revert to form, to our habitual responses, thoughts and feelings.

Even if the change is positive, such as moving to a new or bigger home or a new job, it is still stressful. The current increase in information, made available by high technology, is frequently cited as a source of stress. Some authors claim that we are not physically evolved enough to keep up with the increase in information brought about by new technology. The rate of change has outstripped our ability to adapt and we are in danger of being overwhelmed or stressed by these changes. One way of dealing with stress, of course, is resistance.

Another barrier to change is a deep-seated belief that 'we are who we are' and that our person-alities are fixed. Obviously, this book is not the place to enter into a debate about how 'hard-wired' our characters are, how much of our behaviour is determined by our early experiences or whether in fact there is any truth in the notion that 'character is destiny'. However, coaching is based on the assumption that humans can unlearn maladaptive behaviours and learn more adaptive ones, and grow and develop. The plasticity of the human organism underpins the fundamental principles of coaching. Yet this is not to deny that change is difficult, sometimes painful and frequently uneven and erratic. No one can make another person change. They may induce compliance, but profound, lasting behavioural changes can only originate from within the individual concerned.

Some factors influencing our ability to change

As well as the nature of change itself and our beliefs about change, other factors also impact on how easily we adapt to changing circumstances. For example:

➤ Our attitudes to change even influence our ability to process information. In a world of information overload, the way we deal with this information impacts greatly on our success, particularly in the workplace. Two dimensions of change orientation have been identified: (a) a *tolerance for ambiguity* (the ability to cope with ambiguous situations, rapid or unpredictable change and inadequate or vague information); and (b) the *locus of control* (the extent to which people believe they are in control of their own destinies). Individuals with an internal locus of control believe they are masters of their own destinies, whereas those with an external locus of control see their lives as being determined and controlled by something or someone other than themselves (e.g. fate, destiny or luck). Individuals with a high tolerance for ambiguity and an internal locus of control tend to deal better with change and are more successful managers.

➤ Organisational structures also affect our ability to change. The more rigid or hierarchical the organisation, the more difficult it is to bring about personal and organisational change.

➤ Just as resistance and fear of change can be the greatest obstacles to success, fear of success can be a major obstacle to change. Fear of success may relate back to threatening childhood competitions with our father or siblings, for example. In a coaching relationship, such issues usually would not be explored unless the coachee recognised the patterns from childhood and wished to examine them. In such a case, the coach would be wise to refer the individual out for psychotherapy. Usually, though, fear of success, depending on how debilitating it is, can be looked at within a more cognitive-behavioural framework by examining the individual's beliefs about success and how these impact on his or her behaviour.

➤ Change does not occur in a vacuum. It affects those around us and may irrevocably alter our relationships with some individuals. Being promoted at work, for instance, can result in conflicting feelings about former peers: we wish to assume a position of authority, while at the same time wanting to be liked by subordinates. Change is less likely to cause conflict, either intrapersonally or interpersonally, if we have a support system. A coach is an ideal person to provide such support and encouragement and allow the coachee to ventilate his or her ambivalence about assuming the current role or about adopting any new behaviours that may generate conflict.

The coach's role in change

A coach is a catalyst for change. A coach stimulates and challenges the individual to adopt new behaviours. The coach's task is to maintain a balance between an empathic awareness of the difficulties inherent in change, and championing the new initiatives.

Research has isolated several success factors associated with change agents. As several of these are pertinent to the role of the coach, we shall discuss them briefly.

➤ *Communication effort*   The greater the communication between the client and the agent of change, the greater the success of the change intervention. Good communication skills are the hallmark—we could say the *sine qua non*—of a good coach. The coach provides a trusting, open environment where the individual feels free to communicate any fears or beliefs about coaching and the changes it entails. In turn, the coach communicates his or her enthusiasm and conviction that the client *can* change and that any barriers to change can be overcome.

➤ *Orientation*   The more the change agent is oriented towards the client and the client's needs, as opposed to the needs of the change agency, the more successful the change is likely to be. The coach's focus is always the individual client and his or her goals, needs and agenda. Yet it is possibly naïve to suggest that in the workplace the individual's needs can be met without situating them in the organisational context. The coach's challenge may be to guide the coaching intervention in such a way that there is a win–win outcome for the coachee and the organisation.

➤ *Empathy*   The more empathic the agent of change, the more likely the change project will be successful. As mentioned above, the coach has to balance challenging and championing with an empathic understanding of how change can be difficult for some individuals. Excessive and insufficient empathy can be equally unhelpful. It is therefore particularly important for the coach to reflect on his or her attitudes to change. Coaches who relish change and welcome it as a challenge may tend to lack empathy and be too demanding on their coachees. Conversely, coaches who personally experience change as difficult may be overly empathic and cautious, thereby dampening their coachees' enthusiasm and confidence.

➤ *Credibility*   The more the change agent is perceived as being credible, the greater the likelihood of a successful change outcome. In the context of coaching and change, the coach has credibility when he or she functions as a role model. The coach should be seen as someone who embraces change, who has the flexibility and skills to adapt to the changes occurring within the coaching relationship and, where relevant, within the organisation.

Some responses to change

It is generally considered that people naturally resist change. We find ways of dealing with situations that are effective and we are reluctant to give them up. While individuals vary in their response to change, some authors suggest there is a process that we go through when adapting to change. The process is similar to what we experience when dealing with loss and it involves four stages:

1   *Denial*, where individuals pretend that the changes are not happening or hope that they will go away so they will not have to deal with them. Interestingly, we have found that management and human resources personnel sometimes respond in this fashion to the concept of coaching. They airily dismiss it as another 'fad', despite evidence that it is increasingly accepted as a successful performance enhancement tool throughout the corporate and business worlds.

2   *Resistance or anger* tends to arise when individuals realise the changes will not go away. There may be increased disagreements, frustration, blaming, self-doubt and bargaining.

3   *Emerging acceptance* can result initially in apathy and lack of motivation. Yet gradually people move into negative acceptance (or resignation) or a more positive acceptance of the need for change. Energy starts to flow again and there also can be lack of certainty and chaos, with people feeling overwhelmed by new projects and ideas.

4   *Commitment to change*—at this stage, individuals tend to embrace change, their focus is clearer and they invest their energies in personal and/or organisational growth.

Resistance to coaching

As well as fear of change, there are several other reasons why individuals may be reluctant to be coached. In our experience, this reluctance can take two forms. The first is blatant resistance, with the coachee displaying evident hostility, mistrust and unwillingness to engage with the coach in any meaningful way. The second form of resistance is less obvious and may only become apparent as the coaching sessions proceed. In this instance, the coachee appears to be compliant and even enthusiastic about coaching and the agreed upon goals and strategies. However, the coachee does not change and the goals are never achieved.

Generally, a blatant reluctance to be coached is easier for the coach to deal with than more passive resistance. The coach can confront the hostile coachee and attempt to establish the reason(s) for the individual's resistance. In this situation, most coachees are prepared to talk about their beliefs and feelings about coaching. While it may take several sessions for the coach and coachee to establish a workable and synergistic relationship, there is no reason why a coach with good self-awareness, patience and the ability to contain the coachee's anger cannot deal successfully and productively with the initial resistance.

Dealing with a passive form of reluctance is more difficult. The coachee may be unaware of his or her true motives for resistance or may be unwilling to disclose them. The coach is then faced with several choices:

1   Refuse to work with clients who are reluctant to be coached—this, of course, could jeopardise the coach's position in the organisation.

2   Refer the coachee to a coach who specialises in working with 'difficult/reluctant' clients.

3   Accept 'reluctance' as one of the challenges of coaching.

Some reasons for reluctance

Below are some factors that we and others have isolated as contributing to an individual's reluctance to be coached.

➤ *Personality variables*   It is usually unhelpful to explain an individual's behaviour solely on the basis of personality, which is an elusive concept at best. However, as mentioned in Chapter 4, some personality characteristics can be associated with resistance to coaching. These include a strong need for control, a need to be self-sufficient and an inability to accept perceived criticism.

➤ *Unwillingness to accept scope for improvement*   Some individuals may feel that admitting to weaknesses or areas for improvement could jeopardise their position in the workplace. Some authors even suggest that we have a tendency to resist change and learning by camouflaging our mistakes. Change can present threats to our feelings of competence and our comfort with old systems and processes.

➤ *Mistrust of the organisation*   Some individuals may lack trust in management and feel it has a hidden agenda in suggesting they be coached. They are unsure how management will use the information or reports given to them by the coach, and fear it may impact negatively on their remuneration or career. In our experience, management tends to be motivated by concern for the individual, his or her performance, and its impact on the organisation.

➤ *Fear of failure*   Coaching involves change—a new way of doing something. Embarking on coaching can trigger off memories and anxieties in individuals about past failures and about a lack of belief in their ability to change.

➤ *Drifting*   Some individuals tend to drift through life and work and seem quite content to be unfocused and vague about what they are doing. Change, in the form of coaching, can threaten this pleasant state and force the reluctant individual to focus, establish an agenda and set goals.

Some guidelines for dealing with reluctance

Dealing with a reluctant coachee can be a daunting prospect for the coach. There are various strategies that the coach should adopt in such a situation. For example:

➤ The coach should ask the coachee for his or her reaction to being in the coaching situation.

➤ If the coachee's response is negative, the coach should ask why it is negative.

➤ If the coachee appears reluctant but does not admit to this, the coach should gently confront the person with his or her observations and thoughts and offer some objective evidence for these observations (e.g. the coachee's non-verbal signals, tone of voice, etc.).

➤ If the coachee continues to deny any resistance or lack of interest (but appears reluctant or resentful), the coach should show empathy by suggesting some possible reasons for the behaviour/reluctance.

➤ If the coach does not manage to 'break through' the resistance or establish reasons for the coachee's reluctance, the coach should ask the coachee what he or she thinks he or she could gain from coaching.

➤ If the individual is unable to answer this question, the coach should ask which aspects of work he or she would like to improve or whether he or she has received any feedback which suggested areas for improvement or enhancement.

➤ The coach should truthfully inform the coachee of management's concerns and specify areas management has isolated for coaching.

➤ The coach should acknowledge the coachee's reluctance but reiterate management's wish for the individual to be coached.

➤ The coach should explain and discuss some of the general benefits of coaching and the specific benefits for the individual.

➤ The coach should obtain a commitment and some measure of self-responsibility from the coachee to attend at least three coaching sessions and agree to review the situation after that.

➤ The coach should establish values and purpose as a prelude to goal setting and action planning.

In essence, as shown in Figure 10.1, the coachee's reluctance can be overcome if the coach can establish and clarify the individual's values and purpose, and generate and encourage commitment and self-responsibility.

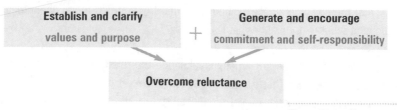

Figure 10.1   How to overcome reluctance

Case Study

Coaching the reluctant client

F. L. was employed by the manager of a medium-sized services industry to coach several key personnel in the context of major structural changes. One of these, A. K., was resistant to coaching from the beginning. He was hostile, withholding and sarcastic. Management had expressed particular concerns about A. K.'s resistance to the organisation's changes and hinted that if his attitude did not alter, they would consider 'letting him go'. Initially, A. K. denied that he was opposed to the restructuring and claimed to be committed to the coaching intervention. The coach continued to confront him regarding his behaviours and non-verbal signals in an attempt to break through his defences. After several sessions wherein little progress appeared to be made, A. K. finally admitted that his opposition to the changes and to coaching were based on his fears and insecurities about his new responsibilities. He was reluctant to approach senior management for fear of embarrassment or possible demotion. Once the reasons for his resistance were clarified, the coach and A. K. worked together to develop competencies for his new position, and strategies to enhance his many strengths and overcome his deficiencies. The coach recommended coaching for leadership and training courses in the areas A. K. felt inadequate.

Self-limiting beliefs

How our beliefs influence our lives

A basic tenet of cognitive-behavioural therapy is that it is our beliefs that influence how we feel and behave, rather than events. Events themselves are essentially neutral. It is how we appraise or interpret events that determine our responses. One person may view an event as devastating, while another person might respond to a similar event with complete indifference. The concept that events are essentially neutral is not new. Buddhists, for instance, have believed this for over 2000 years, and the philosopher Nietzsche claims that there are no moral phenomena, only our interpretations of what is good and what is evil.

Our thinking clearly impacts on our emotions, although the relationship between thoughts and emotions is a complex one. There is an interaction between thoughts and emotions, in that thoughts can determine emotions, and emotional states are associated with or can trigger particular memories and thoughts. While it is somewhat simplistic to view thinking and emotion in a strictly linear, cause and effect fashion, it is sufficient for our purposes to show how our beliefs affect our emotions and behaviours. Figure 10.2 shows the relationship between events, our thoughts or appraisals, our emotions and our responses.

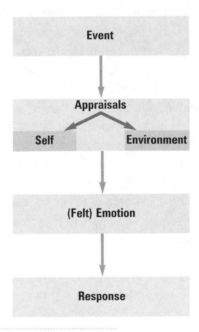

Figure 10.2   The relationship between beliefs, emotions and actions

To illustrate the model: the event is the scenario that a colleague has told us that our presentation was not up to standard. We might think that the person treated us unfairly (an appraisal about the environment) and that we are offended by that person's actions (an appraisal about self). As a result, we feel anger (emotion) and wish to communicate our displeasure (action tendency). Our response then might be to attack verbally the person who criticised us. If, on the other hand, we appraised that person's comments as being constructive, our subsequent emotions and response would be totally different.

How we appraise events, then, is critical in terms of our response. If our beliefs are in any way self-limiting or self-sabotaging, they will present a barrier to our success. They can become self-fulfilling prophecies. This is not to say, however, that we must always think positively or that we 'can walk on water' if we truly believe we can or tell ourselves that we can. Despite exhortations in numerous self-help books to constantly recite positive affirmations, we can waste or expend much energy telling ourselves that we feel great when indeed we feel terrible. It is more helpful to stay with the 'terrible' feeling, experience it bodily, and then examine and challenge any faulty beliefs that may be contributing to the feeling.

Some styles of faulty thinking include:

➤ black and white thinking, which excludes any grey areas and seriously limits our interpretations and our options

➤ setting unrealistic expectations and thereby setting ourselves up for disappointment and failure

➤ selective thinking, such as only thinking about the negative aspects of a situation rather than looking at it from all sides

➤ catastrophising, such as always thinking of the worst possible scenario or calamitous outcome

➤ mistaking feelings for facts

➤ minimising successes and maximising failures.

We recommend that all coaches devote at least one session to examining and challenging self-limiting beliefs with their clients. The following exercise involves a list of statements/beliefs that we find useful to give to our clients early in the coaching process. Of course, this list is not intended in any way to be an exhaustive one. As the session on beliefs usually occupies the third coaching session, the astute coach will already have detected any 'faulty thinking' styles or possible self-limiting beliefs and these could then be included in the list.

Exercise

Instructions

Circle *two* of the following statements/beliefs that play a role in your thinking, feeling and behaviour. Give them a rating on the extent of their influence on your life.

	Not at all					Very much	
	1	2	3	4	5	6	
1	If I expose 'the real me', I might lose control						....
2	Others seem better able to tackle difficult situations than I can						....
3	No one asks for my advice						....
4	I am not capable of completing a task within a designated time frame						....
5	This is the way I am—I cannot change						....
6	I have to be better than others						....
7	I'm a boring person						....
8	If I delegate, I'll lose control						....
9	If you want something done, do it yourself						....
10	Others might judge me unfavourably if I show my true feelings						....
11	If I change, people around me will become upset						....
12	I must have love and approval from all the significant people in my life						....
13	The nicer I am, the better people will behave						....

How to deal with self-limiting beliefs

To follow are some strategies that a coach should adopt when working with a coachee's self-limiting or self-absorbing beliefs.

1   The coach should determine the particular beliefs that are a barrier to change or success either by using the above list shown in the exercise or by developing his or her own.

2   The coach should discuss the frequency and intensity of these beliefs with the coachee. He or she should try to establish where they originated. Much of our thinking is conditioned by our past, by what we were taught at school and by our parents and friends. Often these thoughts become automatic and are no longer appropriate or relevant, yet we act on them and believe that our thoughts are facts.

3   The coach should challenge the coachee's beliefs.

> Is there a rational reason for this belief?

> Could the coachee be mistaken in this belief?

> Could he or she reach the same conclusion about another person in a similar situation?

> Why should the coachee continue to feel and act as though the thought were true if there is no good reason to believe it?

4   The coach should use techniques for dealing with self-limiting thoughts/beliefs. As soon as the coachee notices the thought, he or she should: stop, relax, write down the thought, identify the distortion and counter it with a positive, rational alternative.

The model shown in Figure 10.3 incorporates and summarises the aspects of coaching for personal change as discussed throughout this chapter.

Figure 10.3   A five-step coaching model for personal change

PART FOUR
Specific coaching areas

Coaching in call centres

Key points

➤ The role of coaching in call centres

➤ Some benefits of coaching in call centres

➤ Developing a coaching culture in call centres

➤ The role of the coach

➤ Specific coaching skills for call centre coaches

➤ The team leader as coach

➤ Qualities of a successful call centre coach

The role of coaching in call centres

With the rapid advances in technology and the reduction in telecommunication costs, call centres have come of age. Some estimates predict that around the year 2005 there will be a quarter of a million call centres worldwide. Coaching offers an enormous potential for dealing with some issues specific to the call centre workplace. Individual and team coaching can boost morale, reduce turnover and increase performance and productivity.

It is generally accepted that one of the major training issues in call centres is how to retain and reward talented employees. Turnover figures in the industry are phenomenally high, ranging between 20 and 40 per cent, with some organisations prepared to accept even higher rates. Yet such levels of turnover cost the industry millions of dollars every year. Training is expensive and it can take a new recruit several months to become fully functional and perform at optimal levels. Coaching for career development and job enrichment can increase loyalty and commitment and hence reduce staff turnover levels.

Training costs are also expensive and sometimes difficult to justify. Unless the skills learned in training are transferred to the workplace, much of this investment is indeed wasted. Using coaching as a follow-on to training is one way to ensure that call centres gain the most from their training dollars.

Call centres are about customer service. As well as product knowledge, telephone sales representatives (TSRs) and customer service representatives (CSRs) require advanced communication and interpersonal skills. Coaching provides an ideal forum for call centre employees to develop and enhance their competencies in these areas.

Generally speaking, the principles and models of coaching discussed throughout the book are applicable to call centres. In this chapter we examine some coaching issues specific to call centres. We have also created training and coaching manuals specifically for use in call centres. The manuals contain course material, practical exercises and role-plays designed to ensure that training and coaching strategies are transferred to the workplace.

Some benefits of coaching in call centres

Many of the benefits of coaching are common to all businesses and organisations. However, there are some specific benefits of coaching in call centres. These are:

1   Many companies pay a great deal of attention to recruiting staff, but once the recruit is within the organisation, little attention is paid to developing his or her true potential. Coaches inspire and lead individuals to become top performers and reach their optimal levels of success. In turn, this increases productivity.

2   Coaching justifies the use of limited and precious resources. It focuses on the individual and the team and helps them discover their own motivators. It engages them in a continuous process of learning, change and skill enhancement. Again, this leads to increased productivity.

3   Coaching is about developing self-directed, responsible and committed employees. Ultimately, they are less demanding of the time and attention of managers and supervisors, who can then attend to new recruits and other job responsibilities.

4   Coaching produces a more harmonious, relaxed environment, which stimulates and motivates employees to perform better.

Developing a coaching culture in call centres

Many call centres are busy putting out fires rather than growing staff and examining the reasons for the fires. Coaching, when it occurs, tends to be on a remedial basis and frequently involves 'telling' employees what to do rather than developing their learning and performance capabilities. A coaching culture enables people to thrive and grow while at the same time increasing productivity and consumer satisfaction. Such a culture values professionalism and appreciates the individual's unique contributions, regardless of the task. The organisation is willing to invest in their growth and development.

In our experience, many call centre managers recognise the need to develop the full potential of their staff, but they feel this conflicts with productivity demands from senior management. Such ambivalence is partly a function of the way in which productivity is traditionally measured. Productivity in call centres is frequently measured in seconds and minutes of talk-time, wrap-up time, and so on. An approach such as this tends to lead to a model of management whereby certain minimum standards are set and staff who do not reach these criteria are under threat of losing their jobs. Yet several studies have found that using these productivity levels does not result in true gains in productivity. In fact, employees tend to hover around the set criteria as there is no incentive or impetus to rise above them. As well as lack of productivity, this style of management tends to induce low staff morale, high staff turnover and decreased customer satisfaction.

It is only by adopting a model of management that develops and enhances growth and potential that true productivity occurs. Productivity is not simply a question of the number of calls per so many minutes, but is rather a measure of the improved value of customer interaction with the organisation, as well as call outcomes. It is quality rather than quantity that provides a useful index of productivity in a call centre. Such a model can only be adopted within a culture where staff are encouraged and supported to become self-directed, self-motivated and self-responsible —that is, within a coaching culture.

Who can coach?

To a certain extent, a coaching culture embodies an attitude or approach as much as strategies and techniques. Coaching helps individuals develop and enhance their skills and competencies. Hence, every member of the call centre should be encouraged to develop a philosophy of helping and encouraging each other, and this ethos should ideally be espoused and adopted by all staff from the CEO down. A strong coaching culture embraces peer coaching, which can increase camaraderie, save resources and develop team spirit.

Coaching in call centres can refer to coaching for call monitoring, which is a specific task whereby the coach monitors calls by TSRs and CSRs. Guidelines for call monitoring are discussed later in the chapter. The second type of coaching in call centres is coaching as we have discussed throughout the book, and includes coaching for skills, coaching for team membership and working with the individual employee to improve on weaknesses and develop strengths. Managers, supervisors and team leaders usually assume the formal role of the coach in call centres.

Some reasons why people do not coach in call centres

As with any organisation, there are several reasons why managers and supervisors are reluctant to adopt a coaching profile. These include:

➤ *High staff turnover*. Frequently, managers and organisations claim that it is impossible to justify coaching time and effort on personnel who are likely to leave the organisation. A short-sighted view such as this overlooks the benefits of coaching, for example increased commitment and loyalty.

➤ *Sometimes, telling people what to do is quicker and allows the manager or supervisor more control.*

➤ *Managers and other senior staff have not received coaching themselves.* They may feel somewhat intimidated by the new role and the possibility of failure. On the other hand, some may feel that they had to learn the hard way and that coaching is somehow 'spoiling' staff who should know what to do anyway.

➤ *Coaching is sometimes viewed as too time-intensive, particularly when there are a large number of employees.* Peer coaching is one way to overcome this dilemma.

➤ *The role of the coach is unclear.* Because many senior staff have not had coaching, they are sometimes unsure of the parameters of coaching. Managers and supervisors may fear that coaching will take them away from their 'real jobs'. However, as mentioned earlier, coaching that enables staff to become more competent and therefore more self-reliant in fact frees managers and supervisors to attend to other tasks.

The role of the coach

Although in essence coaching is a style of relating to coachees, there are certain specific roles that a call centre coach can adopt. These include:

➤ *Understanding what it means to adopt a coaching profile* rather than a traditional managerial, supervisory or team leader role. Coaches help staff grow and develop. They use their influence to gain commitment rather than compliance.

➤ *Motivating and encouraging staff to reach their optimum performance levels.* To do this, the coach has to: (a) recognise each individual's needs and motives, because what drives one TSR may be meaningless to another (although most people value security, job stability, recognition and challenge)—recognising each individual's needs, fears, strengths and weaknesses are critical coaching skills; (b) use staff development programs to increase enthusiasm and commitment; and (c) communicate the goals and vision of the company.

➤ *Balancing staff needs with the financial objectives of the centre.* The staff *are* the centre. It is only through recognising their value and treating them as important members of the organisation, as well as asking for and accepting their input, that the financial and 'people' goals of the company will be met.

➤ *Understanding and modelling effective communication skills* (see Chapter 8).

➤ *Providing development opportunities*, such as rotating staff through different sections, offering management and leadership development courses and career direction. Burnout is endemic in call centres and the coach has to be aware of the symptoms and be pro-active in preventing them.

➤ *Developing collaborative performance evaluations* that encourage TSRs and CSRs to develop goals and action plans that will enhance their performance, commitment, and ultimately, their productivity. Staff who are driven by personal results perform markedly better than those motivated by the fear of not reaching some standard criterion.

➤ *Developing a leadership style* (see Chapter 4) that allows flexibility and can be tailored to the needs of the individual employees.

➤ *Counselling employees.* The coach helps staff members identify attitudes and behaviours that present a barrier to reaching their optimal performance. Counselling skills involve active listening, reflecting and asking questions rather than giving advice. Counselling is an opportunity for employees to ventilate any frustrations and difficulties and it also allows them to explore alternatives and develop new problem-solving strategies. The coach does not have to know the answers, but must know which questions to ask. Counselling must be kept strictly confidential and if there are any limits to confidentiality, the coach has an ethical responsibility to discuss these with the employee prior to the commencement of the coaching session. Finally, the coach needs to be aware of resources and services to which he or she can refer the employee for professional help.

Specific coaching skills for call centre coaches

Call monitoring coaching

In the early growth days of call centres, silent call monitoring techniques were used to assess the quality of the calls. Today, many call centres have replaced these techniques with team coaches who sit with TSRs and CSRs and monitor their calls.

However, it is generally recognised that real coaching begins long before the employee makes a call. Coaching is more than feedback. A good call monitoring coach ensures that the employee:

➤ understands the purpose and expected outcome of the call

➤ is knowledgeable about the product and its benefits

➤ believes in the product

➤ understands the needs of the customer

➤ values the customer

➤ has the confidence and skills to perform the task.

These skills include:

1 identifying the needs of the customer by asking appropriate and relevant questions without appearing intrusive

2 guiding the conversation without appearing domineering or impolite and allowing the customer to express his or her wants and needs

3 giving honest, succinct and useful information about the product and the company

4 relating personally to the caller—customers are easily alienated if they feel they are receiving a standardised 'spiel'

5 dealing with angry customers—handling irate callers and rejection are two critical skills for anyone who works in a call centre and the coach has to be aware of each individual's level of sensitivity and their ability to handle frustration

6 dealing with rejection, which is a fact of life in any call centre.

The call monitoring coach is in the front line and is in a position to provide immediate and constructive feedback. He or she can reinforce or reward 'successful' calls and can offer suggestions and opportunities for improvement. Individual call coaching may appear time-intensive, but the benefits include increased customer satisfaction and increased productivity.

Dealing with stress in the workplace

No workplace is without stressors that can impact negatively on employees' motivation and performance. In most call centres, the emphasis is on customer service issues, with little attention given to employee stress. Individuals who are experiencing high levels of stress do not function at their best.

One of the most commonly cited stressors in call centres is monotony. The coach has to appreciate the potential destructiveness of job tedium and, wherever possible, rotate staff. Heavy workloads are another source of stress in call centres. Coaches should encourage staff to discuss their workloads. While it may not be possible to delegate some of the work to less burdened staff, at least the employee has the opportunity to ventilate his or her complaints. In the process, a solution may be found. If staff do not feel free to talk about their workloads, they may build up resentment that can manifest in unproductive work behaviours.

Physical stressors also impact on performance in call centres. Many of us tend to slump forward when sitting at desks for long periods and this impairs breathing, which in turn can affect stress levels as well as voice quality and general levels of alertness and relaxation. Ergonomically designed chairs obviate this problem to a great extent. However, coaches should encourage individuals to 'tune in' to their bodies and to recognise the early signs of stress, tension, anxiety or boredom. Simple breathing exercises can help. A yoga exercise we use with many of our clients involves breathing through the nose to the count of eight, then breathing out through the open mouth for the count of 16. It is a simple but effective technique that 'locates' breathing in the abdomen and immediately rids the body of any tightness or tension. When feeling bored, tired or understimulated, a brisk walk around the office and a few leisurely stretches can restore alertness.

Developing performance measures that motivate and empower staff

Traditional performance measures in call centres focus on quantity, such as volume of sales. Research suggests that call centres of the future will move towards performance measures where the key criterion is quality and where staff are empowered to maximise customer interactions profitably.

Before conducting performance appraisals, the coach should ensure that staff recognise and appreciate the purpose of the assessment. For this to occur, the organisation has to ensure that the appraisal is closely linked to the individual's job and that it is not just a routine process but is seen as an opportunity to expand and enhance existing work skills, as well as acquire new competencies. Follow-on coaching, which includes developing individualised, customised development and training plans for each employee, further places the appraisal process within the context of ongoing growth and development.

One of the major aims and benefits of developing performance appraisal measures is to minimise staff turnover and increase customer satisfaction. While the role of TSRs and CSRs can involve relatively simple tasks, these tasks frequently require advanced customer service skills. Some competencies for TSRs and CSRs that should be included in a skills-based assessment are shown in the following table.

Competencies	
➤ Problem-solving skills	➤ Decision-making skills
➤ Communication skills—establishing rapport, listening, reflecting and asking questions	➤ Courtesy and interest
➤ Matching the customer's style	➤ Dealing with rejection
➤ Product knowledge	➤ Working as a member of a team
➤ Peer coaching skills	➤ Customer satisfaction standards

However, as we note throughout the book, performance measurements are essentially unhelpful unless they are followed up by coaching. Coaching enables staff to isolate areas of weakness, highlight strengths and devise goals and an action plan to reach the targeted goals.

Career development coaching

It is frequently claimed that there is no such thing as a career in call centres. Staff are trained to do a particular task or tasks and then continue to do this (provided they meet 'performance standards') until they burn out or leave. The 'churn and burn' philosophy of many call centre managers contributes to this reputation. It also stems from the inability or unwillingness of many companies to encourage employees to take ownership of, and become involved in, their own growth and development. Training and coaching sessions are sometimes offered, but unless they are aligned with the individual's needs and goals, they will fail to foster any true loyalty or commitment. Some guidelines for career development coaching are as follows:

1 *Initiating new recruits into the organisation*

➤ Explain and discuss the goals, values and mission of the organisation.

➤ Explain the structure of the organisation—who does what, where the recruit fits in. Doing this can foster a sense of belonging and responsibility.

➤ Align personal purpose with job purpose.

➤ Emphasise the importance of the individual's role in the organisation.

➤ Clarify your expectations of the new recruit.

➤ Explain performance measures in terms that highlight the learning and development aspects of the assessment.

2 *Provide training and development to enhance skills*

> Ensure each staff member is aware of the reasons for and the benefits of training.

> Establish their expectations and goals for the training sessions.

> Establish methods (coaching) to ensure that learned skills are transferred to the workplace.

> Carry out reviews to establish what they have learned from training.

> Ask for feedback.

3 *Provide coaching as a follow-on to training*

> Allow time to 'safely' practise new behaviours.

> Provide encouragement.

> Provide support and resources.

4 *Design personalised individual training schedules*

> Identify what the individual needs to learn.

> Establish a time frame to acquire information or skills.

> Emphasise the individual benefits of training and coaching for each coachee.

5 *Develop an individualised action and development plan including short-, medium- and long-term goals*

> Identify required skills, knowledge and competencies.

> Establish benchmarks and time frames to achieve goals.

> Discuss possible obstacles to meeting targeted goals.

> Encourage the employee to generate solutions to overcoming these obstacles.

> Ensure the necessary resources are available.

> Provide regular reviews, feedback and continue to generate stretch goals.

6 *Reward and celebrate individual successes and personal best milestones.*

The team leader as coach

The role of the team leader in a call centre is not different, fundamentally, from the role of team leaders in any other type of organisation (see Chapter 6). In many respects, all team leaders face similar challenges. These include: gaining commitment from team members, targeting and establishing achievable goals, developing strategies to meet these goals, dealing with individual differences, resolving conflict and being familiar with and competent in dealing with the group dynamics and the different stage of group or team formation and functioning.

There are some specific issues for team leaders/coaches in a call centre. These include:

➤ *Being a role model*   How the coach interacts with his or her team members should reflect the standards the coach expects from them when dealing with customers. Each team member deserves the coach's courtesy and respect regardless of his or her personal feelings towards them.

➤ *Showing a personal interest in team members*   The team leader has to be seen as having a genuine interest and concern for members of the team and should be perceived as being 'on their side' and wanting them personally to succeed. Of course, the coach has to balance sensitivity to the individual with organisational goals and productivity demands. Team members are aware of the coach's position and obligations to management and customers as well as to themselves. It is *how* the coach does his or her job as much as the job itself that is important. The coach's interest and concern for individual team members enriches their job.

➤ *Dealing with resistance*   Changes in technology, task requirements and competencies are a feature of most organisations today. Call centres, however, are particularly subject to rapid changes and innovation. The team leader has to be cognisant of the stress involved with change and of the resistance and barriers that some individuals put up as a defence against their fears.

➤ *Receiving feedback*   As well as giving feedback, a good team coach solicits feedback from team members. Sometimes the feedback may be negative, and the coach has to deal effectively with the complaints. Some useful guidelines include:

> The coach should listen carefully to the information/complaint and decide whether it is valid.

> If the coach disagrees with the other person's interpretation of events, he or she should sum up what the person has said and then present his or her viewpoint calmly and logically.

> The coach should not be defensive or show that he or she is 'hurt'.

> The coach should avoid retaliating or using emotive language.

> If the coach considers the person's complaints or feedback to be valid, he or she should accept the comments and acknowledge any personal responsibility. Then the coach should try to solve the problem on the spot in order to reach some mutually acceptable resolution.

➤ *Dealing with day-to-day monotony*   As well as rotating staff whenever possible, the team coach can foster a sense of healthy competition between teams. Such competitions should be in the spirit of fun, and 'prizes' should be attractive and commensurate with the winning team's efforts.

Qualities of a successful call centre coach

The qualities of a successful coach that we have discussed in Chapter 2 and throughout the book apply equally to coaches in call centres. The following brief section aims to discuss some of these characteristics in relation to a call centre environment.

1   *Ability to establish rapport*   Particularly when a coach is monitoring calls, it is crucial that CSRs and TSRs view the coach as a support and a resource rather than a watchdog or critic. The coach can establish trust and confidence by clarifying his or her role in the organisation.

2   *Ability to ask questions*   Questions guide employees to discover different possibilities and new answers for themselves. Self-discovered solutions tend to be more meaningful and longer-lasting than imposed ones. Questions serve to establish the coaching relationship as an alliance in which the coachee is equally responsible for the outcome of the intervention. Some helpful questions include: What is making it work? What do you want to accomplish? How does this fit with your current goal(s)? What could we do differently? How will this benefit your team? What can I do to support you?

3   *Ability to be flexible*   The sheer volume of calls in most call centres can effect a crisis. The system might crash, the centre might be understaffed and employees could be stressed and frustrated. It may not be an appropriate time for coaching. If the coach is contracted from outside the organisation, he or she should be willing to delay coaching until the situation settles down. The team leader or in-house coach could suspend coaching duties and pitch in and help out with the crisis.

4   *Ability to coach the resistant employee*   Working with a resistant call centre employee can present specific challenges to the coach, particularly in a call monitoring situation. In coaching for executive development, for instance, resistance can be discussed and 'worked through'. In a busy call centre this is not usually possible. Some coaches claim it is unwise to pursue coaching with an employee who is clearly resistive. They suggest that the coach asks the employee to tape the calls, and they can then be discussed at a later time when the employee is more receptive. The discussion and coaching could take place away from the telephones and the coach could take the opportunity to discuss resistance if it has not been dispelled.

5   *Knowing when to coach*   The coach has to recognise and believe in the benefits of coaching as well as know when it is most effective. As mentioned earlier, using coaching as a follow-on to training is highly effective. The employee has new information and techniques. The coach has to provide the opportunity for the individual to practise these skills, and to receive feedback and support from someone clearly committed to learning and development.

We have found the model shown in Figure 11.1 to be useful when coaching in call centres.

Step one	**Step two**	**Step three**
Pre-call coaching	Simulated coaching	Feedback
Analyse skill	Demonstrate skill	Repeat role play and ensure
➤ discuss skill	➤ role plays	➤ knowledge
➤ when to use it		➤ competence
➤ why it is important		➤ confidence
➤ determine any obstacles		
➤ provide/discuss solutions		

Step four	**Step five**	**Step six**
Real life coaching	Provide feedback	Ongoing monitoring
Monitor call	Monitor call	Continue to monitor and coach until skill has been mastered
➤ observe skill	Review	
➤ was it used at the appropriate time and for the right reason?		
➤ observe customer's response		

Figure 11.1   A six-step model for coaching TSRs and CSRs

Sales coaching

Key points

➤ Some facts about selling

➤ Benefits of sales coaching

➤ Selling as a mental skill

➤ Selling in the 'flow zone'

➤ Some qualities of a successful sales manager/coach

➤ Some coaching skills for the sales manager/coach

Some facts about selling

In today's extremely competitive global marketplace, selling is more challenging and requires a greater level of skills than ever before. Customers have more choices and are better informed. The quality of the product is no longer sufficient to guarantee sales. Customers demand an honest and trusting relationship with sales professionals who care about them and who can tailor individualised solutions to their problems.

Contemporary sales managers have to coach, lead and empower their sales teams. Rather than controlling or even demanding, the sales manager's role is to inspire sales people to reach their optimum levels of performance.

Selling is a highly skilled profession. It has been claimed that there are over 200 identified competencies in over 30 categories in the selling process. These competencies can be examined within various models of selling skills. Historically, there have been several models of selling skills that have evolved due to changes in the economic climate. These can be roughly divided into five categories. Personal preparation models emphasise the sales person's personality, persistence and mental stamina in selling. Interpersonal skills models focus on relationship building with clients and identify key personality characteristics of the seller (e.g. through the MBTI and DISC Profile). Presentation-based models highlight the presentation aspects of selling, while the application model of the 1980s focused on strategy and partnership. Finally, the value selling matrix model is a relatively new model where the selling is done during the interview rather than the presentation. It is about adding value and cutting costs.

In terms of which models to use, research suggests that most sales professionals use a personal model and an interpersonal model as their foundation for successful selling. Coaching for personal and interpersonal communication skills therefore is clearly warranted, indeed mandatory, if sales staff are to utilise these models to the utmost advantage, both personal and organisational.

Benefits of sales coaching

The benefits of coaching have been discussed throughout this book. While there are general benefits that apply to all individuals or organisations that undertake coaching, some specific advantages apply to the selling profession. Feedback from sales professionals with whom we work suggests the following benefits of sales coaching:

1   Increased productivity, profitability and more efficient cost control.

2   Coaching affects 'the bottom line'. Through coaching, managers can maximise the effectiveness of each individual team member. Coaching can be tailored to each sales person's level of development and can range from 'directive coaching' with a new recruit to mentoring a senior sales professional.

3   Through the use of coaching methods such as goal setting, structuring an action plan, observing and providing feedback, the sales manager can align the goals of the company with those of the individual. The sales person becomes increasingly more self-directed and self-motivated.

4   Sales staff enhance their interpersonal and communication skills so they can relate more effectively to team members and can develop honest, friendly relationships with prospects. They also enhance their ability to develop and sustain mutually beneficial and productive relationships with clients.

5   Staff feel more appreciated and valued as a member of the company. Consequently, they find work more challenging and seek out opportunities for innovative and exciting ways to enhance their selling skills.

Selling as a mental skill

Selling, like sport, is essentially a mental game. It has been suggested that at least 50 per cent of successful sales are due to mental skills, 30 per cent are due to technical skills, and the remaining 20 per cent are based on product knowledge. As mentioned previously, our thoughts determine our feelings and our actions. If a sales person is harbouring negative or distorted thoughts, these will obviously be detrimental to his or her selling performance.

Everyone has negative thoughts. Successful individuals tend to be more skilled at recognising and challenging these impediments to success and wellbeing. Research has established seven main negative beliefs that can act as a barrier to successful sales. These beliefs may be habitual and the individual may be unaware of their existence, least of all their frequency and impact. The sales manager has to be alert to these underlying beliefs and feel confident and competent at challenging them. Briefly, these beliefs include:

1   *Self-blaming*   The individual accepts complete responsibility for a negative event or a sales failure. When successful, these individuals tend to attribute it to good luck or fate.

   The coach's role: The coach has to challenge the coachee's notion that he or she has total control over a buyer. We can have influence over another but not control them. The failure of a sale may be related to product limitations or the current economic landscape rather than the sales person's selling ability. Once the coach has worked with the coachee to tease out the various factors impacting on the sale, they can then collaboratively draw up a plan to improve weaknesses and highlight selling strengths. Emphasising past and current successes and the coachee's active role in these can attenuate self-blaming.

2   *Inaccurate forecasting*   When the individual is in a sales trough, he or she makes excessively pessimistic predictions about future performance.

   The coach's role: Even a top sales person can encounter a slump period. The coach's role is to encourage the individual, while not minimising or denying that performance is down. In order to counteract the belief that sales will never improve, the sales manager can present data (graphs, charts, etc.) that show that selling troughs are a common feature of selling and that they are frequently followed by an upturn in sales. The manner in which the sales professional views the downturn in performance will determine how quickly and how easily he or she regains confidence and control.

3   *Need for immediate results*   Some sales people expect instant, immediate success. They tend to lack perseverance, and become dissatisfied and impatient when there is a slump in sales.

   The coach's role: Expecting instant success can be a function of personality. The coach should recognise the individual's drive and hunger for success as a strength that can, nonetheless, become a limitation in some situations. It may be possible for the coach and coachee to establish an action plan that incorporates a certain number of sales within a specified period. By giving the sales person a time framework in which to achieve success, there may be less emphasis on gaining immediate results.

4   *Exaggerating*   Some individuals have a tendency to turn minor setbacks into major catastrophes. A bad call or an unsuccessful meeting can lead to heightened anxiety and the belief that they will not get the account and will be fired.

   The coach's role: The sales manager has to intervene early in the process or the sales person will lose confidence and possibly the sale. As a coach, the manager has to contain the individual's anxiety and his or her personal disappointment or even anger. A rational, logical approach is required in order to determine what can be done to redeem the situation. Furthermore, the coachee may be an anxious person, so relaxation techniques and strategies to challenge catastrophic thinking may be warranted on an ongoing basis.

5   *Approval seeking*   Individuals who seek approval from everyone are subject to a constant fear of rejection and loss of confidence. Such an attitude can prove a major impediment to selling.

The coach's role: The coach has to challenge rationally the individual's distorted belief that it is possible to please everyone and have everyone like him or her. Some issues the coach can raise with the salesperson include: Is it possible to please everyone? Do you value the person's opinion? Is it you or the product that is being rejected? Is the criticism valid? If the criticism is founded, what can you do about it? Criticism and rejection can be viewed as a learning opportunity.

6   *Comfort seeking*   Some individuals consider that life should be easy and fun, and may resent menial or boring jobs. These somewhat 'entitled' attitudes can lead to resentment, procrastination and avoidance.

The coach's role: The coach may have to be somewhat confrontational when dealing with this type of individual. Essentially, the coach has to challenge the belief that 'life was meant to be easy'. It is a wish rather than a fact. An action plan with a strict time frame could be drawn up to help counteract procrastination and avoidance. Furthermore, the sales manager can point out the repercussions of the person's behaviour, such as dismissal, if there is no change.

7   *Generalising*   The individual believes that one misfortune or one bad incident will inevitably lead to others.

The coach's role: The coach has to challenge the individual's global style of thinking by pointing out that the incidence or failure is an isolated one and is not predictive of future events. By clarifying the factors impacting on the negative event, the coach and coachee can work together to develop strategies to prevent their recurrence or at least minimise their impact. As a result, the coachee will gain greater confidence in his or her ability to control circumstances and to intervene in what was previously considered inevitable.

Selling in the 'flow zone'

Sports psychologists frequently talk about athletes being in the 'flow zone'. It is a state in which all attention is focused on the skills being performed. Mood, distraction and stress do not exist in their consciousness. Although the individual is in a state of high alertness and is vividly aware of the activities being performed, he or she is not aware of the 'self', is not distracted and is not evaluating the performance. Top sales people tend to operate consistently in the flow zone.

The notion of flow and being at one with our experience is exemplified in oriental martial arts, which tend to adopt a Zen-like approach to concentration and performance. According to this philosophy, several factors can interfere with the flow experience, including:

➤ wanting to win

➤ focusing on results and not the experience

➤ being aggressive

➤ trying to impress

➤ wanting to intimidate the opponent

➤ trying so hard to achieve the right state of mind that the individual is distracted.

According to Czikzentmihalyi, we are always in one of three zones. These are the flow zone, the panic zone or the drone zone. When we are in the panic zone, we are anxious, feel things are out of our control and do not function effectively. Not only do we experience these aversive states subjectively, but in a sales environment, customers and colleagues are also aware of how we are feeling.

In the drone zone we are bored, lacking motivation and uninterested in what we are doing. We feel demoralised and 'cannot be bothered'. Some individuals who perform frequently in the panic zone can, because they expend so much energy in a negative or unproductive way, fall into the drone zone through sheer exhaustion.

The characteristics of individuals in the flow zone, the panic zone and the drone zone are shown in Figure 12.1.

The coach's role: working in the three zones

There are a number of things that the coach can do to help individuals to work in the flow zone. First, the coach should be a role model. If the sales manager is anxious and puts undue pressure on his or her staff to achieve, they will tend to model this behaviour and will be more likely to

Flow zone	Panic zone	Drone zone
➤ foouseu	➤ anxious	➤ bored
➤ relaxed	➤ hypervigilant	➤ unmotivated
➤ confident	➤ distorted thinking	➤ demoralised
➤ no self-awareness	➤ distracted	➤ lethargic
➤ no distractions	➤ poor processing skills	➤ unfocused
➤ no evaluation		➤ distracted

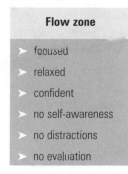 

Figure 12.1   The three performance zones

inhabit the panic zone rather than the flow zone. The sales manager who thinks positively, and is focused, supportive, in control and enjoys the job, is more likely to generate flow zone performers.

Second, the coach should focus on intrinsic motivation. As noted by Montaigne, it is the journey not the arrival that matters. It is the performance itself that matters most to top sales people. They will perform best when what they are doing is in accord with their personal goals and vision. The sales manager has to ensure that the individual's goals are aligned with those of the organisation.

Three coaching methods that are effective with sales people in the panic zone include: (a) empathising with the individual—high anxiety is a very unpleasant, debilitating state; (b) recognising and challenging their negative beliefs—as discussed above; (c) demonstrating and encouraging simple breathing techniques—when we are in the panic zone we tend towards rapid, shallow breathing, rather than breathing from the abdomen, which further escalates anxiety. There is a quick abdominal breathing exercise that serves to centre the person and short-circuit the panic process. It involves breathing in through the right nostril and out through the left nostril three times, breathing in through the left nostril and out through the right nostril three times, and then breathing in through both nostrils and out through both nostrils three times. The exercise is a useful calming technique and can be performed anywhere. Initially, the sales person might require cues to perform the exercise, such as certain times during the day, but with regular practice, the technique becomes habitual. The individual learns to recognise the cues that trigger panic and can intervene before they become immersed in the zone.

When individuals are in the drone zone, they lose their motivation and direction. They tend to lose sight of their goals or cannot relate to the present task. The coach has to work with the sales person to: (a) clarify and restate individual and organisational goals; (b) challenge distorted thinking—monitor negative thoughts, perhaps by writing them down and writing down positive thoughts to replace them; (c) develop a short-term action plan that focuses on an immediate and achievable goal. This involves discussing potential obstacles to reaching the goal and generating solutions and strategies to overcome them. Follow-up must be immediate and frequent. The coach may be required to be more directive than supportive, particularly if the person is deeply immersed in the drone zone. Goals should become more difficult and challenging as the person emerges from the gloom.

Some qualities of a successful sales manager/coach

In order to perform effectively as a coach, the sales manager should cultivate the following attributes:

➤ *Leadership skills*   A top sales manager can develop and communicate a vision that is commensurate with the company's vision, goals and mission. Leaders challenge the status quo, take risks and include and encourage others to make the vision a reality (see the section on leadership in Chapter 4).

➤ *Ability to identify with management*   Successful sales managers see themselves as part of a worthwhile professional management team. They establish and develop solid relationships with other managers and support management decisions. Yet they also maintain trusting and friendly relationships with their sales staff.

➤ *Commitment to the growth and development of others*   Sales managers need to be aware of the skills and competencies that staff need for personal and professional development. They are alert to and commit resources to current training opportunities as well as follow-up coaching, to ensure that what is learned is transferred to the workplace. Successful sales managers have the desire and ability to move sales people beyond their comfort zone to ever increasing levels of performance.

➤ *Achievement-oriented*   Effective sales managers focus on goals that appeal to the intrinsic motivation of staff. They create a positive, motivating environment for their sales team. As with any successful coach, the sales manager collaboratively sets achievable and stretch goals, and develops strategies, benchmarks and action plans for each individual. He or she encourages and models accountability.

➤ *Optimistic*   Top sales managers work from a success model that focuses on strengths rather than deficits. They promote the ability and will to succeed and overcome obstacles by creating a 'can do' attitude.

Some coaching skills for the sales manager/coach

The following list details some of the coaching skills that are particularly relevant to the sales manager.

1   *Use data rather than personal observations/opinions* when dealing with a sales person who is in a slump or is performing below par.

2   *Try to match the individual's style*—for example, when dealing with an impatient, driven, action-oriented type A individual, the coach should be direct and brisk and not waste the individual's time with lengthy explanations. The coach should always aim for a win–win solution. It is important that the coach does not offend the individual's pride. On the other hand, when working with someone who is theoretically-oriented and analytic, the coach can rely on the person's ability to think through the problem and come up with his or her own solutions. Flexibility, as with any type of coaching, is crucial for the sales coach. The onus is on the coach to adapt his or her style to the sales person.

3   *Ask about successes*—that is, the coach should ask the sales person about his or her most effective, successful performance. Some questions to ask include:

> What happened?

> What were you thinking?

> What factors contributed to the success?

> How did the customer respond?

> How were you feeling?

> What is different now from then?

> What can be done to get you back into that successful mode?

4   *Asking questions*—the way the sales manager asks questions serves as a guide to sales people when they are dealing with clients. These questions should establish the individual's needs, goals and aspirations. Similarly, a successful sales professional asks questions that uncover the needs of the prospect or customer. Rather than tell the client what the product offers them, top sales people ask what the client needs, and match the product to meet these needs.

As we have noted before, coaching is 80 per cent listening and 20 per cent talking. The 20 per cent talking, however, also includes asking insightful and astute questions. The rule also applies to selling. Being able to convert the features and benefits of a product into questions allows clients to sell to themselves. Likewise, a coach's questions allow the sales person to generate solutions for himself or herself.

 Coaching the sales person

R. D. is a 32-year-old sales person for a medium-sized manufacturing company. Although highly qualified, enthusiastic and possessing excellent product knowledge, her results are consistently below par. Training courses have failed to lift her performance and management is thinking of letting her go. A coach was employed to work with R. D. in a final effort to upgrade her selling skills. The first assessment found that R. D. was nervous about initial contacts with prospects. She had a tendency to use charm and friendliness as a first line of defence against her anxiety about rejection and failure. Consequently, she would be too friendly, too self-disclosing and would spend too much time establishing rapport rather than trying to understand the prospect's needs. In the coaching sessions, the coach and R. D. first challenged some of her distorted thinking, such as, 'everyone has to like me'. Simple breathing techniques were introduced that allowed her to feel more relaxed and in control when first meeting prospects. Role-plays were enacted with an emphasis on combining R. D.'s natural charm and friendliness with asking focused questions to establish the client's needs. After eight coaching sessions, her performance began to improve dramatically. A three-month follow-up found R. D. performing among the top five sales people in the company.

Career coaching

Key points

➤ Changes in career structure—how coaching can help

➤ Coaching for career blockages

➤ Career coaching in organisations

➤ Executive career coaching

➤ Coaching for different phases of a career

Changes in career structure—how coaching can help

Those of us who are engaged in satisfying, challenging careers that 'fit' with our goals, ambitions and personalities lead productive, fulfilling lives. Being stuck in a 'dead end' job or one for which we are temperamentally ill-suited can lead to stress, anxiety and general misery. Choosing a career, maintaining a career or changing careers in mid-life can present exciting challenges. It can also be fraught with difficulties.

Changes in organisations and in our personal lives mean that the notion of career paths is now almost obsolete—few people look ahead. Careers are shorter and more uncertain. There is very little job security, with short-term jobs becoming the norm. Many people expect to hold a series of jobs and participate in a succession of projects. The notion of full-time employment with a single employer is only one of many options that include 'borderless jobs' and 'virtual work', as well as contractual, consultative and interim arrangements. Part-time, flexi-time and job-sharing options also impact on career choices.

The flattening out of management levels and fewer jobs in companies have resulted in changes in the traditional career path within organisations. Because promotional opportunities are fewer, employees are kept longer in positions before being promoted. Traditionally, the typical career path model was one of upward mobility and employees had the certainty of a structured path for advancement. In the current workplace, there is more emphasis on job rotation, multiskilling and lateral promotions.

Perhaps the most significant change, though, in career structures is that individuals are now responsible for their own careers. Forty or fifty years ago, people found an area or company to work in and stayed there until retirement. A social contract went along with the job, and employers accepted certain responsibilities for their staff. Today, the individual is responsible for identifying his or her career within and between organisations.

As organisations become increasingly less involved in defining career options and individual career paths, the onus is on the individual to become more self-reliant. High incidences of job cuts, euphemistically referred to as 'downsizing', demand that employees have the skills and competencies that will prove invaluable to their employers, both present and future. Career coaching is the ideal vehicle to ensure career enhancement and career success.

Some situations where a career coach can help you

Traditionally, career counselling revolved around interviewing and assessing individuals for their suitability for particular careers. A career coach today, however, can assist individuals in virtually every aspect of their career, from their first job to retirement. Some areas where a career coach can help include:

➤ starting a career

➤ burnout or general career dissatisfaction

➤ transition and change due to company restructuring

➤ executive career development

➤ making a career change in mid-term

➤ re-entering the workforce

➤ preparing for future employment

➤ impression management—preparing resumes, interview skills

➤ redesigning your current position and job description

➤ increasing your visibility and profile in the current workplace

➤ getting ahead

➤ dealing with job loss

➤ retirement coaching

➤ coaching your partner.

What career coaching can do for you

A career coach will advise and assist you in the following aspects:

➤ assessing your situation and objectively evaluating your career opportunities

➤ working with you to clarify your values and aspirations

➤ acting as a resource—providing you with useful and valuable information about how to research particular jobs and careers

➤ assisting you to market yourself effectively

➤ overcoming blockages to attaining a successful and exciting career

➤ coping with rejection

➤ helping you to recognise your personal strengths and weaknesses, and understand how your personality 'type' fits with certain careers and work environments

➤ increasing productivity and status within your current job

➤ developing career goals (short, medium and long term) and an action plan to achieve them

➤ providing ongoing feedback, support and encouragement.

Coaching for career blockages

Several variables have been isolated that can serve to put us off track or short-circuit our careers. A career coach, either personal, in-house or external to the organisation, can work with an individual to develop self-awareness and insight into how these obstacles are impacting on their work life. Unless such issues are dealt with, goals and action plans are unlikely to reach fruition. Some obstacles include:

➤ *A misguided sense of entitlement* or belief that we deserve a career for which we are unqualified and unsuited. While this is not to say that we can, and should, 'aim high', an element of realism has to be brought to career choice activity.

➤ *Expecting fast results and success* without the requisite hard work and perseverance.

➤ *Trying to please others.* From childhood, our attitudes towards work and careers are influenced by our parents' attitudes towards their careers and work in general. While parents can serve as useful guides and role models, some individuals choose careers to please their parents rather than themselves. If there is not genuine interest and suitability for a particular career, lifelong dissatisfaction and resentment can ensue. Some of us are unable to balance our needs and our responsibilities to others, such as family.

➤ *The wrong attitude towards employers.* Some individuals 'parentify' their employer and re-enact a childhood drama, which results in ambivalence towards the boss or a passive dependent stance that excludes autonomy and self-reliance.

➤ *Negative beliefs.* As children many of us receive negative messages about our capabilities and self-worth. These can result in a lifetime of affirming these limitations and an inability to achieve the career we desire and are capable of attaining.

Career coaching in organisations

As noted in Chapter 5, one of the key roles of the manager as coach may be to provide career coaching for employees. The primary purpose of career coaching is to help employees consider alternatives and make decisions regarding their careers. In return, the organisation gains the benefit of knowing about employees' career perspectives and can therefore plan and provide opportunities for them to fulfil their career goals. Of course, human resources personnel can also provide career coaching services. The advantages and disadvantages of in-house and external coaches are discussed in Chapter 5.

Some specific career coaching roles for the manager as coach

In order to assist employees in structuring and pursuing their career strategies, the manager should adopt the roles discussed below.

➤ The manager and human resources personnel can design and implement appraisal systems and standards. They are in an ideal position to give feedback and help employees clarify the opportunities and limits that exist within the company. Future options and directions can be discussed so that the individual can prepare for and adapt to these demands.

➤ The manager should conduct a review of current and future career plans.

➤ While the process of goal setting is essentially similar for all types of coaching, the manager as coach is in a unique position to assess and discuss the employee's level of commitment to his or her career goals. The coach can guide employees in assessing their career motivations and career options and can participate actively in goal setting and action planning.

➤ The manager as coach can provide ongoing support and encouragement during the implementation of the agreed upon career strategies.

➤ The manager as coach can work with employees who may be stressed or dissatisfied with their job. Interpersonal issues at work, such as conflict with colleagues or team members, may adversely affect performance. Coaching for communication skills and ways to resolve conflict can enhance performance and keep the individual focused on his or her career path trajectory.

Executive career coaching

Individual executive coaching sometimes focuses on issues that are related to the individual's career path. However, there are specific coaching areas in which a career coach can guide the executive. Some of these include:

➤ uncertainty over future career—coaching here involves researching the market, identifying present and future skills and dealing with financial issues

➤ career change—working through emotional responses and blockages, researching career opportunities and developing new skills and competencies

➤ coping with promotion (see below)

➤ adapting to lateral moves or redesigning current position

➤ balancing life/work issues (see Chapter 4).

Executive career derailers

Smart has researched career derailers for executives and has isolated several factors that impact negatively on a manager/executive's career prospects. While there are some technical competencies such as delegation skills, most of the deficiencies outlined below are related to self-awareness, impression management and interpersonal skills. All these skills lend themselves to the career coaching alliance. Career derailers for executives include:

➤ inability to upgrade—some executives are afraid to hire someone who is better qualified or more competent than they are

➤ lack of integrity—the executive breaks confidences and is not seen as trustworthy by others in the organisation

➤ inability to empower—an executive may be afraid to delegate, and may be unwilling or unable to be a team player; on the other hand, the individual may be too passive, always delegating upwards and lacking in initiative

➤ likeability—arrogance or rudeness on the part of the executive can overshadow his or her diligence and competence.

Coaching the executive for new appointments

An important aspect of executive career development is that of the newly appointed leader dilemma. Some coaching organisations specialise in providing coaching services during the executive's first 100 days in a new role, job or company. Research suggests that approximately 40 per cent of newly appointed leaders prove to be disappointing, are terminated or leave the job voluntarily within 12 to 18 months of being appointed. Yet little time is afforded the executive to learn the new job.

A personal career coach, either external or in-house, can coach the newly appointed leader in the following areas:

➤ preparing for the new position by conducting a political analysis of powerbrokers in order to build effective partnerships

➤ building strong first impressions

➤ developing an empowering communication strategy

➤ designing a vision and mission and communicating these to all employees

➤ gaining commitment

➤ balancing life and work so that work demands do not jeopardise personal relationships.

Some of the most frequently cited reasons for failure on the part of the newly appointed leader include:

➤ lack of clarity about the appointment charter

➤ failure to identify stakeholders and build key partnerships

➤ learning the job too slowly

➤ failure to mesh with the existing culture or inability to build an appropriate culture

➤ key interpersonal differences

➤ failure to achieve the necessary balance between work and family life

➤ overreliance on existing professional and managerial skills.

Coaching before the appointment is taken up or during the initial phase could serve to prevent or attenuate these failures, which can be damaging to the individual and costly to the organisation.

Coaching the partner

Particularly in the corporate world, the partner and family of the executive are frequently subject to dislocation and change. This can involve moves from one organisation to another or geographical relocation. During these times of transition, the partner particularly can experience isolation, anxiety and lack of support. A career coach can work with the partner to alleviate some of these stressors. Some specific areas of coaching include:

➤ providing emotional support during the adjustment phase

➤ guiding the individual to access and familiarise himself or herself with local resources

➤ networking

➤ understanding local and cultural values.

Coaching for different phases of a career

First job choice

Generally, we seek an initial career that meets our financial needs as well as our professional and personal ambitions and goals. Career coaching assists us to identify our interests and abilities and guides us in clarifying our values and life purpose. Through career coaching we become aware of our personality strengths and our unique skills as well as career opportunities where our talents will flourish.

A career coach works with first job seekers to:

➤ Make a commitment to decide on a future vocation that allows a balanced life and where they can express who they truly are. The coach can help them decide what they have to offer the world and where they want to use their skills. This can involve not putting too much emphasis on job titles and even preparing for careers that do not yet exist.

➤ Assess personality traits and temperament and find a 'goodness of fit' between these and their planned occupation. Research indicates that jobs that demand a work persona or mask prove stressful and, ultimately, unrewarding. Assessments help the first job seeker to pinpoint interests, discover latent and apparent abilities and recognise his or her personality style.

Some common career assessment instruments that can help to access potentialities and possibilities include: the *Self Directed Search (SDS)*, which identifies interests, skills and abilities and focuses on occupations to further explore; the *Strong Interest Inventory (SII)*, which measures occupations and leisure activities; the *Jackson Vocational Interest Survey*, which looks at work role dimensions and work environment preferences; the *Myers-Briggs Temperament Inventory (MBTI)*, which is widely used in career coaching to determine individual style or personality type as it relates to work activities such as decision making, communication and learning; and the *DISC Profile*, which provides the individual with a behaviour analysis and personality profile.

➤ Act as a resource to guide them through libraries, various organisations, the Internet, temporary employment and/or volunteer work. Resume writing, and how to appear polished and confident in an interview situation, are also skills that can be developed and enhanced in a coaching intervention.

Coaching for mid-career change

Today, career decisions are not permanent. Some authors estimate that we can expect four or five career changes in a lifetime. Changing careers is increasingly viewed as a standard feature of growth and development rather than the result of a mistaken choice.

A coach can assist the individual in mid-career change to:

➤ Develop the courage to change and take risks. Some individuals question whether they are courageous enough to leap into what may appear to be a void, whether it is too late to change direction or, indeed, whether it is possible to find true satisfaction and meaning in work. The coach examines and encourages the individual's willingness to stretch boundaries and meet new challenges with enthusiasm and persistence.

➤ Develop skills and competencies to become an independent contractor or a 'portfolio person'.

➤ Change the area or industry in which the individual works. Such a goal includes coaching in the following areas: researching other industries or organisations, networking, using contacts and developing a support group and speaking to professionals who may have got to a position without traditional qualifications.

Coaching and job loss

Career resilience has been defined as the ability to deal with job loss or some other setback in our career. Job loss, particularly, involves trauma. It can adversely affect the individual's feelings of self-worth and confidence and this, in turn, can inhibit the successful pursuit of a new job.

The career coach can:

➤ Assist the individual to manage and resolve feelings of loss, grief, anger and shame. The coach can create a safe environment where the individual can openly discuss his or her feelings and develop strategies to cope with them.

➤ Discuss the expectations, aspirations and the relationships impacting on the individual's present situation.

➤ Conduct a skills assessment and a review of the individual's career history, highlighting successes and aptitudes.

➤ Discuss and advise on future career possibilities via methods to increase awareness of changing work trends.

➤ Advise and offer resources for the individual to conduct occupational career research.

➤ Establish goals and an action plan.

➤ Provide feedback and ongoing support during the job search process.

Pre-retirement and retirement coaching

Approaching retirement, either voluntarily or as the result of downsizing, can demand considerable emotional adjustments and changes in lifestyle. Career coaches, either in-house or external to the organisation, can play a vital role in assisting and guiding the individual through this period of transition.

Certain individuals, particularly those who have invested their life in their work, experience difficulty 'letting go'. The very notion of retiring is anathema to them. Some people may be faced with an existential crisis, and experience feelings of anxiety and panic. On the other hand, change and retirement can be an exciting and joyful time, with new possibilities, new ways of being, new challenges and new opportunities beckoning.

A career coach can work with pre-retirees and retirees in the following areas:

➤ *Planning for positive change*   Letting go of old habits is extremely difficult if an individual is moving into a vacuum. Pre-retirees have to re-examine their values and sense of purpose in the light of their changed status. A person whose identity has been defined chiefly by his or her work may need to work on re-defining who and what he or she wants to be. The process may involve dealing with regrets and loss and the coach has to display patience and empathy during this grieving stage. Traditional beliefs and assumptions may be questioned, with the coach having to confront the coachee regarding distorted or outmoded beliefs which are hindering adaptability and movement. For instance, some individuals may believe that to be a worthwhile person they have to be productive as defined by 'being in the workforce'.

➤ *Financial realities*   Although many pre-retirees and retirees consult financial advisers, a career coach can work through the following financial issues: adjusting to a lower income, investing, perhaps moving to a smaller house or apartment and ways to supplement income.

➤ *Dealing with family reactions*   Adjusting to family life and family expectations is a critical component of the retirement process. Many individuals, particularly males, view themselves as the provider and supporter of the family. Some may have neglected other aspects of family life for a demanding if rewarding career. Now, they may wish to be reabsorbed into the family as their needs for belonging, intimacy, and even power are no longer met by the workplace.

➤ *Dealing with time*   Although retirement affords many benefits, some retirees feel that time weighs heavily on them. The coach and pre-retiree can work together to structure pleasurable and rewarding activities. These may include part-time work, voluntary work, joining associations, pursuing a hobby or taking up study of a lifelong interest that has been put aside because of work demands. Coaching in these areas should begin well before the cessation of work, as emotional issues or the 'shock' of actual retirement can block or delay implementation of strategies and action plans.

 Case Study

Coaching for retirement

G. S. is a 53-year-old senior manager who has worked with the same company for 20 years. His career has plateaued and he is approaching early retirement. He feels that he has neglected his family (his second wife and two adolescent children) during his career. G. S. longs for intimacy, and wants to adjust to being a husband and father. His initial attempts at embracing the role of husband and father received a rather lukewarm reception from his family. Hurt and at a loss, he approached a retirement coach to help him 'reabsorb' into the family. Part of the coaching alliance focused on G. S.'s concept of intimacy and on his definition of himself as

Case Study

someone other than 'the provider'. As a result, G. S. developed a greater self-awareness of his expectations and how these could be at odds with those of his family. His previous attempts had been somewhat overwhelming to his family as he had not really appreciated the independence and autonomy his 'absence' had allowed them. Together, the coach and G. S. worked on an action plan that involved family discussions about the role they wished him to play, and strategies that would enable him to *gradually* assume a more visible and valued position as a member rather than the head of the family.

Bibliography

Adair, J. 1986, *Effective Teambuilding*, Pan, London.

Adilman, A., Maxwell, J. & Wilkinson, S. (eds.) 1994, *Core Lessons for Life Skills Programs*, Province of British Columbia Ministry of Skills, Training and Labour, pp. 172–3.

Alder, H. 1995, *Think Like a Leader: 150 Top Business Leaders Show You How Their Minds Work*, Piatkus, London.

Allen, S., Mehal, M., Palmateer, S. & Sluser, R. 1995, *The New Dynamics of Life Skills Coaching*, YWCA, Toronto.

Andreas, S. & Faulkner, C. 1997, *NLP: The New Technology of Achievement*, Nicholas Brealey Publishing, London.

Aram, E. 1998, 'Virtual Teamworking Using Networking Techniques: An Investigation into its Impact on Organizational Dynamics', Symposium for the Psychoanalytic Study of Organizations.

AREVO (Advocates for Remote Employment and the Virtual Office), 'What Are "Remote Employment" and the "Virtual Office"?', www.globaldialog.com/~morse/arevo.

Argyris, C. 1991, 'Teaching Smart People How to Learn', *Harvard Business Review*, May/June, pp. 99–109.

Arnold, J., Cooper, G. L. & Robertson, I. T. 1995, *Work Psychology: Understanding Human Behaviour in the Workplace*, Second Edition, Pitman Publishing, London.

Balkeman, A. & Malleman, E. 1999, 'Some Barriers to the Development of Self Managing Teams', *Journal of Managerial Psychology*, Vol. 14, No. 2, pp. 134–49.

Bandura, A. 1989, 'Human Agency in Social Cognition Theory', *American Psychologist*, Vol. 44, pp. 1175–84.

Bardwick, J. 1986, *The Plateauing Trap*, Amacom, New York.

Belf, T. 1995, 'In the Beginning...On Purpose', *Being in Action: The Professional and Personal Coaching Association Journal*, Summer, Vol. 4, p. 1.

Belf, T. E. 1996, *Facilitating Life Purpose. A Manual For Coaches*, Success Unlimited Network, pp. 6–7, 9.

Birkel, J. D. & Miller, S. J. 1997, *Career Bounce Back: The Professionals in Transition Guide to Recovery and Reemployment (Professionals in Transition)*, Amacom, New York.

Boak, G. B. & Thompson, D. 1998, *Mental Models for Managers: Frameworks for Practical Thinking*, Century Business, London.

Bolles, R. N. 1999, *What Color is Your Parachute? A Practical Manual for Job-Hunters and Career-Changers*, Ten Speed Press, CA.

Bolton, R. 1997, *People Skills: How to Assert Yourself, Listen to Others, and Resolve Conflicts*, Simon & Schuster, Sydney.

Bridges, W. 1991, 'Change as Beginnings', *Organizations in Transition*, Winter, Vol. 4, No. 1.

Brotman, L. E., Liberi, W. P. & Wasylyshyn, K. M. 1998, 'Executive Coaching: The Need for Standards of Competence', *Consulting Psychology Journal: Practice and Research*, Vol. 50, No. 1, pp. 40–6.

Brown, L. D. 1983, *Managing Conflict at Organizational Interfaces*, Addison Wesley, Reading, Mass.

Burns, R. B. 1997, *Psychology for Effective Managers: Understanding and Managing Human Behaviour in the Workplace*, Business and Professional Publishing, Australia.

Burnside, R. M. & Guthrie, V. A. 1992, *Training for Action: A New Approach to Executive Development*, Center for Creative Leadership, Greensborough, NC.

Butler, R. J. 1996, *Sports Psychology in Action*, Butterworth-Heinemann, Oxford.

Butler, T. & Waldroop, J. 1999, 'Is Your Job Your Calling (Extended Interview)', *Fast Company*, Vol. 13, p. 108.

Caldwell, B. J. & Carter, E. M. A. 1993, *The Return of the Manager: Strategies for Workplace Learning*, The Falmer Press, London, p. 205.

Carlopio, J., Andrewartha, G. & Armstrong, H. 1997, *Developing Management Skills in Australia*, Addison Wesley Longman, Sydney, pp. 463–4.

Carroll, M. 1996, *Workplace Counselling*, Sage Publications, London.

Cherney, E. 1999, 'Women Who Work Are Less Depressed', *Women in Management*, June/July, Vol. 9, No. 4, pp. 1–2.

Church, A. H. 1997, 'Managerial Self-Awareness in High-Performing Individuals in Organizations', *Journal of Applied Psychology*, Vol. 82, No. 2, pp. 281–92.

Clemmer, J. 1999, 'Blocks to Customer Focus', www.clemmer.net./htm.

Coffey, R. E., Cook, C. W. & Hunsaker, P. L. 1994, *Management and Organizational Behavior*, Austin Press/Irwin, Burr Ridge, ILL.

Coleman, D. 1998, 'Working with Tough-Minded Executives: A Coach's Lessons Learned', in Proceedings of the 1998 Leadership Conference, The Art and Practice of Coaching Leaders, UMUC: National Leadership Institute. p. 291.

Comfort, M. 1997, *Portfolio People: How to Create a Workstyle As Individual As You Are*, Century Business Books, UK.

Cooper, R. & Sawaf, A. 1997, *Executive EQ: Emotional Intelligence in Business*, Orion Business Books, London, p. xii.

Corey, G. 1997, *Theory and Practise of Counseling and Psychotherapy*, Fourth Edition, Brooks/Cole Publishing Company, CA.

Covey, S. R. 1998, *The Seven Habits of Highly Effective People*, The Business Press, Melbourne.

Crane Consulting, 'High Performance Team Building', www.craneconsulting.com/teams.htm.

Czikzentmihalyi, M. 1990, *Flow*, Harper Perennial.

Dalton, M. A. 1998, *Becoming a more versatile learner,* Greensborough, NC: Center for Creative Leadership.

De Groot, R. 1999, 'The 12 Models of Selling', *www.saleshelp.com/GuestEntrance/Newsletters.html*.

Divine, L. & Flaherty, J. 1998, 'Coaching Essential Competencies For Leaders', in Proceedings of the 1998 Leadership Conference, The Art and Practice of Coaching Leaders, UMUC: National Leadership Institute, pp. 95–104.

Dwyer, J. 1997, *The Business Communication Handbook*, Fourth Edition, Prentice Hall, Sydney.

Eales-White, R. 1995, *Building Your Team*, The *Sunday Times* Business Skills Series, Kogan Page, London.

Ekman, P. & Friesen, W. V. 1971, 'Constants Across Cultures in the Face and Emotion', *Journal of Personality and Social Psychology*, Vol. 17, pp. 124–9.

Erikson, E. 1982, *The Life Cycle Completed,* Norton, New York.

Ernst, R. L. 1999, *Real Time Coaching: How to Make the Minute by Minute Decisions that Unleash the Power in Your People*, Leadership Horizons, LLC, Carmel, IN, p. 3.

Farber, B. J. & Wycoff, J. 1992, *Breakthrough Selling*, Prentice Hall, Englewood Cliffs, NJ.

Ferguson, Adele, 1999, 'A World of Shifting Goal Posts', *Management Today*, January/February, pp. 14–19.

Fernandez, E., Clark, T. S. & Rudick-Davis, D. 1998, 'A Framework for Conceptualization and Assessment of Affective Disturbance in Pain', in A. R. Block, E. F. Kremer & E. Fernandez (eds.), *Handbook of Pain Syndromes: Biopsychosocial Approaches*, Erlbaum, Mahwah, NJ, pp. 123–47.

Filipczak, B. 1998, 'The Executive Coach: Helper or Healer', *Training*, March, p. 30.

Fishman, C. 1999, 'Change', http://orionlearning.com/Change.htm.

Flaherty, J. 1998, *Coaching: Evoking Excellence in Others*, Butterworth, Woburn, MA.

Folkman, J. 1998, *Making Feedback Work: Turning Feedback From Employee Surveys into Change*, Executive Excellence Publishing, Provo, UT, p. 9.

Fontana, D. 1985, 'Learning and Teaching', in C. L. Cooper & P. Makin (eds.), *Psychology and Managers*, BPS & Macmillan, London.

Foster, B. & Seeker, K. R. 1997, *Coaching for Peak Employee Performance: A Practical Guide to Supporting Employee Development*, Richard Chang Associates, Irvine, CA, p. 18.

Friend, F. 1999, *Coaching at the Executive Level (How to Coach the Coach)*, Center for Coaching and Mentoring, www.coachingandmentoring.com/Articles/ExecutiveCoaching/htm.

Friend, F. 1999, 'The "outside" Coach: Developing a Personal-Professional Relationship', www.thecoach.com/Articles/outsidecoaching/htm.

Fritz, S., Brown, F. W., Lunde, J. P. & Banset, E. A. 1999, *Interpersonal Skills For Leadership*, Prentice Hall, Englewood Cliffs, NJ, pp. 120–7.

Gallway, W. T. 1974, *The Inner Game of Tennis*, Random House, New York.

Gilley, J. W. & Boughton, N. W. 1996, *Stop Managing, Start Coaching!: How Performance Coaching Can Enhance Commitment and Improve Productivity*, Irwin Professional Publishing, Chicago, pp. 187–204.

Goldstein, I. L. 1993, *Training in Organizations*, Third Edition, Brooks/Cole, Monterey, CA, p. 115.

Goleman, D. 1996, *Emotional Intelligence: Why it Can Matter More Than IQ*, Bloomsbury, London.

Gollan, P. 1998, 'I'm ok, You're ok, the Company's ok: Only People Can Excel', *Management Today*, June, p. 6.

Hargrove, R. 1995, *Masterful Coaching: Extraordinary Results by Impacting People and the Way They Think and Work Together*, Jossey-Bass Pfeiffer, San Francisco.

Harrison, R. P. & Dunnells, N. P. 1998, 'The Newly Appointed Leader Dilemma' in Proceedings of the 1998 Leadership Conference, The Art and Practice of Coaching Leaders, UMUC: National Leadership Institute, pp. 249–57.

Harvey, E. H. 1998, 'A Holistic Approach to Coaching', in Proceedings of the 1998 Leadership Conference, The Art and Practice of Coaching Leaders, UMUC: National Leadership Institute, pp. 229–35.

Heifetz, R. A. & Laurie, D. L. 1997, 'Leaders Don't Need to Know All the Answers. They Do Need to Ask the Right Questions', *Harvard Business Review*, January/February, pp. 124–34.

Hill, J. 1997, *Managing Performance: Goals, Feedback, Coaching, Recognition*, Gower Publishing Limited, Aldershot, UK.

Honey, P. & Mumford, A. 1987, *A Manual of Learning Styles*, P. Honey Publications, Maidenhead, UK.

Horsburgh, L. 1998, Coping With Stress. *TELCALL*, Vol. 2, No. 9.

Howatt, W. A. 1999, 'Peak Performance Coaching for Business and Personal Success: Can You Afford Not to be a Peak Performer?', www.hindlecanada.com/peak/peakimain.htm.

Huber, G. 1991, 'Organizational Learning: The Contributing Processes and Literature', *Organizational Science*, Vol. 2, pp. 88–115.

Hurley, K. V. & Dobson, T. E. 1991, *What's My Type? Using the Enneagram System of Nine Personality Types to Discover Your Best Self*, Harper Collins, San Francisco.

Jarvenpaa, S. L. & Leidner, D. E. 1998, 'Communication and Trust in Global Virtual Teams', *Journal of Computer-Mediated Communication*, Vol. 3, No. 4.

Judge, W. Q. & Cowell, J. 1997, 'The Brave New World of Executive Coaching', *Business Horizons*, July/August, pp. 71–7.

Kamp, D. 1997, *Sharpen Your Team's Skills in People Skills*, The McGraw-Hill Companies, London, pp. 56–63.

Kander, R. E. 1998, *An Introduction to Business Coaching*, Work Resources Inc.

Kastenbaum, P. 1999, 'The inner search for greatness', www.eds.com/about_eds/homepage/home_page_inner-search.shtml.

Katzenbach, J. R. 1998, *Teams at the Top: Unleashing the Potential of Both Teams and Individual Leaders*, Harvard Business School Press, Boston.

Katzenbach, J. R. 1997, 'The Myth of the Top Management Team', *Harvard Business Review*, November/December, pp. 83–91.

Kidder, P. 1998, 'Coaching Experientially: Using Life Content to Produce Excellence', in Proceedings of the 1998 Leadership Conference, The Art and Practice of Coaching Leaders, UMUC: National Leadership Institute, pp. 105–13.

Kiel, F., Rimmer, E., Williams, K. & Doyle, M. 1996, 'Coaching at the Top', *Consulting Psychology Journal: Practice and Research*, Vol. 48, No. 2, p. 68.

Kilburg, R. 1996, 'Toward a Conceptual Understanding and Definition of Executive Coaching', *Consulting Psychology Journal: Practice and Research*, Vol. 48, No. 2, pp. 134–44.

Kiser, A. G. 1998, *Masterful Facilitation: Becoming a Catalyst for Meaningful Change*, Amacom, New York.

Knight, S. 1995, *NLP at Work: The Difference That Makes a Difference in Business*, Nicholas Brealey Publishing, London.

Knowles, M. 1980, *The Modern Practise of Adult Education: From Pedagogy to Andragogy*, Revised Edition, Prentice Hall, Englewood Cliffs, NJ.

Knudsen, M. J. & Kandola, B. 1998, 'Maximising Coaching Effectiveness at Digital: The Strategic Use and Implementation', in Proceedings of the Coaching and Mentoring Conference, Amsterdam, pp. 464–524.

Kolb, D. 1984, *Experiential Learning*, Prentice Hall, Englewood Cliffs, NJ.

Koonce, R. 1994, *Career Power: 12 Winning Habits to Get You From Where You Are to Where You Want to Be*, Amacom, New York.

Kraut, R., Steinfield, C., Chan, A., Butler, B. & Hoag, A. 1998, 'Coordination and Virtualization: The Role of Electronic Networks and Personal Relationships', *Journal of Computer-Mediated Communication*, Vol. 3, No. 4.

Landsberg, M. 1997, *The Tao of Coaching: Boost Your Effectiveness at Work by Inspiring and Developing Those Around You*, Harper Collins Business, London.

Landsberg, M. 1998, 'How to Design and Develop a World-Class Coaching Programme', in the Proceedings of the Coaching and Mentoring Conference, Amsterdam, p. 137.

Lauderbaugh, J. J. 1999, 'Coaching and Developing Call Center Staff', www.jjlauderbaugh.com/Articles/callcenter.html.

Leider, R. J. 1994, *Life Skills: Taking Charge of Your Personal and Professional Growth*, Prentice Hall, Englewood Cliffs, NJ.

LeKander, R. 1999, *An Introduction to Business Coaching*, WorkGroup Resources, Inc.

Levinson, H. 1975, *Executive Stress: Learn to Overcome the Pressures of Corporate Life*, A Mentor Book: New American Library, New York, p. 44.

Levinson, H. 1996, 'Executive Coaching', *Consulting Psychology Journal: Practice and Research*, Vol. 48, No. 2, p. 116.

Lewis, G. 1996, *The Mentoring Manager: Strategies for Fostering Talent and Spreading Knowledge*, Pitman Publishing, London.

Leyland, P. & Rosinki, P. 1998, 'Coaching Teams for High Performance at Baxter-Renal', in Proceedings of the Coaching and Mentoring Conference, Amsterdam.

Littrell, J. H. 1998, *Brief Counseling in Action*, W.W. Norton & Co, New York.

Locke, E. A. 1991, 'Problems with Goal-Setting Research in Sport – and Their Solution', *Journal of Sport and Exercise Psychology*, Vol. 13, pp. 311–16.

London, M. & Smithers, J. W. 1995, 'Can Multi-Source Feedback Change Perceptions of Goal Accomplishment, Self-Evaluations, and Performance-Related Outcomes? Theory-Based Applications and Directions for Research', Special Issue: Theory and Literature, *Personnel Psychology*, Vol. 48, No. 4, pp. 803–39.

Lowe, P. 1995, *Coaching and Counselling Skills*, McGraw-Hill, London.

Maddux, R. 1992, *Team Building: An Exercise in Leadership*, Revised Edition, Crisp Publications, CA, p. 5.

Magrid, R. Y. & Codkind, L. 1995, *Work and Personal Life: Managing the Issues*, Crisp Publications, CA, pp. 72–3.

Majchrzak, A. & Wang, Q. 1996, 'Breaking the Functional Mindset in Process Organisations', *Harvard Business Review*, September/October, pp. 90–6.

Marchese, T. 1998, 'The New Conversations about Learning: Insights from Neuroscience and Anthropology, Cognitive Science and Work-Place Studies', *The Adult Learner* (on-line journal), available at http://www.newhorizons.org/lrnbus_marchese.html.

Martens, R. 1987, *Coach's Guide to Sport Psychology*, Human Kinetics, Champaign, ILL.

Martin, I. 1996, *From Couch to Corporation: Becoming a Successful Corporate Therapist*, John Wiley & Sons, New York.

McGregor, D. 1960, *The Human Side of the Enterprise*, McGraw-Hill, London.

Mill, C. R. 1976, 'Feedback: The Art of Giving and Receiving Help', in L. Porter & C. R. Mill (eds.), *The Reading Book For Human Relations Training*, NTL Institute for Applied Behavioral Science, Bethel, ME, pp. 18–19.

Mills, H. 1996, *The Mental Edge: Unlocking the Secrets of Inner Selling*, Simon & Schuster, Sydney.

Mobley, S. A., Gravenstein, K., Isaacson, S., Perrelli, C. & Salmon, G. L. 1998, 'Coaching as Part of an Organisation Development', in Proceedings of the 1998 Leadership Conference, The Art and Practice of Coaching Leaders, UMUC: National Leadership Institute.

Neideffer, R. M. 1992, *Psyched to Win: How to Master Mental Skills to Improve Your Physical Performance*, Human Kinetics, Champaign, ILL.

Nelson-Jones, R. 1992, *Lifeskills: A Textbook of Practical Counselling and Helping Skills*, Holt, Rhinehart & Winston, Sydney.

Nevis, E. C., DiBella, A. J. & Gould, J. M. 1999, 'Understanding Organizations as Learning Systems', http://learning.mit.edu/res/wp/learning_sys.html.

Nilson, C. 1999, *The Performance Consulting Toolbook*, McGraw-Hill, New York, p. 187.

Olalla, J. 1998, 'The Mind, Body, and Spirit of Coaching', in Proceedings of the 1998 Leadership Conference, The Art and Practice of Coaching Leaders, UMUC: National Leadership Institute, pp. 19–36.

Olivero, G., Bane, K. D. & Kopelman, R. E. 1997, 'Executive Coaching as a Transfer of Training Tool: Effects on Productivity in a Public Agency', *Public Personnel Management*, Vol. 26, No. 4, pp. 461–9.

Open-Book Management, 'Coaching for Success', www.obm.com/index.htm.

Orlick, T. 1998, *Psyching for Sport*, Human Kinetics, Champaign, ILL.

Orlick, T. 1998, *Embracing Your Potential: Steps to Self-Discovery, Balance, and Success in Sports, Work, and Life*, Human Kinetics, Champaign, ILL.

Pedler, M., Burgoyne, J. & Boydell, T. 1994, *A Manager's Guide to Self-Development*, Third Edition, The McGraw-Hill Companies, London, p. 244.

Petersen, D. B. 1996, 'Executive Coaching at Work: The Art of One-On-One Change', *Consulting Psychology Journal: Practice and Research*, Vol. 48, No. 2, pp. 78–86.

Peterson, D. B. & Hicks, M. D. 1998, 'Professional Coaching: State of the Art, State of the Practice', in Proceedings of the 1998 Leadership Conference, The Art and Practice of Coaching Leaders, UMUC: National Leadership Institute, pp. 37–46.

Pfeiffer, J. 1998, *The Human Equation: Building Profits by Putting People First*, Harvard Business School Press, Boston.

Richardson, L. 1996, 'Sales Coaching', www.businesssavvy.com.html; www.Saleshelp.com/guests.3htm.

Robbins, S. P. & Hunsaker, P. L. 1996, *Training in Interpersonal Skills: Tips for Managing People at Work*, Second Edition, Prentice Hall, Englewood Cliffs, NJ.

Rockport Institute, 'How to Choose or Change Your Career for a Lifetime of Satisfaction and Success', www.rockportinstitute.com/brochure.html.

Rolfe-Flett, A. 1996, *Tailor Made Mentoring for Organisations*, Synergetic Management Pty Ltd, Australia, p. 3.

Root, B. 1999, 'The Hidden Organisation: The Failings of Hierarchical Management in the Information Age', http://orionlearning.com/hiddenorg.html.

Saporito, T. J. 1996, 'Business-Linked Executive Development: Coaching Senior Executives', *Consulting Psychology Journal: Practice and Research*, Vol. 48, No. 2, pp. 96–103.

Shea, G. 1997, *Mentoring: A Practical Guide*, Crisp Publications, Australia, p. 9.

Skiffington, S. & Zeus, P. 1998, 'Time of Transition Looms as Managers Become Leaders', *HR Monthly*, October, pp. 45–6.

Skiffington, S. & Zeus, P. 1999, 'Cultivating the Learning Organization Through Coaching', *Management Today*, March, p. 40, http://www.coachinglogic.com.

Skiffington, S., Fernandez, E. & McFarland, K. 1998, 'Towards a Validation of Multiple Features in the Assessment of Emotions', *European Journal of Psychological Assessment*, Vol. 14, No. 3, pp. 202–10.

Skliros, S. 1999, 'Achieving Peak Performance', *TELCALL*, Vol. 3, No. 5, p. 31.

Smart, B. D. 1999, *Topgrading: How Leading Companies Win by Hiring, Coaching and Keeping the Best People*, Prentice Hall, Englewood Cliffs, NJ.

Smith, D. K. & Katzenbach, J. R. 1993, *The Wisdom of Teams*, Boston Business School Press.

Snyder, A. 1995, 'Executive Coaching: The New Solution', *Management Review*, March, pp. 29–30.

Sperry, L. 1996, *Corporate Therapy and Consulting*, Brunner/Mazel, New York.

Staples, D. S., Hulland, J. S. & Higgins, C. A. 1998, 'A Self-Efficacy Theory Explanation for the Management of Remote Workers in Virtual Organizations', *Journal of Computer-Mediated Communication*, Vol. 3, No. 4.

Stimson, N. 1995, *Coaching Your Employees*, Kogan Page, London, p. 78.

Stone, F. M. 1999, *Coaching, Counseling & Mentoring: How to Choose the Right Technique to Boost Employee Performance*, Amacom, New York.

Stowell, S. J. & Starcevich, M. M. 1998, *The Coach: Creating Partnerships for a Competitive Edge*, Centre for Management and Organization Effectiveness, Utah, pp. 46–9.

Strassmann, P. A. 1994, 'How We Evaluated Productivity', *Computerworld*, Premier 100 Issue, September, p. 45.

Stroul, N. A. & O'Brien, M. 1998, 'Coaching: The Provocative Question', in Proceedings of the 1998 Leadership Conference, The Art and Practice of Coaching Leaders, UMUC: National Leadership Institute, pp. 141–5.

Thomas, K. W. & Velthouse, B. A. 1990, 'Cognitive Elements of Empowerment: An Interpretive Model of Intrinsic Task Motivation', *Academy of Management Review*, Vol. 15, pp. 666–81.

Thompson, P. & McHugh, D. 1995, *Work Organizations: A Critical Introduction*, Second Edition, Macmillan Business, London.

Tice, L. & Quick, J. 1997, *Personal Coaching For Results: How to Mentor and Inspire Others to Amazing Growth*, The Nelson Publishers, Nashville.

Tobias, L. L. 1996, 'Coaching Executives', *Consulting Psychology Journal: Practice and Research*, Vol. 48, No. 2, pp. 87–95.

Uren, D. 1999, 'Smart Thinkers Bring Passion to Power Roles', *The Weekend Australian*, 9–10 October, p. 50.

Verespi, M. A. 1990, 'Yea, Teams? Not Always', *Industry Week*, 18 June, pp. 103–5.

Walker, J. W. 1992, *Human Resource Strategy*, McGraw-Hill, New York, p. 211.

Walker, L. & Breeze, C. 1998. 'Coaching for Increased Business Performance', in Proceedings of the Coaching and Mentoring Conference, Amsterdam, pp. 249–68.

Walther, J. B. 1997, 'Group and Interpersonal Effects in International Computer-Mediated Collaboration', *Human Communication Research*, Vol. 23, No. 3, pp. 342–69.

Whitmore, J. 1998, *Coaching for Performance*, Second Edition, Nicholas Brealey Publishing, London, p. 46.

Whitworth, L., Kimsey-House, H. & Sandahl, P. 1998, *Co-Active Coaching: New Skills For Coaching People Toward Success in Work and Life*, Davies-Black Publishing, CA, p. 110.

William Bridges & Associates 1998, 'Why Change Management isn't Enough', *Newsletter*, Fall, Vol. 9, No. 4.

Williams, H. 1996, *The Essence of Managing Groups and Teams*, Prentice Hall, London.

Witherspoon, R. & White, R. P. 1998, 'Four Essential Ways to Coach Executives: A Progress Report and Reflections on Our Practice', in Proceedings of the 1998 Leadership Conference, The Art and Practice of Coaching Leaders, UMUC: National Leadership Institute, pp. 219–20.

WorkGroup Resources, Inc, 'The WorkGroup Method: A New Paradigm for Organisational Effectiveness, www.business-coaching.com/Method.htm.

Wycoff, J. 1991, *Mindmapping: Your Personal Guide to Exploring Creativity and Problem-Solving*, Berkley Books, New York.

Wylie, P. & Grothe, M. 1993, *Dealing with Difficult Colleagues: How to Improve Troubled Business Relationships*, Piatkus, London, p. 158.

Young, P. 1996, 'The Coaching Paradigm: Developing the Next Generation of Managers', *The Practising Manager*, October, p. 50.

Zemke, R. & Anderson, K. 1997, *Coaching Knock Your Socks Off Service*, Amacom, New York.

Zeus, P. 1999, 'Coaching in the New Century', *Coaching News*, Vol. 2, No. 7, http://www.ozcallcentres.com.

Index

goals, 40, 94, 110, 125, 161
    benofits of, 162
    in life skills coaching, 162–3
    steps in establishing, 163–6
Goleman, D., 81, 101
guidelines for making recommendations to
    clients, 61

Hargrove, R., 142, 165
Hill, J., 112
Honey, D., 190

impermanence, 198
in-house coaching, some advantages of, 124–5

Jackson Vocational Interest Survey, 243

Katzenbach, J. R., 131, 138
Kilburg, R., 11, 64
Knight, S., 47
Knowles, M., 184
Kolb, D., 187

leaders, versus managers, 82
leadership
    coaching for, 81–2
    issues in coaching for, 85
    transformational, 83–4
    types of, 82–3
leadership and influencing skills questionnaire, 84
learning, 182, 184
    characteristics of adult learners, 186
    coaching and, 182–3
    Kolb's model of, 188
    model for coaches, 188–9
    model for organisational learning, 193–5
    obstacles to, 186
    organisations and, 193–5
    styles of, 190–2
learning styles questionnaire (LSQ), 190–2

learning and development audit, 108, 193
Leider, R. J., 157
LeKander, R., 42
Levinson, H., 11, 75
Lewis, G., 17
life issues in executive coaching, 96–9
    the coach's role in working with, 97–9
life skills coaching
    benefits of, 7
    choosing the right coach, 31–3
    definitions of, 7
listening, 173–6
Littrell, J. M., 165

management consulting, compared with
    coaching, 15–17
manager as coach, 101–3
    benefits of, 105–6
    coaching skills for, 116–17
    feedback model for, 114
    managing time and stress, 118–19
    managing conflict, 120–1
    model for, 103
    obstacles to, 106–7
    roles of, 108–10, 125–6
Maddux, R., 130
Maslow, A., 10, 24, 155
McGregor, D., 83
McPhee Andrewartha Influence Dimensions (ID),
    85
mentoring, compared with coaching, 17–19
Milton Index of Personality Styles (MIPS), 78
Mumford, A., 190
Myers–Briggs Type Inventory (MBTI), 77, 84,
    143, 226, 243

negotiation, 51–5
    coaching and, 51
    emotional competence in, 54
    obstacles to success in, 52